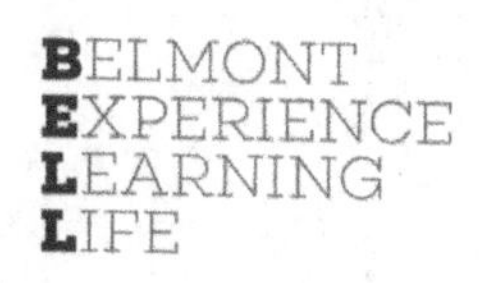

BELMONT UNIVERSITY

Ways of Knowing

The First-Year Seminar Anthology

SEVENTH EDITION

Editor: Daniel Schafer
Introduction: Noel Boyle

XanEdu

Printed in the United States of America

ISBN 13: 978-1-71149-409-8

Acknowledgments:

pp. 16–17: Association of American Colleges & Universities (AACU), "Statement on Liberal Learning" (October 1998). Reprinted with permission from the Association of American Colleges and Universities. Copyright © 1998.

pp. 18–24: Plato, "The Allegory of the Cave" from *Republic*, Book VII, translated by G. M. A. Grube and edited by John M. Cooper. Copyright © 1992 by Hackett Publishing Company, Inc. Reprinted by permission of Hackett Publishing Company, Inc. All rights reserved.

pp. 25–35: "Who Are You and What Are You Doing Here? A Word to the Incoming Class," from *Why Teach? In Defense of a Real Education*, by Mark Edmundson. Copyright © 2013 by Mark Edmundson. Reproduced by permission of Bloomsbury Publishing, Inc.

pp. 36–56: From *Love Your Enemies* by Arthur C. Brooks. Copyright © 2019 by the American Enterprise Institute. Reprinted by permission of HarperCollins Publishers.

pp. 57–60: "Don't Dismiss 'Safe Spaces'" by Michael S; Roth, *The New York Time*s, August 29, 2019. Copyright © 2019 by The New York Times. All rights reserved. Used under license. https://nytimes.com

pp. 61–66: Octavia E. Butler, "Lost Races of Science Fiction." Originally published in *Transmission Magazine*, summer 1980. Reprinted in Octavia E. Butler, *Kindred, Fledgling, Collected Stories*. Edited by Gerry Canavan. The Library of America, 2021

XanEdu

4750 Venture Drive, Suite 400
Ann Arbor, MI 48108
800-562-2147

Contents

Introduction

Noel Boyle

***Noel Boyle** (b. 1973) is a professor in Belmont's Philosophy Department, where he specializes in philosophy of mind and philosophy of science. In addition to teaching introductory and upper-level philosophy courses, he regularly teaches First-Year Seminar. In his scholarly work, he examines consciousness through physical and phenomenological approaches. From 2017 to 2020 he served as Director of the BELL Core, Belmont's distinctive general education program.*

***Why we are reading this:** As you embark upon the First-Year Seminar, your introduction to liberal education at Belmont, Dr. Noel Boyle answers some questions that you may have. What exactly IS a liberal education and what is it for? Do I really want one? Can I get it at Belmont? What might stand in the way? Along the way, he will introduce you to some major thinkers – both ancient and modern – who have thought deeply about these issues.*

Welcome to Belmont, and to First-Year Seminar, the flagship course of the BELL Core, which is the liberal arts foundation of a Belmont education. As the BELL Core is a liberal arts program, it seems you'll be asking at least three questions. What is a liberal education? Do I want a liberal education? Am I going to get a liberal education at Belmont? I'll approach each question in turn, trying to give direct responses and explanations.

What is a liberal education?

Answer #1: Socrates is a good example for conveying the ideals of a liberal education.

Socrates was literate, but write nothing of philosophical significance, preferring oral discourse. Most of what we know about Socrates we infer from the writings of Plato, a young friend of Socrates.

The *Apology* is Plato's account of Socrates' defense while on trial.[1] In it, Socrates relates the story of Chaerephon being told by the sacred

[1] Plato, *Apology* in *Plato: Complete Works*, ed. John Cooper (Indianapolis: Hackett Publishing, 1997). See the complete text of the *Apology* below on pages 72-93.

Delphic oracle that there is no one in Athens wiser than Socrates. Socrates did not understand. He was painfully aware that he did not possess substantive wisdom, which is why he sought wisdom. The oracle's response left Socrates in a bind. Knowing he lacked wisdom, he could not accept the oracle's declaration. Deeply and sincerely religious, he could not reject it.

Socrates searched for someone with wisdom to bring before the oracle so he could seek clarification. He found that those who were considered wise, or who claimed to be wise, were demonstrably lacking wisdom. Socrates eventually concluded that he was wiser than these because he knew that he did not know the things he did not know. Put differently, Socrates was wiser than others because he knew something others didn't: that neither he nor any other human understood fundamental matters; only the gods actually possess wisdom. Socrates eventually concluded that the highest wisdom possible for human beings is knowledge of the limits of their knowledge. He inferred that the gods intended him to dedicate his life to showing his fellow Athenians that they were not as wise as they think they were, imploring them to seek knowledge and virtue. Today, the phrase "Socratic wisdom" means knowing that you don't know, being aware of your ignorance regarding a certain matter. Socratic wisdom is both a beginning and a purpose in enquiry. It takes a great deal of hard work to figure out that the world is not as it once seemed, while realization of one's ignorance inspires an ongoing desire to overcome one's ignorance.

Socrates said, "the unexamined life is not worth living."[2] We enter adult life with various beliefs that are unquestioned, that we assume to be true. Most people live unexamined lives, in which they never identify and test their beliefs to see if they are worth holding. Many will only discuss fundamental questions of religion, morality, and politics with those they know will agree with them. As a result, most people go through life rarely questioning if their beliefs are actually true, never growing in their basic understanding of the world.

In Plato's famous "Allegory of the Cave," we are asked to imagine a group of people imprisoned, able to see only a series of shadows cast on a cave wall.[3] They become absorbed in the procession of shadows, unaware of the real life that exists outside the cave. We are no different. Where and when we are born almost entirely determine what we believe and value. No one entirely escapes conflating their own subjective prejudices with objective reality. As prisoners in Plato's cave, we assume that appearance

---

[2] Plato, *Apology*, 38a.

[3] See the complete "Allegory of the Cave" below on pages 18-24.

(how the world seems to us) and reality (what the world actually is) are aligned. But we are wrong. Things are not what they seem. The world is far grander, more complex, more disturbing, and more beautiful than it seems to be.

Socrates' method for seeking knowledge can be called a "Socratic conversation." A conversation is neither a debate nor a speech; the goal isn't to win the day for your view. The purpose is to interact toward a more insightful end than any saw at the beginning. During conversations, Socrates brought attention to unquestioned beliefs of others, and subjected them to logical examination. He never claimed to know the answer to the deepest question on the table, though he frequently shared views of his own (and criticisms of those views). Socrates' goal in these conversations was to move closer toward the truth, realizing that whatever view he had as a mere mortal, it was not the absolute truth of the matter as the gods understand them.

Contrary to the impulse of too many today, Socrates actively sought out those whose views differed from his own, seeking a different perspective from which to look upon his own view. After Callicles launched a forceful and personal criticism of Socrates' core values, Socrates responded gleefully. He had finally found someone with the "knowledge, good will, and frankness" to truly test his basic beliefs and see if they hold up to scrutiny.[4] A long conversation ensues between Callicles and Socrates. It eventually descends into a mere debate, with each trying to win the argument. But Plato is a careful writer: readers can reasonably disagree about whether Socrates or Callicles made the stronger case.

Plato's dialogues abound with examples of Socrates probing others toward critical self-examination, demonstrating that knowledge emerges through a process of dynamic interaction between alternative and diverse ideas. In conversation with Socrates, Nicias and Laches were unable to articulate a consistent view regarding the nature of courage, despite being prominent generals renowned for their courage.[5] Lysis and Menexenus were young friends when they discussed friendship with Socrates, and found themselves unable to navigate puzzles about what friendship is for.[6] Euthyphro was a zealous priest who claimed knowledge of everything regarding the gods, but found himself unable to answer questions about such things as how prayer benefits the gods.[7] The interlocutors initially thought Socrates' questions were easy to answer. What is courage? What

---

[4] Plato, *Gorgias* in *Plato: Complete Works*, 487a.
[5] Plato, *Laches* in *Plato: Complete Works*.
[6] Plato, *Lysis* in *Plato: Complete Works*.
[7] Plato, *Euthyphro* in *Plato: Complete Works*.

is friendship? What is piety? In each case, simplistic and conventional answers were exposed as incoherent, building toward more complex and insightful answers, only for those answers to be shown inadequate as well, with the dialogue ending on a suggestion that they need to keep learning, and ought to continue the conversation another day.

It may seem futile. *They never get anywhere; they don't know anything more at the end than they did at the beginning!* This response misunderstands the Socratic view of knowing. Knowledge, human knowledge anyways, is not a matter of settling on the right beliefs and holding firm. Knowing involves always growing toward a deeper understanding, through ongoing dynamic interaction between various views. For Socrates, knowledge is not merely a matter of having true beliefs. Aligning one's beliefs with absolute truth is, after all, an unattainable ideal for a mere mortal. More central to knowledge than correct belief is *justification*. Why do you hold the views that you do? Do you have good reasons for those beliefs? Have you come to them through a process involving critical self-examination?

In 399 B.C.E., Socrates was convicted of corrupting the youth and being an atheist. He was executed by poison. Though he was no atheist, I suppose there was something to the charge of corrupting the youth. He taught youth to pursue wisdom and virtue as the center of their lives, ignoring the attractions of money and power. He taught them to have the courage and discipline to live according to their convictions. He taught the youth to speak truth to the face of tyranny, without fear for their lives, because suffering injustice is not as bad as doing injustice.[8] He taught young people to question what they had been told by teachers, parents, priests, and all other authority figures. Some still consider it a form of corruption to teach young people to be so rebellious and disobedient. They are wrong. It is the best advice that a young person can get.

Answer #2: The trivium and quadrivium are still useful in understanding the liberal arts.

Socrates helps explain the *values and ideals* of a liberal education, but not the *content*.

Traditionally, there were seven liberal arts, in two groups. The *trivium* consisted of grammar, rhetoric, and logic. Through the *trivium*, students

---

[8] The phrase "speak truth to tyranny" is typically used metaphorically. Here, it is intended quite literally, and tyrants are nameable: Critias and Charmides were among the leaders of the Thirty Tyrants who briefly and brutally ruled Athens in 404 BCE. Though Socrates publicly defied them, he somehow lived. He was executed by the restored democracy in 399 BCE.

learned how to construct linguistic expressions properly, with beauty and persuasive appeal, and in accord with reason. The *quadrivium* consisted of arithmetic, geometry, music, and astronomy. The relation between these four is fascinating. Arithmetic is the study of number; geometry is the study of number in space; music is the study of number in time; astronomy, the crown jewel, is the study of number in time and space simultaneously. Considering all seven arts together, a liberal education can be summarized as an education in words and numbers.

Such historical understanding helps avoid a common misconception: that the natural sciences (such as physics, chemistry, biology) are not among the liberal arts. Many mistakenly think the liberal arts include only the humanities (such as philosophy, literature, religion), or that the liberal arts are the humanities along with the social sciences (such as history, sociology, political science). There is a misguided rivalry between the natural sciences and the humanities, but that is a distinction *within* the liberal arts, one roughly akin to the older distinction between the *trivium* and the *quadrivium*.

In today's university, the natural sciences are probably the best exemplars of the liberal arts. Notice how similar scientific methods are to a Socratic conversation: belief should emerge from evidence; claims must be subject to peer-review; all conclusions are tentative and subject to later revision; insights that disrupt the established order are especially prized; and the only recognized forms of authority are evidence and logic. The resulting accomplishment is breathtaking: a massive body of endlessly fascinating scientific knowledge that ranges from quarks to black holes, with plenty of unexplored terrain open to the restlessly curious.

Despite the complexity of its range, a liberal education is still an education in words and numbers, in literacy and calculation. To list today's liberal arts would be impossible for any number of reasons. Nevertheless, a functional definition is at hand: the liberal arts are those academic disciplines that can count for BELL Core credit.

Answer #3: Knowledge as its own end is the essence of liberal education.

Even understanding the *values* and the *content* of a liberal education leaves the *purpose* to be explained.

John Newman described a kind of knowledge that is worth having "for its own sake."[9] Some knowledge we seek for its *instrumental value,* as an instrument to achieve something else. Knowing how to fix cars is useful

[9] Cardinal John Henry Newman, *The Idea of a University* (Notre Dame: Notre Dame University Press, 1982). Originally published in 1854.

for fixing a car, or for making money fixing cars. The knowledge associated with liberal education is prized for its *intrinsic value*; we want to know simply because we want to know. There is something inherently fascinating about the inner happenings of black holes, the structure of a Bach symphony, the politics of ancient Sparta, and the social life of elephant tribes. Satisfying curiosity is not an idle or trivial matter. Deep yet wandering curiosity is a basic feature of human nature. The world should be experienced as a fascinating place, because it is our nature to be fascinated by the world.

It is sometimes said that a liberal education is "useless." Brand Blanshard explained the flaw in such thinking.[10] Some things, appropriately called "useful," are desired for the sake of other things. Some things, however, are not desired because they are useful, but as ends, as the final purpose. Happiness, security, and love are all useless. But we don't desire love because it useful; we desire love directly. Love isn't a tool used to achieve human flourishing; it partly constitutes human flourishing. Useless things such as love and happiness have a value that transcends usefulness, becoming useful in a higher sense. Blanshard called it "the transcendent usefulness of useless things."

Knowledge of the world and our place in it is a transcendently useful thing. Knowledge of what there is, and how the world works, is worthwhile as a source of direct and genuine satisfaction in human life. Education is best treasured not as the means of making of a living, but as the end to which those are directed. Too often, we value education as a way to make money. This is almost backwards. Money should be valued strictly as an instrumental good, not an end in itself, and knowledge should be valued as an intrinsic good.

Why should I want a liberal education?

Answer #1: Liberal education can help you become free from ignorance, prejudice, and ideology.

As children, we don't know how the world works and therefore we don't know what to do. We latch on to the guidance of our parents and their circle of influence. Even then, most of us reach early adulthood largely ignorant of world cultures, history, or the building blocks of the natural world. Fundamentally, it stinks not to understand what is going on in the

---

[10] Brand Blanshard, "The Uses of a Liberal Education," in *The Uses of a Liberal Education: And Other Talks to Students* (Chicago: Open Court Publishing, 1977), 27-43.

world around you, and a liberal education can free you from some of that frustration.

Liberally educated people can accurately describe something of genetics, neuroscience, geological timeframes, and astronomical distances. They can intelligently converse about things like ancient Greek family structures, Hindu religious beliefs, or the emergence of modern Israel. Liberally educated people can intelligently participate in a discussion ranging over authors like Jane Austen, Shakespeare, Gabriel Garcia Marquez, or Toni Morrison. Liberally educated people have encountered landmark figures of intellectual history such as Plato, Thomas Aquinas, Copernicus, Rene Descartes, Newton, Friedrich Nietzsche, Karl Marx, and Charles Darwin. This knowledge secures a degree of freedom from ignorance about the world that we live in, and a direct source of satisfaction in a complex world.

A Socratic pursuit of such knowledge offers partial inoculation against the human tendency toward insular and ideological thinking. Ideological thinking is characterized by a rigid commitment to pre-established conclusions that reinforce one's own established worldview, judging the evidence based on whether it conforms to your prejudices, instead of the other way around. Insular thinking is only engaging with those who share your basic beliefs. We tend to be in love with our own opinions; Socrates treated his opinions as sources of probable falsehood, not as absolute principles of conscience.

Liberal education teaches you how to detect what Harry Frankfurt might have called "baloney" (he chose a more evocative word).[11] Baloney makers seek to persuade with utter disregard for what is true and what is false; only the degree to which their claims serve an ideological agenda matters. This differs from lying in that a lie is still wrapped within a conception of objective truth, and hiding falsity is paramount to a liar. There is a great deal of baloney in our culture, especially our political culture. Irrational conspiracy theories show up in our houses of congress. Cancel culture chills certain forms of discourse, setting retroactive purity as a condition for entrance into the conversation. Various forms of science rejection, from creationism to climate-denial, serve thinly veiled ideological or economic agendas, undermining the public good. The critical thinking skills central to liberal education equip you to detect such abuses of reason.

Answer #2: Liberal education can help you become free to, *not merely* free from.

---

[11] Henry Frankfurt, *On Bullshit* (Princeton: Princeton University Press, 2005).

Freedom from the constraints of ignorance and ideology is mere pre-requisite for *being free to* manifest your chosen existence.

Consider the U.S. constitution and American freedom. Americans have freedom of speech, for instance. If you want to say that the president is a shape-shifting alien colonizer, then go ahead (though no one has to listen). This can be called *freedom from*, freedom from external constraint. Properly understood, privately considered, external freedom is a tool and not an end in itself.

John Dewey cherished *freedom to*, requiring not only the absence of external constraint, but also the presence of an internal capacity to deliberatively form and act upon a purpose of one's own deliberative construction.[12] The constitution enshrines your right to say more or less whatever you wish. Now it is incumbent on you to form in yourself something worth saying and listening to, something worthy of your unique presence in the world. You have to decide what to do with your constitutional freedoms. A liberal education can free you to live a life of your own deliberative construction, forged by your own examined values.

We say democracy is good, but we rarely ask why. Democracy is rule by the people. Presumably, democracy is only good if the people rule well, being both capable and willing. Otherwise, a democracy will not be fertile ground for human flourishing. Plato opposed democracy, considering it a form of government wherein ignorant masses of people are easy prey for those who would manipulate them, shaping public opinion to serve their pursuit of power, wealth, or fame.[13]

Notice that Plato presumes the mass of people are ignorant, and that knowledge is in the hands of the few. Rotated to a different perspective, Plato's critique of democracy asserts a requirement for a functioning democracy: the people need to know what they are doing. Understanding some science is necessary for constructively contributing to a conversation about energy policy. Economic science should guide tax policy. The history of a particular region is the foundation for any pragmatic discussion of international disputes within the region. Voters need to understand what is going on. If they don't, the result will be as Plato saw: the people will rule themselves into disaster, either through their own terrible and well-intentioned decisions or by manipulation into empowering tyrannical ambitions.

---

[12] John Dewey, *Experience and Education* (New York: Free Press, 1997). Originally published in 1938.

[13] Plato, *Gorgias* in *Plato: Complete Works*, 464d/ 490a.

Answer #3: A liberal education bequeaths to you your cultural heritage as a world citizen.

Socrates preferred the spoken word to the written word because words on a page lack the dynamic interplay of a conversation. They are dead, never saying anything new. Plato recognized the weakness in Socrates' position: spoken words aren't preserved. Compromising between writing treatises and only having conversations, Plato wrote dialogues in which historical persons are featured in fictional philosophical conversations. Good readers of Plato's dialogues try to insert themselves into these conversations, considering alternate ways participants might have answered certain questions, suggesting questions they would ask.

In this sense, it starts to become clear what might be meant by the term "The Great Conversation." As Plato joined an ongoing conversation in which Parmenides and Pythagoras had already spoken, medieval intellectuals responded to the Greeks, the Enlightenment thinkers built on both ancient and medieval scholarly traditions, and so on. As Isaac Newton put it, "if I have seen farther than others, it is because I have stood on the shoulders of giants." The metaphor is clichéd because it is effective: consider that any Belmont freshman, with what you know now, could have amazed Aristotle for endless hours by describing what you know of the natural world. Cells, galaxies, genes, dinosaurs, germs, tectonic plates, koala bears, black holes. He had no idea.

The ideal of liberal education can be imagined as a great human conversation constituting the whole of what has been written, spoken, created or calculated. We enter the conversation by getting a sense of what has come before, and we make our own contribution as we are able. The topic of the conversation ranges, in principle, over all that is or has been, all occurrences and experiences. As contemporary people, especially with our extraordinary digital information platforms, we each inherit the whole that has been handed down to us.

The problem is that this image is historical fantasy. Even the term, "Great Conversation," emerges from a movement within liberal education, and a literal series of books, titled (in full) *The Great Books of the Western World.* The list of books are the landmark products of the great conversation that is the Western intellectual tradition. Reading them still constitutes a rigorous liberal education.[14] The range of thinkers and ideas included is largely isomorphic with a standard liberal arts general education program, such as the BELL Core.

---

[14] St. John's College offers a rigorous liberal arts curriculum that is rooted in the Great Books.

A critical feature of a conversation is membership. Who is in the conversation? Who has been left out? Why? The authors of *The Great Books of the Western World* are almost entirely white European aristocratic men. Why?

The traditional content of a liberal education has been profoundly shaped by the twin legacies of colonialism and slavery, as well as their historical ripples through discrimination, racism, segregation, and mass incarceration. The situation differed in important ways across history and geography, but certain processes seem identifiable. Most directly, people of color have often been oppressed and brutalized. Laws against educating Black children, or systematically undermining that education, enforce a white-only intellectual conversation as a matter of public policy. Women have also been routinely denied an education, and similarly excluded. Apparently oblivious to the stark hypocrisy, many central figures associated with Enlightenment ideals of egalitarianism and individual freedom were white-supremacists who defended slavery and sexism. Even the author of America's Bill of Rights was a slaver.

Through colonialism, many non-European voices, rich cultural tapestries, were annihilated nearly to the point of being erased from history. Greece of twenty-six hundred years ago is better understood and vastly easier to study than South America of six hundred years ago. Existent non-European voices have typically been excluded from the discussion, sometimes as a mere matter of definition, as when philosophy is defined as the intellectual tradition emanating from early Greek thinkers, leading to the absurd conclusion that Confucius was not a philosopher. Or when the study of African History is considered distinct from World History, and only appropriate for more advanced students (or, worse, presumed to be of interest only to Black students).

Nevertheless, the intellectual heritage left by women and people of color is as rich and complex as it is, too often, overlooked. In all human societies, there are traditions of systematic attempts to understand the world, and for the people to express themselves in it. Any number of other figures could, in principle, have served instead of Socrates as the example at the beginning of this essay: Confucius, Alhazen, W.E.B. Dubois, Marie Curie… There is nothing inherently white, male, or European about the liberal arts ideal of encountering the world with curiosity and humility. That the liberal arts tradition is often, and too easily, equated with Western civilization is a dark consequence of world history, a tragic legacy of brutality and hubris.

We cannot undo the past; we cannot make the conversation as we inherit it other than it actually was. Instead, moving forward, we shape the conversation in ways that are more broadly inclusive and, therefore, more productive. Historical contributions by women and people of color were often not acknowledged in their own day, but the written word persists and can be read even generations later. Figures such as seventeenth-century Ethiopian philosopher Zera Yacob or nineteenth-century Native American writer Sarah Winnemucca can be brought into the conversation. The intellectual and cultural traditions devastated by colonialism must be, to the extent possible, preserved and reconstructed, not merely as anthropological relics but as vibrant sources to enhance our own understanding of the world. Finally, the historical facts of the oppression, destruction, and systematic exclusion of women, people of color, and other historically marginalized groups needs to become part of the curriculum. In our times, a central task in the pursuit of knowledge is understanding how our intellectual inheritance carries the legacy of historical systems of exclusion, and taking bold measures toward a genuinely inclusive conversation.

Answer #4: Liberal education will help you adapt and prosper over a long career.

Though liberal education does not exist for the sake of professional preparation, it will benefit your professional career. You will be a better nurse if you have studied comparative theology and understand the variety of spiritual responses to suffering and death. You will be a better civil engineer if you have studied political science and understand how science informs, or fails to inform, public policy decisions. You will be a better business executive if you study a foreign language, take courses in cultural anthropology, and become adept at working and thinking across cultural divides.

Health care and teaching are particularly clear examples of professions which benefit from a broad and robust liberal education. To thrive as nurse or teacher, you need to be able to reach a diversity of people going through often tumultuous experiences and emotions. If a pediatric nurse cannot gain the parents' trust because of an inability or unwillingness to comprehend their culture, care standards will be impaired. If a teacher cannot understand the psycho-social factors in children's lives, he might not understand why his students don't thrive.

Admittedly, the likelihood of such direct application varies across professions, and might be rare for some professions. More important than such direct application, however, is developing what are sometimes called transfer skills. These skills develop in one context but can be transferred and applied in other contexts. A liberal education greatly improves written and oral communication, critical thinking, abstract reasoning, integrating new information, avoiding the rush to judgment, working with others, disagreeing productively, and staying on track to meet long-term goals. Those are core skills no matter what profession you pursue. Studying the liberal arts is not the only way to acquire such skills, but it is the surest and most efficient.[15]

Immanuel Kant was an eighteenth-century transcendental idealist. Reading one of his treatises is not easy. It requires learning and navigating a vast technical vocabulary, seeing how seemingly disparate ideas fit together into a larger whole, on topics that are dizzyingly abstract. The content of Kant's treatise won't help you in a professional setting, but the intellectual skills you acquired by reading the treatise will. The skills transfer to any context in which there is technical language and a complex whole. My college roommate and fellow philosophy major now works for a tech firm, managing of a team of network… something or other. Honestly, I don't know enough about computers to understand. He has no formal university training in computers or in management. There is no overlap whatsoever between the *content* of his professional work and the *content* of his college coursework. Yet, he laughs off any suggestion that he is "not using" his philosophy degree. He says that anyone who can read Kant can figure out a programming manual.

Am I going to get a liberal education at Belmont?

Answer #1: It is on offer.

You will not automatically get a liberal education at Belmont or anywhere else, but the BELL Core is a good start (if you approach the classes seriously and engage with them rigorously). Though most Belmont graduates earn degrees in other areas, Belmont has quality programs across the core liberal arts and distinguished graduates to prove it. In our philosophy department, our former students have gone to become professors, attorneys, ministers, and many other things. One of our graduates is a former director of Amnesty International in North America. Another was a researcher on the Mars Rover project at NASA. Another is soon headed to medical school. The other liberal arts departments at Belmont all have similar stories. Most Belmont students can add a second major or a minor in the liberal arts without extending their time until graduation or adding to their costs. Many students discover a passion in a

---

[15] For a defense of the professional value of a liberal education, see Fareed Zakaria, *In Defense of a Liberal Education* (New York: W.W. Norton and Company, 2015).

general education course, and choose to follow their curiosity into a second major or a minor. It is the best way to use what are otherwise called "free electives."

Answer #2: There will be many challenges to overcome.

The most basic challenges you already know: college is expensive; the need to have a job might limit study hours; students increasingly have family obligations; the pervasiveness of social media is a relentless distraction; to top it all, we've been enduring the worst pandemic in a century.

Abstract challenges are more difficult to see, but are no less real. We live in a culture that fundamentally misunderstands the nature and purpose of education, and this has almost certainly impacted your educational history and your understanding of education. Standardized tests present education as merely a matter of learning certain facts and skills, not something that might transform the whole person. Authoritarian pedagogies reinforce a passive and obedient model of learning, instead of one rooted in active curiosity.

It is worse than that. Understanding the value of a college education in terms that reduce it to financial cost-benefit analysis is deeply engrained in the culture. Too many think: "the degree will cost *x* number of dollars; it will be worth the expense only if grows my lifetime earnings by more than *x*." Such considerations offer a horrible way to choose a major, and a worse way to choose a vocation. While college graduates have substantially higher lifetime earnings, the value of an education cannot be measured economically. Similarly, your vocational choice should include higher values than financial gain.

Assess the value of your education in the context of your whole life, not merely your vocational and financial life. Learn to see your education as the process of shaping and cultivating yourself into who you decide to become. You will have to walk against the herd of students. You will need to seek out the places where the real stuff of intellectual life is happening: the lively and unpredictable classroom conversations, the groups of students extending learning beyond the class, the dormitory spaces where students wonder out loud together about the biggest questions. Those spaces do exist, but I will not pretend that they are the norm at Belmont, or anywhere else.

The free speech crisis on American college campuses also presents a challenge.[16] Though misrepresented by partisan media, there are growing

---

[16] For an account of the nature and extent of the problem, see Greg Lukianoff and

calls from students and administrators to censor content they believe offensive or upsetting. While deliberately abusive or deceptive speech is anathema to academic values, so is censorship. Freedom of speech is not only a constitutional right; it is also an academic value of first rate. Truth grows from the dynamic interaction between differing views and understandings. Refusing to admit certain voices or topics into the conversation because they seem vulgar, overly provocative, or out of line with religious orthodoxies harms the learning process. Shielding views and values from critical examination does not strengthen commitment to them. The opposite is more nearly true; unexamined beliefs are more fragile than those strengthened by testing.

It is not enough to avoid controversy and stick to "polite" matters. Learning requires dwelling in the uncomfortable, engaging with the provocative, and seeking to learn from a diversity of worldviews. A willingness to listen to some point of view is not an endorsement of that view. It is engagement in a conversation, and one in which you are invited to passionately disagree. You will have to find the spaces in which people demonstrate the courage to discuss difficult and even offensive things. Again, such places exist, at Belmont and elsewhere, but you will have to seek them out.

Perhaps the biggest challenge is the consumerist culture that increasingly pervades higher education. It warps the mission of the institution when students are seen as the customers of the university, here to be provided an economic service. It would be nearer to say the university's customer is the society at large, and the transformation of the students into better educated persons is the product provided.

Students adopting a consumerist mentality make fundamental mistakes in their educational journey. General education is not something to be "gotten out of the way," and whether a class was enjoyable (or easy) is different than whether it was valuable. Instead of asking what the university is giving you, ask how you are transforming yourself in the sea of opportunities the university creates. Although a degree can be seen as a consumer object, there is all the difference in the world between getting a *degree* and getting an *education*. Many of those who get their degree arrive at graduation little transformed by a genuine education. Having sought the easiest path, their journey was the least meaningful. There is, of course, a different and more "Socratic" path, but you will have to seek it out.

Jonathan Haidt, *The Coddling of the American Mind: How Good Intentions and Bad Ideas are Setting Up a Generation for Failure* (New York: Penguin Press, 2018).

How? Start by treating your general education courses as the core of your education that they are intended to be, understanding that a liberal education is both map and fuel for attempting an escape from Plato's cave.

Statement on Liberal Education

Association of American Colleges & Universities

"Statement on Liberal Education," adopted by the Board of Directors of the Association of American Colleges & Universities on October 1, 1998. Available from https://www.aacu.org/about/statements/liberal-education

The Association of American Colleges & Universities *is a national organization headquartered in Washington, D.C. Its mission is to "advance the vitality and public standing of liberal education by making quality and equity the foundations for excellence in undergraduate education in service to democracy." The AAC&U is a sponsor of academic conferences, institutes, and publications on topics related to liberal education.*

Why we are reading this: *This statement, adopted by the Board of Directors in 1998, provides a concise description of the ideals and goals of liberal education in the United States. How does this account differ from the description of liberal education laid out by Noel Boyle in the introduction to this volume? In what ways do they overlap?*

A truly liberal education is one that prepares us to live responsible, productive, and creative lives in a dramatically changing world. It is an education that fosters a well-grounded intellectual resilience, a disposition toward lifelong learning, and an acceptance of responsibility for the ethical consequences of our ideas and actions. Liberal education requires that we understand the foundations of knowledge and inquiry about nature, culture and society; that we master core skills of perception, analysis, and expression; that we cultivate a respect for truth; that we recognize the importance of historical and cultural context; and that we explore connections among formal learning, citizenship, and service to our communities.

We experience the benefits of liberal learning by pursuing intellectual work that is honest, challenging, and significant, and by preparing ourselves to use knowledge and power in responsible ways. Liberal learning is not confined to particular fields of study. What matters in liberal education is substantial content, rigorous methodology and an active engagement with the societal, ethical, and practical implications of our learning. The spirit and value of liberal learning are equally relevant to all forms of higher education and to all students.

Because liberal learning aims to free us from the constraints of ignorance, sectarianism, and myopia, it prizes curiosity and seeks to expand the boundaries of human knowledge. By its nature, therefore, liberal learning is global and pluralistic. It embraces the diversity of ideas and experiences that characterize the social, natural, and intellectual world. To acknowledge such diversity in all its forms is both an intellectual commitment and a social responsibility, for nothing less will equip us to understand our world and to pursue fruitful lives.

The ability to think, to learn, and to express oneself both rigorously and creatively, the capacity to understand ideas and issues in context, the commitment to live in society, and the yearning for truth are fundamental features of our humanity. In centering education upon these qualities, liberal learning is society's best investment in our shared future.

The Allegory of the Cave

Plato

From *The Republic*, Book VII. In *Plato: Complete Works*. Translated by G. M. A. Grube and edited by John M. Cooper. Indianapolis: Hackett Publishing Company, 1997.

***Plato** (429-347 BCE) is a foundational figure in the intellectual history of humanity. Born into a prominent Athenian family during a time when Athens was the center of Greek cultural and political life, Plato became a student and follower of the great philosopher Socrates. After Socrates' death in 399 BC, Plato founded the Academy, a school that endured for several centuries and served as the source of the word "academic." He was also a teacher of the influential thinker Aristotle. Plato's works are often written as imagined dialogues between Socrates and his followers.*

***Why we are reading this:** In this well-known passage from Plato's* Republic, *Socrates converses with his student Glaucon, who also happened to be Plato's elder brother. Plato has Socrates describe the nature of education through an extended metaphor about people trapped in a cave and unable to imagine the world outside. One common interpretation of the story is that humans often work from false assumptions of which they are entirely unaware, assumptions that may draw them toward complacency, smugness, or dogmatism about the way things are. His allegory also spotlights the difficulties that may come when one "leaves the cave" to see the world as it actually is, as well as the great opportunities that emerge when one commits to moving beyond one's limited worldview to pursue truth and reality. Of course, other interpretations are possible. What does the story of the cave mean to you?*

SOCRATES: Next, I said, compare the effect of education and of the lack of it on our nature to an experience like this: Imagine human beings living in an underground, cavelike dwelling, with an entrance a long way up, which is both open to the light and as wide as the cave itself. They've been there since childhood, fixed in the same place, with their necks and legs fettered, able to see only in front of them, because their bonds prevent them from turning their heads around. Light is provided by a fire burning far above and behind them. Also behind them, but on higher ground, there is a path stretching between them and the fire. Imagine that along this path a low wall has been built, like the screen in front of puppeteers above which they show their puppets.

GLAUCON: I'm imagining it.

SOCRATES: Then also imagine that there are people along the wall, carrying all kinds of artifacts that project above it – statues of people and other animals, made out of stone, wood, and every material. And, as you'd expect, some of the carriers are talking, and some are silent.

GLAUCON: It's a strange image you're describing, and strange prisoners.

SOCRATES: They're like us. Do you suppose, first of all, that these prisoners see anything of themselves and one another besides the shadows that the fire casts on the wall in front of them?

GLAUCON: How could they, if they have to keep their heads motionless throughout life?

SOCRATES: What about the things being carried along the wall? Isn't the same true of them?

GLAUCON: Of course.

SOCRATES: And if they could talk to one another, don't you think they'd suppose that the names they used applied to the thing they see passing before them?

GLAUCON: They'd have to.

SOCRATES: And what if their prison also had an echo from the wall facing them? Don't you think they'd believe that the shadows passing in front of them were talking whenever one of the carriers passing along the wall was doing so?

GLAUCON: I certainly do.

SOCRATES: Then the prisoners would in every way believe that the truth is nothing other than the shadows of those artifacts.

GLAUCON: They must surely believe that.

SOCRATES: Consider, then, what being released from their bonds and cured of their ignorance would naturally be like, if something like this came to pass. When one of them was freed and suddenly compelled to stand up, turn his head, walk, and look up toward the light, he'd be pained and dazzled and unable to see the things whose shadows he'd seen before. What do you think he'd say, if we told him that what he'd seen before was inconsequential but that now – because he is a bit closer to the things that are and is turned towards things that are more – he sees more correctly? Or, to put it another way, if we pointed to each of the things passing by, asked him what each of them is, and compelled him to answer, don't you think he'd be at a loss and that he'd believe that the things he saw earlier were truer than the ones he was now being shown?

GLAUCON: Much truer.

SOCRATES: And if someone compelled him to look at the light itself, wouldn't his eyes hurt, and wouldn't he turn around and flee towards the things he's able to see, believing that they're really clearer than the ones he's being shown?

GLAUCON: He would.

SOCRATES: And if someone dragged him away from there by force, up the rough, steep path, and didn't let him go until he had dragged him into the sunlight, would he be pained and irritated at being treated that way? And when he came into the light, with the sun filling his eyes, would he be unable to see a single one of the things now said to be true?

GLAUCON: He would be unable to see them, at least at first.

SOCRATES: I suppose, then, that he'd need time to get adjusted before he could see things in the world above. At first, he'd see shadows most easily, then images of men and other things in water, then the things themselves. Of these, he'd be able to study the things in the sky and the sky itself more easily at night, looking at the light of the stars and the moon, than during the day, looking at the sun and the light of the sun.

GLAUCON: Of course.

SOCRATES: Finally, I suppose, he'd be able to see the sun, not images of it in water or some alien place, but the sun itself, in its own place, and be able to study it.

GLAUCON: Necessarily so.

SOCRATES: And at this point he would infer and conclude that the sun provides the seasons and the years, governs everything in the visible world, and is in some way the cause of all the things that he used to see.

GLAUCON: It's clear that would be his next step.

SOCRATES: What about when he reminds himself of his first dwelling place, his fellow prisoners, and what passed for wisdom there? Don't you think that he'd count himself happy for the change and pity the others?

GLAUCON: Certainly.

SOCRATES: And if there had been any honors, praises, or prizes among them for the one who was sharpest at identifying the shadows as they passed by and who remembered which usually came earlier, which later, and which simultaneously, and who could thus best divine the future, do you think that our man would desire these rewards or envy those among the prisoners who were honored and held power? Instead, wouldn't he feel, with Homer, that he'd much prefer to "work the earth as a serf to another, one without possessions," and go through any sufferings, rather than share their opinions and live as they do?

GLAUCON: I suppose he would rather suffer anything than live like that.

SOCRATES: Consider this too. If this man went down into the cave again and sat down in his same seat, wouldn't his eyes – coming suddenly out of the sun like that – be filled with darkness.

GLAUCON: They certainly would.

SOCRATES: And before his eyes had recovered – and the adjustment would not be quick – while his vision was still dim, if he had to compete again with the perpetual prisoners in recognizing the shadows, would he invite ridicule? Wouldn't it be said of him that he'd returned from his upward journey with his eyesight ruined and that it isn't worthwhile even to try to travel upward? And, as for anyone who tried to free them and lead them upward, if they could somehow get their hands on him, would they kill him?

GLAUCON: They certainly would.

SOCRATES: This whole image, Glaucon, must be fitted together with what we said before. The visible realm should be linked to the prison dwelling, and the light of the fire inside it to the power of the sun. And if you interpret the upward journey and the study of things above as the upward journey of the soul to the intelligible realm, you'll grasp what I hope to convey, since that is what you wanted to hear about. Whether it's true or not, only the god knows. But this is how I see it: In the knowable realm, the form of the good is the last thing to be seen, and it is reached only with difficulty. Once one has seen it, however, one must conclude that it is the cause of all that is correct and beautiful in anything, that it produces both light and its source in the visible realm, and that in the intelligible realm it controls and provides truth and understanding, so that anyone who is to act sensibly in private or public must see it.

GLAUCON: I have the same thought, at least as far as I'm able.

SOCRATES: Come, then, share with me this thought also: It isn't surprising that the ones who get to this point are unwilling to occupy themselves with human affairs and that their souls are always pressing upwards, eager to spend their time above, for, after all, this is surely what we'd expect, if indeed things fit the image I described before.

GLAUCON: It is.

SOCRATES: What about what happens when someone turns from divine study to the evils of human life? Do you think it's surprising, since his sight is still dim, and he hasn't yet become accustomed to the darkness around him, compelled, either in the courts or elsewhere, to contend about the shadows of justice or the statutes of which they are the shadows and to dispute about the way these things are understood by people who have never seen justice itself?

GLAUCON: That's not surprising at all.

SOCRATES: No, it isn't. But anyone with any understanding would remember that the eyes may be confused in two ways and from two causes, namely, when they've come from the light into the darkness *and* when they've come from the darkness into the light. Realizing that the same applies to the soul, when someone sees a soul disturbed and unable to see something, he won't laugh mindlessly, but he'll take into consideration whether it has come from a brighter life and is dimmed through not having yet become accustomed to the dark or whether it has come from greater ignorance into greater light and is dazzled by the increased brilliance. Then he'll declare the first soul happy in its experience and life, and he'll pity the latter – but even if he chose to make fun of it, at least he'd be less ridiculous than if he laughed at a soul that has come from the light above.

GLAUCON: What you say is very reasonable.

SOCRATES: If that's true, then here's what we must think about these matters: Education isn't what some people declare it to be, namely, putting knowledge into souls that lack it, like putting sight into blind eyes.

GLAUCON: They do say that.

SOCRATES: But our present discussion, on the other hand, shows that the power to learn is present in everyone's soul and that the instrument with which each learns is like an eye that cannot be turned around from darkness to light without turning the whole body. This instrument cannot be turned around from that which is coming into being without turning the whole soul until it is able to study that which is and the brightest thing that is, namely, the one we call the good. Isn't that right?

GLAUCON: Yes.

SOCRATES: Then education is the craft concerned with doing this very thing, this turning around, and with how the soul can most easily and effectively be made to do it. It isn't the craft of putting sight into the soul. Education takes for granted that sight is there but that it isn't turned the right way or looking where it ought to look, and it tries to redirect it appropriately.

GLAUCON: So it seems.

SOCRATES: Now, it looks as though the other so-called virtues of the soul are akin to those of the body, for they really aren't there beforehand but are added later by habit and practice. However, the virtue of reason seems to belong above all to something more divine, which never loses it power but is either useful and beneficial or useless and harmful, depending on the way it is turned. Or have you never noticed this about people who are said to be vicious but clever, how keen the vision of their little soul is and how sharply it distinguishes the things it is turned towards? This shows that its sight isn't inferior but rather is forced to serve evil ends, so that the sharper it sees, the more evil it accomplishes.

GLAUCON: Absolutely.

SOCRATES: However, if a nature of this sort had been hammered at from childhood and freed from the bonds of kinship with becoming, which have been fastened to it by feasting, greed, and other such pleasures and which, like leaden weights, pull its vision downwards – if, being rid of these, it turned to look at true things, then I say that the same soul of the same person would see these most sharply, just as it now does the things it is presently turned towards.

GLAUCON: Probably so.

SOCRATES: And what about the uneducated who have no experience of truth? Isn't it likely – indeed, doesn't it follow necessarily from what was said before – that they will never adequately govern a city? But neither would those who've been allowed to spend their whole lives being educated. The former would fail because they don't have a single goal at which all their actions, public and private, inevitably aim; the latter would fail because they'd refuse to act, thinking that they had settled while still alive in the faraway Isled of the Blessed.

GLAUCON: That's true.

SOCRATES: It is our task as founders, then, to compel the best natures to reach the study we said before is the most important, namely, to make the ascent and see the good. But when they've made it and looked sufficiently, we mustn't allow them to do what they're allowed to do today.

GLAUCON: What's that?

SOCRATES: To stay there and refuse to go down again to the prisoners in the cave and share their labors and honors, whether they are of less worth or of greater.

GLAUCON: Then are we to do them an injustice by making them live a worse life when they could live a better one?

SOCRATES: You are forgetting again that it isn't the law's concern to make any one class in the city outstandingly happy but to contrive to spread happiness throughout the city by bringing the citizens into harmony with each other through persuasion or compulsion and by making them share with each other the benefits that each class can confer on the community. The law produces such people in the city, not in order to allow them to turn in whatever direction they want, but to make use of them to bind the city together.

GLAUCON: That's true, I had forgotten.

SOCRATES: Observe, then, Glaucon, that we won't be doing an injustice to those who've become philosophers in our city and that what we'll say to them, when we compel them to guard and care for the others, will be just. We'll say: "When people like you come to be in other cities, they're justified in not sharing in their city's labors, for they've grown there spontaneously, against the will of the constitution. And what grows of its own accord and owes no debt for its upbringing has justice on its side when it isn't keen to pay anyone for that upbringing. But we've made you kings in our city and leaders of the swarm, as it were, both for yourselves and for the rest of the city. You're better and more completely educated than the others and grow accustomed to seeing in the dark. When you are used to it, you'll see vastly better than the people there. And because you've seen the truth about fine, just, and good things, you'll know each image for what it is and also that of which it is the image. Thus, for you and for us, the city will be governed, not like the majority of cities nowadays, by people who fight over shadows and struggle against one another in order to rule – as if that were a great good – but by people who are awake rather than dreaming, for the truth is surely this: A City whose prospective rulers are least eager to rule must of necessity be most free from civil war, whereas a city with the opposite kind of rulers is governed in the opposite way."

GLAUCON: Absolutely.

SOCRATES: Then do you think that those we've nurtured will disobey us and refuse to share the labors of the city, each in turn, while living the greater part of their time with one another in the pure realm?

GLAUCON: It isn't possible, for we'll be giving just orders to just people. Each of them will certainly go to rule as to something compulsory, however, which is exactly the opposite of what's done by those who now rule in each city.

SOCRATES: This is how it is. If you can find a way of life that'sbetter than ruling for the prospective rulers, your well-governed city will become a possibility, for only in it will the truly rich rule – not those who are rich in gold but those who are rich in the wealth that the happy must have, namely, a good and rational life. But if beggars hungry for private good go into public life, thinking that the gòod is there for the seizing, then the well-governed city is impossible, for then ruling is something fought over, and this civil and domestic war destroys these people and the rest of the city as well.

GLAUCON: That's very true.

SOCRATES: Can you name any life that despise political rule besides that of the true philosopher?

GLAUCON: No, by god, I can't.

SOCRATES: But surely it is those who are not lovers of ruling who must rule, for if they don't, the lovers of it, who are rivals, will fight over it.

GLAUCON: Of course.

SOCRATES: Then who will you compel to become guardians of the city, if not those who have the best understanding of what matters for good government and who have other honors than political ones, and a better life as well?

GLAUCON: No one.

Who Are You and What Are You Doing Here?
A Word to the Incoming Class

Mark Edmundson

From Mark Edmundson, *Why Teach? In Defense of Real Education*. New York: Bloomsbury, 2013, pp. 51-67.

Mark Edmundson *(b. 1952) is a professor English at the University of Virginia. He earned a PhD in English from Yale University in 1985 with a specialty in nineteenth-century British and American poetry. He is the author of books on diverse topics: Sigmund Freud, the relationship between literature and philosophy, Gothic culture, rock & roll, and American football. His best-known works articulate and defend the value of traditional liberal learning in American higher education and the contemporary relevance of that vision. The following essay was first published in 2011 in the literary magazine* Oxford American *and was anthologized in* The Best American Essays of 2012.

Why we are reading this: *Edmundson frames his defense of liberal learning in a personal way as a letter to incoming university students. He reflects on his own college experience, acknowledges the challenges and risks of pursuing a liberal arts education, and urges his readers to take responsibility for their own education. Does this work speak to you in some way? Does the essay seem to be aimed at some kinds of college students more than others? Do you find anything in this essay surprising? Encouraging? Discouraging? Inspiring?*

WELCOME AND CONGRATULATIONS: Getting to the first day of college is a major achievement. You're to be commended, and not just you, but the parents, grandparents, uncles, and aunts who helped get you here.

It's been said that raising a child effectively takes a village: Well, as you may have noticed, our American village is not in very good shape. We've got guns, drugs, wars, fanatical religions, a slime-based popular culture, and some politicians who – a little restraint here – aren't what they might be. Merely to survive in this American village and to win a place in the entering class has taken a lot of grit on your part. So, yes, congratulations to all.

You now may think that you've about got it made. Amid the impressive college buildings, in company with a high-powered faculty, surrounded by the best of your generation, all you need is to keep doing what you've done before: Work hard, get good grades, listen to your teachers, get along with the people around you, and you'll emerge in four years as an educated young man or woman. Ready for life.

Do not believe it. It is not true. If you want to get a real education in America, you're going to have to fight – and I don't mean just fight against the drugs and the violence and against the slime-based culture that is still going to surround you. I mean something a little more disturbing. To get an education, you're probably going to have to fight against the institution that you find yourself in – no matter how prestigious it may be. (In fact, the more prestigious the school, the more you'll probably have to push.) You can get a terrific education in America now – there are astonishing opportunities at almost every college – but the education will not be presented to you wrapped and bowed. To get it, you'll need to struggle and strive, to be strong, and occasionally even to piss off some admirable people.

I came to college with few resources, but one of them was an understanding, however crude, of how I might use my opportunities there. This I began to develop because of my father, who had never been to college – in fact, he'd barely gotten out of high school. One night after dinner, he and I were sitting in our kitchen at 58 Clewley Road in Medford, Massachusetts, hatching plans about the rest of my life. I was about to go off to college, a feat no one in my family had accomplished in living memory. "I think I might want to be prelaw," I told my father. I had no idea what being prelaw was. My father compressed his brow and blew twin streams of smoke, dragonlike, from his magnificent nose. "Do you want to be a lawyer?" he asked. My father had some experience with lawyers, and with policemen, too; he was not well disposed toward either. "I'm not really sure," I told him, "but lawyers make pretty good money, right?"

My father detonated. (That was not uncommon. He detonated a lot.) He told me that I was going to go to college only once, and that while I was there I had better study what I wanted. He said that when rich kids went to school, they majored in the subjects that interested them, and that my younger brother Philip and I were as good as any rich kids. (We were rich kids minus the money.) Wasn't I interested in literature? I confessed that I was. Then I had better study literature, unless I had inside information to the effect that reincarnation wasn't just hype, and I'd be able to attend college thirty or forty times. If I had such info, prelaw would be fine, and maybe even a tour through invertebrate biology could also be tossed in. But until I had the reincarnation stuff from a solid source, I better get to work and pick out some English classes from the course catalog. "How about the science requirements?" I asked. "Take 'em later," he said.

"You never know."

My father, Wright Aukenhead Edmundson, Malden High School class of 1948 (by a hair), knew the score. What he told me that evening at the Clewley Road kitchen table was true in itself, and it also contains the germ of an idea about what a university education should be. But apparently almost everyone else – students, teachers, trustees, and parents – see the matter much differently. They have it wrong.

Education has one salient enemy in present-day America, and that enemy is education – university education in particular. To almost everyone, university education is a means to an end. For students, that end is a good job. Students want the credentials that will help them get ahead. They want the certificate that will grant them access to Wall Street, or entrance into law or medical or business school. And how can we blame them? America values power and money, big players with big bucks. When we raise our children, we tell them in multiple ways that what we want most for them is success – material success. To be poor in America is to be a failure. It's to be without decent health care, without basic necessities, often without dignity. Then there are those backbreaking student loans: People leave school as servants, indentured to pay massive bills, so that first job better be a good one. Students come to college with the goal of a diploma in mind – what happens to them in between, especially in classrooms, is often of no deep and determining interest to them.

In college, life is elsewhere. Life is at parties, at clubs, in music, with friends, in sports. Life is what celebrities have. The idea that the courses you take should be the primary objective of going to college is tacitly considered absurd. In terms of their work, students live in the future and not the present; they live with their prospects for success. If universities stopped issuing credentials, half of the clients would be gone by tomorrow morning, with the remainder following fast behind.

The faculty, too, is often absent: Their real lives are also elsewhere. Like most of their students, they aim to get on. The work they are compelled to do to advance – get tenure, promotion, raises, outside offers – is, broadly speaking, scholarly work. No matter what anyone says, this work has precious little to do with the fundamentals of teaching. The proof is that virtually no undergraduate students can read and understand their professors' scholarly publications. The public senses this disparity and so thinks of the professors' work as being silly or beside the point. Some of it is. But the public also senses that because professors don't pay full-bore attention to teaching, they don't have to work very hard – they've created a massive feather bed for themselves and called it a university.

This is radically false. Ambitious professors, the ones who, like their students, want to get ahead in America, work furiously. Scholarship, even if pretentious and almost unreadable, is nonetheless labor-intense. One can slave for a year or two on a single article for publication in this or that refereed journal. These essays are honest: Their footnotes reflect real reading, real assimilation, and real dedication. Shoddy work – in which the author cheats, cuts corners, copies from others – is quickly detected. The people who do the work have highly developed intellectual powers, and they push themselves hard to reach a certain standard. That the results have almost no practical relevance for students, the public, or even, frequently, other scholars is a central element in the tragicomedy that is often academia.

The students and the professors have made a deal: Neither of them has to throw himself heart and soul into what happens in the classroom. The students write their abstract, overintellectualized essays; the professors grade the students for their capacity to be abstract and overintellectual – and often genuinely smart. For their essays can be brilliant, in a chilly way; they can also be clipped from the Internet, and often are. Whatever the case, no one wants to invest too much in them – for life is elsewhere. The professor saves his energies for the profession, while the student saves his for friends, social life, volunteer work, making connections, and getting in position to clasp hands on the true grail, the first job.

No one in this picture is evil; no one is criminally irresponsible. It's just that smart people are prone to look into matters to see how they might go about buttering their toast. Then they butter their toast.

As for the administrators, their relation to the students often seems based not on love but fear. Administrators fear bad publicity, scandal, and dissatisfaction on the part of their customers. More than anything else, though, they fear lawsuits. Throwing a student out of college for this or that piece of bad behavior is very difficult, almost impossible. The student will sue your eyes out. One kid I knew (and rather liked) threatened on his blog to mince his dear and esteemed professor (me) with a samurai sword for the crime of having taught a boring class. (The class was a little boring – I had a damn cold – but the punishment seemed a bit severe.) The dean of students laughed lightly when I suggested that this behavior might be grounds for sending the student on a brief vacation. I was, you might say, discomfited, and showed up to class for a while with my cell phone jiggered to dial 911 with one touch.

Still, this was small potatoes. Colleges are even leery of disciplining guys who have committed sexual assault, or assault plain and simple. Instead of being punished, these guys frequently stay around, strolling the quad and swilling the libations, an affront (and sometimes a terror) to their victims.

You'll find that cheating is common as well. As far as I can discern, the student ethos goes like this: If the professor is so lazy that he gives the same test every year, it's okay to go ahead and take advantage – you've got better things to do. The Internet is amok with services selling term papers, and those services exist, capitalism being what it is, because people purchase the papers – lots of them. Fraternity files bulge with old tests from a variety of courses. Periodically, the public gets exercised about this situation and there are articles in the national news. But then interest dwindles and matters go back to normal.

One of the reasons professors sometimes look the other way when they sense cheating is that it sends them into a world of sorrow. A friend of mine had the temerity to detect cheating on the part of a kid who was the nephew of a well-placed official in an Arab government complexly aligned with the U.S. Black limousines pulled up in front of his office and disgorged decorously suited negotiators. Did my pal fold? No, he's not the type. But he did not enjoy the process.

What colleges generally want are well-rounded students, civic leaders, people who know what the system demands, how to keep matters light and not push too hard for an education or anything else; people who get their credentials and leave professors alone to do their brilliant work so they may rise and enhance the rankings of the university. Such students leave and become donors and so, in their own turn, contribute immeasurably to the university's standing. They've done a fine job skating on surfaces in high school – the best way to get an across-the-board outstanding record – and now they're on campus to cut a few more figure eights.

In a culture where the major and determining values are monetary, what else could you do? How else would you live if not by getting all you can, succeeding all you can, making all you can?

The idea that a university education really should have no substantial content, should not be about what John Keats was disposed to call "Soul-making," is one that you might think professors and university presidents would be discreet about. Not so. This view informed an address that Richard Brodhead gave to the senior class at Yale before he departed to become president of Duke. Brodhead, an impressive, articulate man, seems to take as his educational touchstone the Duke of Wellington's precept that the Battle of Waterloo was won on the playing fields of Eton. Brodhead suggests that the content of the course isn't really what matters. In five years (or five months, or minutes), the student is likely to have forgotten how to do the problem sets and will only hazily recollect what happens in the ninth book of *Paradise Lost*. The legacy of their college years will be a legacy of difficulties overcome. When they face equally arduous tasks later in life, students will tap their old resources of determination, and they'll win.

All right, there's nothing wrong with this as far as it goes – after all, the student who writes a brilliant forty-page thesis in a hard week has learned more than a little about her inner resources. Maybe it will give her needed confidence in the future. But doesn't the content of the courses matter at all?

On the evidence of this talk, no. Trying to figure out whether the stuff you're reading is true or false and being open to having your life changed is a fraught, controversial activity. Doing so requires energy from the professor – which is better spent on other matters. This kind of perspective-altering teaching and learning can cause the things that administrators fear above all else: trouble, arguments, bad press, et cetera. After the kid-samurai episode, the chair of my department not unsympathetically suggested that this was the sort of incident that could happen when you brought a certain intensity to teaching. At the time I found this remark a tad detached, but maybe he was right.

So, if you want an education, the odds aren't with you: The professors are off doing what they call their own work; the other students, who've doped out the way the place runs, are busy leaving their professors alone and getting themselves in position for bright and shining futures; the student-services people are trying to keep everyone content, offering plenty of entertainment and building another state-of-the-art workout facility every few months. The development office is already scanning you for future donations.

So why make trouble? Why not just go along? Let the profs roam free in the realms of pure thought, let yourselves party in the realms of impure pleasure, and let the student-services gang assert fewer prohibitions and newer delights for you. You'll get a good job, you'll have plenty of friends, you'll have a driveway of your own.

You'll also, if my father and I are right, be truly and righteously screwed. The reason for this is simple. The quest at the center of a liberal arts education is not a luxury quest; it's a necessity quest. If you do not undertake it, you risk leading a life of desperation – maybe quiet; maybe, in time, very loud – and I am not exaggerating. For you risk trying to be someone other than who you are, which, in the long run, is killing.

By the time you come to college, you will have been told who you are numberless times. Your parents and friends, your teachers, your counselors, your priests and rabbis and ministers and imams have all had their say. They've let you know how they size you up, and they've let you know what they think you should value. They've given you a sharp and protracted taste of what they feel is good and bad, right and wrong. Much is on their side. They have confronted you with scriptures – holy books that, whatever their actual provenance, have given people what they feel to be wisdom for thousands of years. They've given you family traditions – you've learned the ways of your tribe and community. And, too,you've been tested, probed, looked at up and down and through. The coach knows what your athletic prospects are, the guidance office has a sheaf of test scores that relegate you to this or that ability quadrant, and your teachers have got you pegged. You are, as Foucault might say, the intersection of many evaluative and potentially determining discourses: You, boy, you, girl, have been made.

And – contra Foucault – that's not so bad. Embedded in all of the major religions are profound truths. Schopenhauer, who despised belief in transcendent things, nonetheless taught Christianity to be of inexpressible worth. He couldn't believe in the divinity of Jesus or in the afterlife, but to Schopenhauer, a deep pessimist, a religion that had as its central emblem the figure of a man being tortured on a cross couldn't be entirely misleading. To the Christian, Schopenhauer said, pain was at the center of the understanding of life, and that was just as it should be.

One does not need to be as harsh as Schopenhauer to understand the use of religion, even if one does not believe in an otherworldly God. And all those teachers and counselors and friends – and the prognosticating uncles, the dithering aunts, the fathers and mothers with their hopes for your fulfillment, or their fulfillment in you – should not necessarily be cast aside or ignored. Families have their wisdom. The question "Who do they think you are at home?" is never an idle one.

The major conservative thinkers have always been very serious about what goes by the name of common sense. Edmund Burke saw common sense as a loosely made but often profound collective work in which humanity deposited its hard-earned wisdom – the precipitate of joy and tears – over time. You have been raised in proximity to common sense, if you've been raised at all, and common sense is something to respect, though not quite – peace unto the formidable Burke – to revere.

You may be all that the good people who raised you say you are; you may want all they have shown you is worth wanting; you may be someone who is truly your father's son or your mother's daughter. But then again, you may not be.

For the power that is in you, as Emerson suggested, may be new in nature. You may not be the person that your parents take you to be. And – this thought is both more exciting and more dangerous – you may not be the person that you take yourself to be, either. You may not have read yourself aright, and college is the place where you can find out whether you have or not. The reason to read Blake and Dickinson and Freud and Dickens is not to become more cultivated or more articulate or to be someone who, at a cocktail party, is never embarrassed (or can embarrass others). The best reason to read them is to see if they know you better than you know yourself. You may find your own suppressed and rejected thoughts following back to you with an "alienated majesty." Reading the great writers, you may have the experience Longinus associated with the sublime: You feel that you have actually created the text yourself. For somehow your predecessors are more yourself than you are.

This was my own experience reading the two writers who have influenced me the most, Sigmund Freud and Ralph Waldo Emerson. They gave words to thoughts and feelings that I had never been able to render myself. They shone a light onto the world, and what they saw, suddenly I saw, too. From Emerson I learned to trust my own thoughts, to trust them even when every voice seems to be on the other side. I need the wherewithal, as Emerson did, to say what's on my mind and to take the inevitable hits. Much more I learned from the sage – about character, about loss, about joy, about writing and its secret sources, but Emerson most centrally preaches the gospel of self-reliance, and that is what I have tried most to take from him. I continue to hold in mind one of Emerson's most memorable passages: "Society is a joint-stock company, in which the members agree, for the better securing of his bread to each shareholder, to surrender the liberty and culture of the eater. The virtue in most request is conformity. Self-reliance is its aversion. It loves not realities and creators, but names and customs."

Emerson's greatness lies not only in showing you how powerful names and customs can be, but also in demonstrating how exhilarating it is to buck them. When he came to Harvard to talk about religion, he shocked the professors and students by challenging the divinity of Jesus and the truth of his miracles. He wasn't invited back for decades.

From Freud I found a great deal to ponder as well. I don't mean Freud the aspiring scientist, but the Freud who was a speculative essayist and interpreter of the human condition like Emerson. Freud challenges nearly every significant human ideal. He goes after religion. He says that it comes down to the longing for the father. He goes after love. He calls it "the overestimation of the erotic object." He attacks our desire for charismatic popular leaders. We're drawn to them because we hunger for absolute authority. He declares that dreams don't predict the future and that there's nothing benevolent about them. They're disguised fulfillments of repressed wishes.

Freud has something challenging and provoking to say about virtually every human aspiration. I learned that if I wanted to affirm any consequential ideal, I had to talk my way past Freud. He was – and is – a perpetual challenge and goad.

Never has there been a more shrewd and imaginative cartographer of the psyche. His separation of the self into three parts, and his sense of the fraught, anxious, but often negotiable relations among them (negotiable when you come to the game with a Freudian knowledge), does a great deal to help one navigate experience. (Though sometimes – and I owe this to Emerson – it seems right to let the psyche fall into civil war, accepting barrages of anxiety and grief for this or that good reason.)

The battle is to make such writers one's own, to winnow them out and to find their essential truths. We need to see where they fall short and where they exceed the mark, and then to develop them a little, as the ideas themselves, one comes to see, actually developed others. (Both Emerson and Freud live out of Shakespeare – but only a giant can be truly influenced by Shakespeare.) In reading, I continue to look for one thing – to be influenced, to learn something new, to be thrown off my course and onto another, better way.

My father knew that he was dissatisfied with life. He knew that none of the descriptions people had for him quite fit. He understood that he was always out of joint with life as it was. He had talent: My brother and I each got about half the raw ability he possessed, and that's taken us through life well enough. But what to do with that talent – there was the rub for my father. He used to stroll through the house intoning his favorite line from Groucho Marx's ditty "Whatever It Is, I'm Against It." (I recently asked my son, now twenty-one, if he thought I was mistaken in teaching him this particular song when he was six years old. "No!" he said, filling the air with an invisible forest of exclamation points.) But what my father never managed to get was a sense of who he might become. He never had a world of possibilities spread before him, never made sustained contact with the best that has been thought and said. He didn't get to revise his understanding of himself, figure out what he'd do best that might givethe world some profit.

My father was a gruff man but also a generous one, so that night at the kitchen table at 58 Clewley Road he made an effort to let me have the chance that had been denied to him by both fate and character. He gave me the chance to see what I was all about, and if it proved to be different from him, proved even to be something he didn't like or entirely comprehend, then he'd deal with it.

Right now, if you're going to get a real education, you may have to be aggressive and assertive.

Your professors will give you some fine books to read, and they'll probably help you understand them. What they won't do, for reasons that perplex me, is ask you if the books contain truths you could live your life by. When you read Plato, you'll probably learn about his metaphysics and his politics and his way of conceiving the soul. But no one will ask you if his ideas are good enough to believe in. No one will ask you, in the words of Emerson's disciple William James, what their "cash value" might be. No one will suggest that you might use Plato as your bible for a week or a year or longer. No one, in short, will ask you to use Plato to help you change your life.

That will be up to you. You must put the question of Plato to yourself. You must ask whether reason should always rule the passions, philosophers should always rule the state, and poets should inevitably be banished from a just commonwealth. You have to ask yourself if wildly expressive music (rock and rap and the rest) deranges the soul in ways that are destructive to its health. You must inquire of yourself if balanced calm is the most desirable human state.

Occasionally – for you will need some help in fleshing out the answers – you may have to prod your professors to see if they will take the text at hand – in this case the divine and disturbing Plato – to be true. And you will have to be tough if the professor mocks you for uttering a sincere question instead of keeping matters easy for all concerned by staying detached and analytical. (Detached analysis has a place, but in the end, you've got to speak from the heart and pose the question of truth.) You'll be the one who pesters your teachers. You'll ask your history teacher about whether there is a design to our history, whether we're progressing or declining, or whether, in the words of a fine recent play, *The History Boys*, history's "just one fuckin' thing after another." You'll be the one who challenges your biology teacher about the intellectual conflict between evolutionist and creationist thinking. You'll not only question the statistics teacher about what numbers can explain but what they can't.

Because every subject you study is a language, and since you may adopt one of these languages as your own, you'll want to know how to speak it expertly and also how it fails to deal with those concerns for which it has no adequate words. You'll be looking into the reach of every metaphor that every discipline offers, and you'll be trying to see around their corners.

The whole business is scary, of course. What if you arrive at college devoted to premed, sure that nothing will make you and your family happier than life as a physician, only to discover that elementary-school teaching is where your heart is?

You might learn that you're not meant to be a doctor at all. Of course, given your intellect and discipline, you can still probably be one. You can pound your round peg through the very square hole of medical school, then go off into the profession. And society will help you. Society has a cornucopia of resources to encourage you in doing what society needs done but that you don't much like doing and are not cut out to do. To ease your grief, society offers alcohol, television, drugs, divorce, and buying, buying, buying what you don't need. But all those, too, have their costs.

Education is about finding out what form of work for you is close to being play – work you do so easily that it restores you as you go. Randall Jarrell once said that if he were a rich man, he would pay money to teach poetry to students. (I would, too, for what it's worth.) In saying that, he (like my father) hinted in the direction of a profound and true theory of learning.

Having found what's best for you to do, you may be surprised by how far you rise, how prosperous, even against your own projections, you become. The student who eschews medical school to follow his gift for teaching small children spends his twenties in low-paying but pleasurable and soul-rewarding toil. He's always behind on his student-loan payments; he still lives in a house with four other guys, not all of whom got proper instructions on how to clean a bathroom. He buys shirts from the Salvation Army, has intermittent Internet, and vacations where he can. But lo – he has a gift for teaching. He writes an essay about how to teach, then a book – which no one buys. But he writes another – in part out of a feeling of injured merit, perhaps – and that one they do buy.

Money is still a problem, but in a new sense. The world wants him to write more, lecture, travel more, and will pay him for his efforts, and he likes this a good deal. But he also likes staying around and showing up at school and figuring out how to get this or that little runny-nosed specimen to begin learning how to read. These are the kinds of problems that are worth having, and if you advance, as Thoreau asked us to do, in the general direction of your dreams, you may have them. If you advance in the direction of someone else's dreams – if you want to live someone else's dreams rather than yours – then get a TV for every room, buy yourself a lifetime supply of your favorite quaff, crank up the porn channel, and groove away. But when we expend our energies in rightful ways, Robert Frost observed, we stay whole and vigorous and we don't get weary. "Strongly spent," the poet says, "is synonymous with kept."

The Culture of Contempt

Arthur C. Brooks

Chapter 1 in Arthur C. Brooks, *Love Your Enemies: How Decent People Can Save America from the Culture of Contempt*. New York: Broadside Books, 2019, pp. 19-43. Slightly edited for length and clarity.

***Arthur C. Brooks** (b. 1964) is an American economist, political commentator, and professor of the practice of public leadership at the Harvard Kennedy School. After high school he pursued a career as a professional French hornist before earning degrees in economics and a PhD in policy analysis. Brooks has taught at Syracuse University and Georgia State University, and he served as head of the American Enterprise Institute for more than a decade. He is the author of several books on charitable giving, free enterprise, and economic policy.*

***Why we are reading this:** This is the first chapter of a book that Brooks published in 2019 to address the toxic atmosphere of today's politics. In recent years, people have blamed this divisive climate on different things – social media, cable news channels, economic and cultural divisions, changing demographics, economic distress, cynical political actors, and even university professors. People on the political right tend to blame the Left, while those on the left often blame the Right. Brooks does not provide a complete explanation of how we got to this point, but he provides an interesting diagnosis. For Brooks, our problem is a pervasive "culture of contempt," which he argues is more corrosive of social relations than anger, fear, or other such emotions. Brooks suggests a few ways to break out of the culture of contempt in order to have more fulfilling and productive conversations and relationships with people with whom we disagree. He develops these themes further in later chapters of his book (not included here), which focus less on systematic or institutional change and more on how each individual can strive to improve their relationships with others. What do you think of Brooks' diagnosis and his prescription for the ailment? Brooks seems most interested in contempt between Democrats and Republicans. Are there other kinds of contempt that you see in our society, directed against other kinds of groups?*

The year was 2006. I was a professor at Syracuse University, and I had just released my first commercial book, *Who Really Cares*. It was about charitable giving – about the people in America who give the most to charity, broken down by categories such as politics and religion.

Sounds like a real page-turner, doesn't it? Frankly, I didn't expect it to get much attention. I would have been happy if it had sold a couple thousand copies. Why? My past work had consisted mostly of dense academic journal articles with blood-pumping titles like "Genetic Algorithms and Public Economics" and "Contingent Valuation and the Winner's Curse in Internet Art Auctions." *Who Really Cares* was a little more interesting, but not much. I published the book, and waited for the phone to not ring.

Instead, it rang. And rang. As sometimes happens with academic books, it hit the popular zeitgeist in just the right way. For whatever reason, it was a hot news story that some people gave a lot to charity and some didn't, and my book appeared to explain why. A few famous people talked about the book, and before I knew it, I was on TV and the book started selling hundreds of copies a day.

Weirdest of all for me, total strangers began to reach out. I quickly got used to e-mails from people I had never met, pouring out intimate details of their lives, because, I learned, when people read a whole book by you, they feel that they know you. Moreover, if they don't like the book, they don't like *you*.

One afternoon a couple of weeks after the book came out, I got an e-mail from a man in Texas that began "Dear Professor Brooks: You are a fraud." Tough start. But my Texan correspondent didn't stop there. His e-mail was about five thousand words long, criticizing in vitriolic detail every chapter in the book and informing me of my numerous inadequacies as a researcher and person. It took me twenty minutes just to get through his screed.

OK now, put yourself in my position. What would you do at this point? Here are three options:

Option 1. Ignore him. He's just some random guy, right? Why waste *my* time, even if he wasted *his* lambasting my book, chapter and verse?

Option 2. Insult him. Say, "Get a life, man. Don't you have something better to do than reach out and bother a stranger?"

Option3. Destroy him. Pick out three or four of his most glaring, idiotic errors and throw them in his face, adding, "Hey, blockhead, if you don't know economics, best not to embarrass yourself in front of a professional economist."

More and more, these three alternatives (or a combination of them) are the only ones we feel are available to us in modern ideological conflicts. Few other options come to mind when we're confronted with disagreement. Notice that they all grow from the same root: contempt. They all express the view that my interlocutor is unworthy of my consideration.

Each option will provoke a different response, but what they all have in common is that they foreclose the possibility of a productive discussion. They basically guarantee permanent enmity. You might note that *he started it.* True – although you could probably say I started it by writing the book. Either way, just as the rejoinder "he started it" never cut any ice for me when my kids were little and fighting in the back seat of the car, it has no moral weight here, where our goal is to undercut the culture of contempt.

Later, I'll tell you which of the three options – ignore, insult, or destroy – I chose in responding to my Texan correspondent. But before I do so, we have a trip to make through the science and philosophy of contempt.

In 2014, researchers at Northwestern University, Boston College, and the University of Melbourne published an article in the *Proceedings of the National Academy of Sciences,* a prestigious academic journal.[1] The subject was human conflict due to "motive attribution asymmetry" – the phenomenon of assuming that your ideology is based in love, while your opponent's ideology is based in hate.

The researchers found that a majority of Republicans and Democrats today suffer from a level of motive attribution asymmetry that is comparable to that of Palestinians and Israelis. In both cases, the two sides think that they are driven by benevolence, while the other side is evil and motivated by hate. Therefore, neither side is willing to negotiate or compromise. As a result, the authors found, "political conflict between American Democrats and Republicans and ethnoreligious conflict between Israelis and Palestinians seem intractable, despite the availability of reasonable compromise solutions in both cases."

Think about what this means: We are headed to the point where achieving bipartisan compromise, on issues from immigration to guns to confirming a Supreme Court justice, is as difficult as achieving Middle East peace. We may not be engaging in daily violence against each other, but we can't make progress as a society when both sides believe that they are motivated by love while the other side is motivated by hate.

People often characterize the current moment as being "angry." I wish

---

[1] Adam Waytz, Liane L. Young, and Jeremy Ginges, "Motive Attribution Asymmetry for Love vs. Hate Drives Intractable Conflict," *Proceedings of the National Academy of Sciences of the United States of America* 111, no. 44 (Nov. 2014): 15687-92, doi: 10.1073/pnas.1414146111.

this were true, because anger tends to be self-limiting. It is an emotion that occurs when we want to change someone's behavior and believe we can do so. While anger is often perceived as a negative emotion, research shows that its social purpose is not actually to drive others away but rather to remove problematic elements of a relationship and bring people back together.[2] Believe it or not, there is little evidence that anger in marriage is correlated with separation or divorce.[3]

Think about a fight you've had with a close friend, sibling, or spouse. If you were upset and got angry, was your goal to push her out of your life entirely? Did you suppose that the person was motivated by her *hatred* for you? Of course not. Whether anger is the right strategy or not, we get angry because we recognize that things are not as they should be, we want to set them right, and we think we can.

Motive attribution asymmetry doesn't lead to anger, because it doesn't make you want to repair the relationship. Believing your foe is motivated by hate leads to something far worse: contempt. While anger seeks to bring someone back into the fold, contempt seeks to exile. It attempts to mock, shame, and permanently exclude from relationships by belittling, humiliating, and ignoring. So while anger says, "I care about this," contempt says, "You disgust me. You are beneath caring about."

Once I asked a psychologist friend about the root of violent conflict. He told me it was "contempt that is poorly hidden." What makes you violent is the perception that you are being held in contempt. This rips families, communities, and whole nations apart. If you want to make a lifelong enemy, show him contempt.

The destructive power of contempt is well documented in the work of the famous social psychologist and relationship expert John Gottman. He is a longtime professor at the University of Washington in Seattle and cofounder with his wife, Julie Schwartz Gottman, of the Gottman Institute, which is dedicated to improving relationships. In his work, Gottman has studied thousands of married couples. He'll ask each couple to tell their story – how they met and courted, their highs and lows as a couple, and how their marriage has changed over the years – before having them discuss contentious issues.

After watching a couple interact for just one hour, he can predict with

---

[2] Agneta H. Fischer and Ira J. Roseman, "Beat Them or Ban Them: The Characteristics and Social Functions of Anger and Contempt," *Journal of Personality and Social Psychology* 93, no. 1 (July 2007): 103-15, doi: 10.1037/0022-3514.93.1.103.

[3] John M. Gottman, "A Theory of Marital Dissolution and Stability," *Journal of Family Psychology* 7, no. 2 (June 1993): 57-75, doi: 10.1037/0893-3200.7.1.57.

94 percent accuracy whether that couple will divorce within three years.[4] How can he tell? It's not from the anger that the couples express. Gottman confirms that anger doesn't predict separation or divorce.[5] The biggest warning signs, he explains, are indicators of *contempt*. These include sarcasm, sneering, hostile humor, and – worst of all – eye-rolling. These little acts effectively say "You are worthless" to the one person you should love more than any other. Want to see if a couple will end up in divorce court? Watch them discuss a contentious topic, and see if either partner rolls his or her eyes.

What does all this have to do with American politics? I asked him that. At this question, Gottman – an ebullient, happy person – becomes somber.

> There's been a denigration of respect in the dialogue in this country. It's always us versus them.... We see Republicans thinking they're better than Democrats, Democrats thinking they're better than Republicans, people from the coast thinking they're better than people inland. It goes on and on, and I think it's very harmful. This "us versus them" is what gets our medial prefrontal cortex – that's the part of the brain between our eyes – to not respond with understanding and compassion. And that's not what our country's about.

The pandemic of contempt in political matters makes it impossible for people of opposing views to work together. Go to YouTube and watch the 2016 presidential debates: they are masterpieces of eye-rolling, sarcasm, and sneering derision. For that matter, listen as politicians at all levels talk about their election opponents, or members of the other party. Increasingly, they describe people unworthy of any kind of consideration, with no legitimate ideas or views. And social media? On any contentious subject, these platforms are contempt machines.

Of course this is self-defeating in a nation in which political competitors must also be collaborators. How likely are you to want to work with someone who has told an audience that you are a fool or a criminal? Would you make a deal with someone who publicly said you are corrupt? How about becoming friends with someone who says your opinions are idiotic? Why would you be willing to compromise politically with such a person? You can resolve problems with someone with whom you disagree,

---

[4] Kim T. Buehlman, John M. Gottman, and Lynn F. Katz, "How a Couple Views Their Past Predicts Their Future: Predicting Divorce from an Oral History Interview," *Journal of Family Psychology* 5, nos. 3-4 (Mar.-June 1992): 295-318, doi: 10.1037/0893-3200.5.3-4.295.

[5] John M. Gottman, "A Theory of Marital Dissolution and Stability," *Journal of Family Psychology* 7, no. 2 (June 1993): 57-75, doi: 10.1037/0893-3200.7.1.57.

even if you disagree angrily, but you can't come to a solution with someone who holds you in contempt or for whom you have contempt.

Contempt is impractical and bad for a country dependent on people working together in politics, communities, and the economy. Unless we hope to become a one-party state, we cannot afford contempt for our fellow Americans who simply disagree with us.

Nor is contempt morally justified. The vast majority of Americans on the other side of the ideological divide are not terrorists or criminals. They are people like us who happen to see certain contentious issues differently. When we treat our fellow Americans as enemies, we lose friendships, and thus, love and happiness. That's exactly what's happening. One poll shows that a sixth of Americans have stopped talking to a family member or close friend because of the 2016 election. People have ended close relationships, the most important source of happiness, because of politics.

In one particularly sad example of this in the run-up to the 2018 midterm election, *six siblings* of an incumbent congressman made a television advertisement for his opponent.[6] One sister called him a racist. A brother said, "He just doesn't appear to be well." Another brother impugned his motives for his policies, saying his views on regulation must be motivated by money from industry. The congressman's public response? His siblings "are related by blood to me but like leftists everywhere, they put political ideology before family. Stalin would be proud."[7]

In 1960, only 5 percent of Americans said they would be displeased if their child married someone from the other political party. By 2010, that number was 40 percent, and no doubt has risen from there.[8] We have become far removed indeed from Thomas Jefferson's admonition that a "difference in politics should never be permitted to enter into social intercourse, or to disturb its friendships, its charities or justice."[9]

---

[6] Joseph Flaherty, "Arizona Congressman Paul Gosar's Siblings Endorse Rival in New Campaign Ads," *Phoenix New Times,* Sept. 21, 2018, https://www.phoenixnewtimes.com/news/arizona-congressman-paul-gosars-siblings-endorse-opponent-10849863.

[7] Paul Gosar (@DrPaulGosar), "My siblings who chose to film ads against me are all liberal Democrats who hate President Trump. These disgruntled Hillary supporters are related by blood to me but like leftists everywhere, they put political ideology before family. Stalin would be proud. #Azo4 #MAGA2018," Twitter, Sept. 22, 2018, 11:24 a.m.

[8] David A. Graham, "Really, Would You Let Your Daughter Marry a Democrat?" *Atlantic,* Sept. 27, 2012, https://www.theatlantic.com/politics/archive/2012/09/really-would-you-let-your-daughter-marry-a-democrat/262959/.

[9] Thomas Jefferson, "From Thomas Jefferson to Henry Lee, 10 August 1824,"

Gottman calls contempt "sulfuric acid for love." However, it doesn't just destabilize our relationships and our politics. Gottman tells me that it also causes a comprehensive degradation of our immune systems. It damages self-esteem, alters behavior, and even impairs cognitive processing.[10] According to the American Psychological Association, the feeling of rejection, so often experienced after being treated with contempt, increases "anxiety, depression, jealousy, and sadness" and "reduces performance on difficult intellectual tasks."[11] Being treated with contempt takes a measurable physical toll. Those who routinely feel excluded "have poorer sleep quality, and their immune systems don't function as well" as those of people who don't suffer contemptuous treatment.[12]

As important, contempt isn't just harmful for the person being treated poorly. It is also harmful for the contemptuous person, because treating others with contempt causes us to secrete two stress hormones, cortisol and adrenaline. The consequence of constantly secreting these hormones – the equivalent of living under significant consistent stress – is staggering. Gottman points out that people in couples who are constantly battling die *twenty years earlier,* on average, than those who consistently seek mutual understanding. Our contempt is inarguably disastrous for *us,* let alone the people we are holding in contempt.

In truth, contempt is *not* what we really want. How do I know this? To begin with, that's what I hear all day, every day. I travel constantly, and for my job I talk about policy and politics. Not a day goes by when someone doesn't bemoan the fact that we are coming apart as a country, unable to have a respectful airing of political views like civilized adults. People are exhausted.

That's exactly what Tim Dixon, cofounder of the organization More in Common, calls the "exhausted majority": Americans who are tired of the constant conflict and worried about the future of the country. In a groundbreaking study on political attitudes in the US, he finds that 93 percent of Americans say that they are tired of how divided we have

---

Rotunda, http://rotunda.upress.virginia.edu/founders/default.xqy?keys=FOEA-print-04-02-02-4451.

[10] Agneta H. Fischer and Ira J. Roseman, "Beat Them or Ban Them: The Characteristics and Social Functions of Anger and Contempt."

[11] Kirsten Weir, "The Pain of Social Rejection," American Psychological Association, *Monitor on Psychology* 43, no. 4 (Apr. 2012), 50, http://www.apa.org/monitor/2012/04/rejection.aspx.

[12] Weir, "Pain of Social Rejection."

become as a country; 71 percent believe this "strongly." Large majorities say privately that they believe in the importance of compromise, reject the absolutism of the extreme wings of both parties, and are not motivated by partisan loyalty.[13]

A lot of other evidence backs up Dixon's claim that a majority of Americans dislike the culture of contempt. A 2017 *Washington Post*-University of Maryland poll asked, "Do you think problems in America's politics right now are similar to most periods of partisan disagreement, or do you think problems have reached a dangerous low point?" Seventy-one percent of respondents chose the latter.[14] Almost two-thirds of Americans say that the future of the country is a very or somewhat significant source of stress, more than the percentage who say they are stressed by money concerns or work.[15] Even more disconcerting, 60 percent of Americans consider our current political moment the lowest point in U.S. history that they can remember – a figure, the American Psychological Association points out, that spans "every generation, including those who lived through World War II and Vietnam, the Cuban missile crisis and the September 11 terrorist attacks."[16] More than 70 percent of Americans believe that the country will be greatly hurt if opposing parties don't work together.[17]

This defies the idea that America is split between two big groups of hyperpartisans intent on vanquishing the other side. On the contrary, most are quite nuanced in their views and don't fit into a neat ideological camp. As just one illustrative example, Dixon's exhausted majority is significantly more likely than the highly partisan minority to believe that hate speech in America is a problem, but that political correctness is *also* a problem. In other words, this majority wants our country to address the

---

[13] Stephen Hawkins, et al., "Hidden Tribes: A Study of America's Polarized Landscape," More in Common, 2018, https://static1.squarespace.com/static/5a70a7c3010027736a2274of/t/5bbcea6b7817f7bf7342b718/1539107467397/hidden_tribes_report-2.pdf.

[14] John Wagner and Scott Clement, "'It's Just Messed Up': Most Think Political Divisions as Bad as Vietnam Era, New Poll Shows," *Washington Post,* Oct. 28, 2017, https://www.washingtonpost.com/graphics/2017/national/democracy-poll/?utm_term=.c6b95de49f42.

[15] "APA Stress in America Survey: US at 'Lowest Point We Can Remember'; Future of Nation Most Commonly Reported Source of Stress," American Psychological Association, Nov. 1, 2017, http://www.apa.org/news/press/releases/2017/11/lowest-point.aspx.

[16] "APA Stress in America Survey."

[17] "Many See Potential Harm from Future Gridlock, for the Nation and Personally," Pew Research Center, Dec. 11, 2014, http://www.people-press.org/2014/12/11/few-see-quick-cure-for-nations-political-divisions/12-11-2014_02.

former, but not by embracing the latter.

You might be thinking I have some explaining to do here. On the one hand, I am asserting that our culture, especially our political culture, is overrun with contempt. On the other hand, I'm saying it's not what a pretty big majority of us want. But don't we get what we want in democracies and free markets?

Yes and no. There are lots of cases in which people demand something they hate. Have you ever met a problem drinker? Every morning, he berates himself for his lack of self-discipline and resolves not to drink that night. When night rolls around, filled with anxiety and cravings, he says, "Eh, I'll quit tomorrow." Similarly, most smokers say they wish they didn't smoke, yet they voluntarily continue, spending their money and wrecking their health in the process.

What's going on here? The answer is addiction, of course. Addiction clouds our ability to make long-run choices in our own interest. Personally, I have a terrible sweet tooth. I know perfectly well that I should cut refined sugar out of my diet. I *want* to get off the sweet stuff. But Ijust know that tonight, around eight p.m., I'll lose my resolve and hit the Oreos. (It's my wife's fault for buying them.) You probably have your own weakness, out of which you demand something in the short run that you don't really want in the long run. Maybe it's a bad relationship you just can't quit, or gambling, or buying clothes you can't afford.

Economists carve out a special sort of demand for addictive things. They note that we make decisions that are deeply suboptimal in the long run because the pain of breaking the habit is so high in the short run. Therefore, we really wish we didn't drink, but we put off the discomfort of quitting, day after day.

America is addicted to political contempt. While most of us hate what it is doing to our country and worry about how contempt coarsens our culture over the long term, many of us still compulsively consume the ideological equivalent of meth from elected officials, academics, entertainers, and some of the news media. Millions actively indulge their habit by participating in the cycle of contempt in the way they treat others, especially on social media. We wish our national debates were nutritious and substantive, but we have an insatiable craving for insults to the other side. As much as we know we should ignore the nasty columnist, turn off the TV loudmouth, and stop checking our Twitter feeds, we indulge our guilty urge to listen as our biases are confirmed that the other guys are not just wrong, but stupid and evil.

We are responsible for our contempt addiction, of course, just as meth addicts are ultimately accountable for their addiction. But there are also our pushers – the political meth dealers. Knowing our weakness, dividing leaders on both the left and right seek power and fame by setting American against American, brother against brother, compatriot against compatriot. These leaders assert that we must choose sides, then argue that the other side is wicked – not worthy of any consideration – rather than challenging them to listen to others with kindness and respect. They foster a culture of contempt.

There is an "outrage industrial complex" in American media today, which profits handsomely from our contempt addiction. This starts by catering to just one ideological side. Leaders and media on the left and right then keep their audiences hooked on contempt by telling audiences what they want to hear, selling a narrative of conflict and painting gross caricatures of the other side. They make us feel justified in our own beliefs while affirming our worst assumptions about those who disagree with us – namely that they are, in fact, stupid, evil, and not worth giving the time of day.

In a battle for public attention, elite opinion makers on both the right and left increasingly describe our political disagreements as an apocalyptic struggle between good and evil, comparing the other side to animals and using metaphors of terrorism. Open your favorite newspaper or browse the prime-time cable lineup and you will find example after example. The result of hyperbolic rhetoric becoming commonplace? A deepening culture of contempt, a growing threat of actual violence, and – of course – record profits. (Hey, you saw *Breaking Bad,* right? Meth is very profitable, too.)

Social media intensifies our addiction by allowing us to filter out the news and opinions we disagree with, thus purifying the contempt drug. According to the Brookings Institution, the average Facebook user has five politically like-minded friends for every friend on the other side of the political spectrum.[18] Researchers from the University of Georgia have shown that Twitter users are unlikely to be exposed to cross-ideological content because the users they follow are politically homogeneous.[19] Even in the world of dating apps, scholars have found that people sort themselves based on political affiliation.[20] These companies give us

---

[18] Joshua Bleiberg and Darrell M. West, "Political Polarization on Facebook," May 13, 2015, https://www.brookings.edu/blog/techtank/2015/05/13/political-polarization-on-facebook.

[19] Itai Himelboim, Stephen McCreery, and Marc Smith, "Birds of a Feather Tweet Together: Integrating Network and Content Analysis to Examine Cross-Ideology Exposure on Twitter," *Journal of Computer-Mediated Communication* 18, no. 2 (Jan. 2013): 40-60, doi: 10.1111/jcc4.12001.

[20] Neil Malhotra and Gregory Huber, "Dimensions of Political Homophily: Isolating Choice Homophily along Political Characteristics," Stanford Graduate

platforms to create feedback loops where we are exposed only to those who think similarly, and where people can hide behind a cloak of anonymity and spew hateful, vitriolic commentary.

"Ideological siloing" means we stop interacting entirely with those who hold opposing views. Polls show that a majority of both Republicans and Democrats have "just a few" or no friends who are members of the other party.[21] By contrast, just 14 percent of Republicans and 9 percent of Democrats have "a lot" of close friends from the opposing party.[22] The results of not knowing people of opposing viewpoints and seeing them only through the lens of hostile media is predictable. Today, 55 percent of Democrats have a "very unfavorable" view of Republicans, and 58 percent of Republicans hold that view of Democrats. This represents a threefold increase since 1994.[23]

There is evidence that as we become less exposed to opposing viewpoints, we become less logically competent as people. Author David Blankenhorn has noted a rise in several modes of weak political thinking in the past decade.[24] Notable among these modes are: extreme binary opinions ("I am completely right, so you are completely wrong"); seeing any uncertainty as a mark of weakness; motivated reasoning (looking only for evidence that supports your own opinion – which is easier when one can curate one's news and social media); *argumentum ad hominem* ("You have selfish and immoral reasons for your opinion"); and a refusal to agree on any basic facts ("Your news is fake news").

The structure of party politics is also driving the culture of contempt. Every two years, 435 seats in the House of Representatives are up for election. In the last three national elections, more and more of those seats have become noncompetitive, with incumbents winning reelection at rates of 90 percent, 95 percent, and 97 percent.[25] Both political parties draw up

---

School of Business Working Paper No. 3108 (Oct. 2013), https://www.gsb.stanford.edu/faculty-research/working-papers/dimensions-political-homophily-isolating-choice-homophily-along.

[21] "Partisan Animosity, Personal Politics, Views of Trump," Pew Research Center, Oct. 5, 2017, http://www.people-press.org/2017/10/05/8-partisan-animosity -personal-politics-views-of-trump.

[22] "Partisan Animosity."

[23] "Partisanship and Political Animosity in 2016," Pew Research Center, June 22, 2016, http://www.people-press.org/2016/06/22/partisanship-and-political-animosity-in-2016.

[24] David Blankenhorn, "The Top 14 Causes of Political Polarization," *American Interest,* May 16, 2018, https://www.the-american-interest.com/2018/05/16/the-top-14-causes-of-political-polarization.

[25] "Reelection Rates over the Years," Open Secrets, Center for Responsive Politics, https://www.opensecrets.org/overview/reelect.php. Election results are

gerrymandered districts that are filled with true believers, dividing theirs into many districts and lumping opponents into few so as to decrease their legislative representation. As a result, politicians increasingly have to appeal only to members of their own party for votes. Primaries often devolve into a competition to see who can take the most extreme positions in order to prove party fealty and turn out the hard-core base. The inevitable result is the demonization of the other side.

Members of Congress often say that a big change over the past decade is that they no longer spend much social time with members of the opposing party. Not only do they disagree about politics; they hardly know one another as people. You have probably heard many times that in decades past, Democrats and Republicans would argue vigorously on the floor by day, and then go out to dinner together by night. This was part of how they ultimately got business done. By sharing life together outside of work, they developed the trust and goodwill necessary to make difficult choices for the good of all, including those beyond their own political camps.

Politicians often tell me they have felt the need to avoid these friendships for self-preservation; they worry about being seen as too chummy with the other side. In an environment of gerrymandered ideological purity and extreme political contempt, a primary challenger's dream is finding an incumbent fraternizing with the "enemy."

This isn't bad for just our politics; it's bad for politicians as people. Of course, some politicians on both sides like the polarized status quo – it has made their careers possible. Perhaps I would have believed this is the norm before I moved to Washington, DC, ten years ago, but today I know that's not the case at all. I have gotten to know many members of Congress as friends, and – as surprising as it might seem to some readers – my admiration for politicians has grown enormously. They are some of the most patriotic, hardworking people I have ever met. They love America and hate our culture of contempt as much as you and I. They tell me they regret how polarized things have become and wish they knew how to fight the trend. Like us, they are victims of America's political contempt addiction.

One of their biggest regrets is that important issues that require cooperation become a political Ping-Pong match. One side gains power and imposes its vision on strict party-line voting, and then the other side gains power and tries to impose its vision in the same way. The people

---

for 2012, 2014, and 2016; at the time of writing, final results for the 2018 midterms are not available, but the incumbent reelection rate will likely be similar to recent reelection rates of at least 90 percent.

caught in the middle are those with the least power.

Take health care in America. The Affordable Care Act of 2010 – aka Obamacare – changed how health care was purchased and delivered for millions of low-income Americans. It was passed on party-line Democratic votes in the House and Senate, with no Republican support at all. This, of course, set it up to be rolled back the minute the Republicans took over both houses and the White House, which they did in 2016. While getting rid of Obamacare proved harder than Republicans planned, they did succeed in dismantling large parts of it, once again changing how poorer Americans got their health care, and doing so on strict party-line terms. No one doubts that when (not *if*) the Democrats take full control once again, the political Ping-Pong match will continue, wherein low-income Americans' health care is the ball.

As an old African proverb has it, "When elephants fight, it's the grass that suffers." The weak get hurt in conflicts between the powerful. Americans at the bottom of the income scale are always the ones who lose when contempt crowds out cooperation at the top. The politics of contempt never hurts the rich very much. It hurts people in poverty. We should all be able to agree that that's bad.

Contempt is driving us apart and making us miserable. It is holding us hostage. What exactly do we want instead?

For the answer to this, let me start by turning back to my opening story – about my correspondent in Texas who hated my book and let me know in vivid terms. My response options seemed to be (1) ignore, (2) insult, or (3) destroy.

Instead, I accidentally picked a fourth option, and it created a huge epiphany for me. Here's what happened: As I read his e-mail, I was insulted and felt attacked. But I also kept thinking, *He read my book!* I was filled with gratitude. As an academic, I was used to writing things that almost no one would read. I had put my whole heart into that project for two years, and this guy had taken the time to read the whole thing. That amazed me. I became conscious of that particular sentiment, and for whatever reason, I decided to tell him that. I wrote back and said I realized he really hated my book, but that it had taken me a lot of work to write, and I deeply appreciated his time and attention to every detail.

Fifteen minutes later, a second message from the guy popped up in my in-box. I opened the e-mail and braced myself. But instead of another salvo, he said he was shocked that I'd read his note and the next time I was in Dallas we should grab some dinner. This message was completely friendly. From enemy to friend in a matter of minutes! Did he suddenly like my book? Of course not. He simply learned that he liked *me* because

I had taken the time to read his e-mail and was nice in the way I responded. Don't get the wrong impression here. I'm not some saint who always reacts that way when personally attacked. Perhaps our unexpected rapprochement that day was just dumb luck. But here's what I learned from that lucky interaction: contempt is no match for love. The cycle of contempt depended on me, and I broke it with just a few words of gratitude. Doing so felt great for me, and it changed another person's heart. I saw firsthand that contempt transmuted into friendliness when it was met with an overt expression of kindness and respect. From this, I saw for myself that kindness, reconciliation, and connection – not contempt, division, and isolation – are what our hearts really desire. I have since sought to understand the science behind this, reading all the scholarship I could find, and getting to know scholars on this topic.

One of the leading experts is Matthew Lieberman, a social psychologist at the University of California-Los Angeles. Lieberman has spent decades exploring the neuroscience of human relationships. He contends that we have an innate desire for positive social connections with one another, and that our brains experience deep pleasure when we achieve these connections.

You can think about this in dollars and cents. In his book, *Social: Why Our Brains Are Wired to Connect,* Lieberman observes that simply having a friend you see on most days gives the equivalent happiness boost of earning an additional $100,000 of income each year.[26] Seeing your neighbors on a regular basis gives as much happiness as an extra $60,000. Meanwhile, the experience of breaking a critical social tie, such as with a family member, is like experiencing a large income decline.[27] I suppose the congressman I mentioned before (who was denounced by his six siblings) effectively suffered bankruptcy.

In a similar study, psychologists from Brigham Young University examined the habits and social connections of more than three hundred thousand participants, and found that a lack of strong relationships increases the risk of premature death from all causes by 50 percent.[28] A Harvard University publication notes that this lack of communion through social connections is roughly equivalent in health effects to that of smoking fifteen cigarettes a day.[29]

---

[26] Matthew D. Lieberman, *Social: Why Our Brains Are Wired to Connect* (New York: Crown, 2013), 247.

[27] Lieberman, *Social,* 247.

[28] Julianne Holt-Lunstad, Timothy B. Smith, and J. Bradley Layton, "Social Relationships and Mortality Risk: A Meta-analytic Review," *PLOS Medicine* 7, no. 7 (July 2010): doi: 10.1371/journal.pmed.1000316.

[29] "The Health Benefits of Strong Relationships," *Harvard Women's Health*

Here's what these facts and figures mean to you and me. We all want to earn a lot more, and no one wants a big loss in income. We can't always control that, but we can affect something just as valuable for our well-being: our connections with others. Would you trade away $100,000 of your salary, or years of healthy life, over a political disagreement? Probably not. So don't sacrifice a friendship or family relationship over one either, and don't pass up a possible new friendship just because of politics.

A number of recent studies have asked why we crave connection and have found physiological answers. As neuroscientists from Emory University have discovered, social cooperation activates the parts of our brain that are linked to reward processing.[30] Using brain scans, they demonstrate that when we experience the pleasure of connection, these reward circuits are activated, proving that "social cooperation is intrinsically rewarding to the human brain."[31] By contrast, when we experience exclusion or rejection, the brain's pain centers are activated. In fact, the brain processes relational rejection the same way it processes physical pain. As Lieberman has found in his research, a broken heart can in many ways feel like a broken leg.[32]

Once again, ask yourself: Would I be willing to break a bone to be "right," politically?

We probably shouldn't need brain scans to tell us that building relationships is far preferable to the consequences of contempt and division. After all, the great thinkers and religions of the world have been counseling the wisdom of unity for millennia.

In Plato's *Republic,* the great philosopher writes, "Can there be any greater evil than discord and distraction and plurality where unity ought to reign? Or any greater good than the bond of unity? There cannot."[33] Aristotle believed the same thing. If separated from the unifying bonds of friendship, he wrote in his *Nicomachean Ethics,* "no one would choose to live, though he had all other goods."[34]

Watch, Dec. 2010, https://www.health.harvard.edu/newsletter_article/the-health-benefits-of-strong-relationships.

[30] "Emory Brain Imaging Studies Reveal Biological Basis for Human Cooperation," Emory Health Sciences Press Release, July 19, 2002, http://whsc.emory.edu/_releases/2002july/altruism.html.

[31] "Emory Brain Imaging Studies."

[32] Matthew D. Lieberman, *Social: Why Our Brains Are Wired to Connect* (New York: Crown Publishers, 2013).

[33] Plato, *The Republic*, trans. Benjamin Jowett (Los Angeles: Madison Park, 2010), 75.

[34] Aristotle, *Nicomachean Ethics*, trans. W. D. Ross (Stilwell: Digireads.com,

This theme is consistent throughout the sacred texts of the world's religions, too. Psalm 133 proclaims, "How good and pleasant it is when God's people live together in unity!"[35] In Matthew's Gospel, Jesus warns, "Every kingdom divided against itself will be ruined, and every city or household divided against itself will not stand."[36] And the Bhagavad Gita, one of the ancient holy books of Hinduism, teaches that knowledge that "sees in all things a single, imperishable being, undivided among the divided" is *sattvic* – meaning pure, good, and virtuous.[37]

The Founding Fathers knew that social harmony would form the backbone of America. In his celebrated pamphlet *Common Sense,* Thomas Paine held that "it is not in numbers, but in unity, that our great strength lies."[38] James Madison, in the fourteenth Federalist Paper, warned that the "most alarming of all novelties, the most wild of all projects, the most rash of all attempts, is that of rendering us in pieces, in order to preserve our liberties and promote our happiness."[39] John Adams believed that the cancer of faction in America was to be "dreaded as the greatest political Evil, under our Constitution."[40] In his farewell address, George Washington famously warned against "the baneful effects" of political enmity.[41]

We try to have it both ways, of course – love for our friends and contempt for our enemies. Indeed, sometimes we even try to build unity around the common bonds of contempt for "the other." But it doesn't work, any more than an alcoholic can have "just a little drink" to take the edge off. Drunkenness crowds out sobriety. Contempt crowds out love because it becomes our focus. If you have contempt for "them," more and more people will become "them." Monty Python made this point hilariously in the movie *Life of Brian,* where the bitterest of enemies are

---

2005), 8.1.

[35] Psalms 133:1 (New International Version).

[36] Matthew 12:25 (New International Version).

[37] Bhagavad Gita, trans. Stephen Mitchell (New York: Harmony Books, 2000), 186.

[38] Thomas Paine, *Common Sense*, Project Gutenberg, June 9, 2008, https://www.gutenberg.org/files/147/147-h/147-h.htm.

[39] James Madison, *The Federalist Papers*, No. 14, Avalon Project, Lillian Goldman Law Library, Yale University, 2008, http://avalon.law.yale.edu/18th_century/fed14.asp.

[40] John Adams, "From John Adams to Jonathan Jackson, 2 October 1780," Founders Online, National Archives, last modified June 13, 2018, https://founders.archives.gov/documents/Adams/06-10-02-0113.

[41] George Washington, "Washington's Farewell Address," Avalon Project, Lillian Goldman Law Library, Yale University, 2008, http://avalon.law.yale.edu/18th_century/washing. asp.

two rival Jewish dissident groups: the Judean People's Front and the People's Front of Judea.

From the philosophers of ancient Greece to the world's great religions to our own Founding Fathers to the psychology research of the modern era, we are exhorted to choose our heart's true desire: love and kindness. All warn unambiguously that division, if allowed to take permanent root, will be our misery and downfall.

Two caveats are in order here. First, unity does not necessarily mean agreement. I will devote a whole chapter later in this book to the importance of respectful *dis*agreement. Second, unity is always an aspiration; we will never be 100 percent unified. Even in times of war, our nation has not been unanimously behind the effort. Nevertheless, though not perfectly attainable, the goal to be *more* unified is still the right one to give us more of what we want as people.

We want love. How do we get it? We have to start by saying that it *is* what we really want. That is easier said than done. A famous Bible story makes this point:

> As Jesus and his disciples, together with a large crowd, were leaving the city, a blind man, Bartimaeus, was sitting by the roadside begging. When he heard that it was Jesus of Nazareth, he began to shout, "Jesus, Son of David, have mercy on me!"... "What do you want me to do for you?" Jesus asked him. The blind man said, "Rabbi, I want to see."[42]

At first, it seems kind of silly. A blind man, Bartimaeus, wants a miracle from Jesus. Jesus asks, "What do you want?" As my kids might say, "Duh – he wants to see." And, in fact, that is pretty much what the blind man answers.

This story is profound because, while people *do* know what they really want, they often *don't* ask for it. Think about the last time you had a real conflict with someone you love. You badly wanted the conflict to end and affection to return, but you kept fighting anyway. I have a friend who didn't talk to his daughter for twenty years and didn't even know his grandchildren's names. He badly wanted to reconcile but couldn't bring himself to do it. Maybe you have never done anything this extreme, but at one time or another, we have all experienced the pain of a relational fracture that our pride prevents us from fixing.

Once again, there's the addiction. Addicts *all* want to be free from addiction, and there is a lot of help out there to set them free. All they have

---

[42] Mark 10:46-51 (New International Version).

to do is let go of the thing they hate, and ask for what they truly want. But they don't, sometimes even until death. Why not? Most say the short-term agony of quitting is just too great, or that booze or other drugs, as terrible as they are, are the only thing that give real satisfaction in an empty life.

We have a cultural addiction to contempt – an addiction abetted by the outrage industrial complex for profit and power – and it's tearing us apart. Most of us don't want that, though. We want love, kindness, and respect. *But* we have to ask for it, choose it. It's hard; we are prideful, and contempt can give a sense of short-term purpose and satisfaction, like one more drink. No one ever said that breaking an addiction was easy. But make no mistake: Like Bartimaeus, we *can* choose what we truly want, as individuals and as a nation.

How? It's not good enough to leave it up to chance, hoping we accidentally react as I did to my Texan e-mailer. What can we do starting today to reject contempt and embrace love?

For an answer, I asked two experts.

The first is Dr. John Gottman, whom we met earlier in this chapter. I asked him how he thought we could use his ideas on marital harmony to improve our national discourse. If you want a more unified America based on bonds of love, how should you treat others with whom you disagree politically?

Gottman paused when I asked him this, because he had never answered this question before. Professors are always reluctant to go outside the range of their data and specific expertise. Nevertheless, he told me that he loved America, was brokenhearted by the contempt spreading across the country, and wanted to bring us back together. So he gave me four rules:

1. Focus on other people's distress, and focus on it empathetically. When others are upset about politics, listen to them respectfully. Try to understand their point of view before offering your own. Never listen only to rebut.
2. In your interactions with others, particularly in areas of disagreement, adopt the "five-to-one rule," which he gives couples. Make sure you offer five positive comments for every criticism. On social media, that means five positive messages for every one others might see as negative.
3. No contempt is *ever* justified, even if, in the heat of the moment, you think someone deserves it. It is unjustified more often than you know, it is always bad for you, and it will never convince anyone that she is wrong.
4. Go where people disagree with you and learn from them. That

means making new friends and seeking out opinions you know you don't agree with. How to act when you get there? See rules 1 to 3!

The second person I consulted about how to fight contempt is the wisest man I know, who also happens to be one of the world's experts on bringing people together through bonds of compassion and love: His Holiness the Dalai Lama.

The Dalai Lama is the spiritual leader of the Tibetan Buddhist people and one of the most respected leaders in the world today. We have had a collaboration for a number of years, and although I am a Catholic and not a Buddhist, for me he is a mentor and guide. I was visiting him at his monastery in Dharamshala, India, in the Himalayan foothills, when I was starting to work on this book. "Your Holiness," I asked him, "what do I do when I feel contempt?" He responded, "Practice warm-heartedness."

To be honest, at first I thought, *You got anything else?* It sounded more like an aphorism than useful counsel. But when I thought about it, I saw it was actually tough and practical advice. He was not advocating surrender to the views of those with whom we disagree. If I believe I am right, I have a duty to stick to my views. But my duty is also to be kind, fair, and friendly to all, even those with whom I have great differences.

Difficult? Sure. The Dalai Lama would be the first to note that warm-heartedness is for strong people, not weak people. It is advice he has taken himself. At the age of just fifteen, he became the leader of the Tibetan Buddhist people after China's invasion of Tibet in 1950.[43] Following brutal suppression of his people, the Dalai Lama escaped into exile in 1959, and has since led a poor and dispossessed Tibetan community from his home in Dharamshala. The Dalai Lama and his people have been treated with contempt worse than most of us will ever experience in our lives – driven from their homes and barely recognized as people.

How has he responded? The Dalai Lama begins each day by offering up prayers for China, its leaders, and its people.[44] He practices warm-heartedness toward the very regime that drove him and his followers into exile and continues to oppress the people of Tibet. That is strong, not weak. Warm-heartedness is not for the faint-hearted.

My next question to him was: How do I do that? Give me some practical tips, Your Holiness. He told me: Think back to a time in your life when you answered contempt with warm-heartedness. Remember how it

---

43 "Brief Biography," Office of His Holiness the Dalai Lama, https://www.dalailama.com/the-dalai-lama/biography-and-daily-life/brief-biography.

44 Pico Iyer, *The Open Road: The Global Journey of the Fourteenth Dalai Lama* (New York: Borzoi Books, 2008).

made you feel, and then do it again. It was at that moment that I realized that warm-heartedness is exactly what transformed my e-mail exchange at the beginning of this chapter. I accidentally answered contempt with warm-heartedness and watched the contempt melt away in an instant.

Kindness and warm-heartedness are the antivenom for the poisonous contempt coursing through the veins of our political discourse. Contempt is what we saw when Tommy Hodges and Hawk Newsome – the Trump rally organizer and the Black Lives Matter activist – arrived on the National Mall. By inviting Hawk up onstage, Tommy did more than give Hawk a platform to speak. He acknowledged his dignity as a fellow American. He effectively said, *I may not agree with you, but what you have to say matters.* That simple demonstration of respect broke through the wall of mutual contempt that had separated them and completely transformed their interaction.

Hawk then responded in kind, by engaging his audience in a positive, warm-hearted way. He expressed moral common cause with his listeners – declaring that he was an American who loves his country and who wants to make America great – while challenging them to think differently about the plight of African Americans. His approach was deeply unifying. He made a moral case for compassion and fairness, and appealed to something that everyone had written on their hearts.

That doesn't mean that everyone in the audience agreed with what he said; they didn't. Something more profound happened than mere political agreement: a human connection that led to a respectful, productive competition of ideas.

This is exactly what America needs. It is what our hearts desire. And it does not have to be a flash in the pan. It's actually something that we can engineer and replicate all over America if we have the courage and will to do so.

How? Start with your own interactions. When you are treated with contempt, don't see it as a threat but as an opportunity. In the Dhammapada, one of the primary collections of the teachings of the Buddha, the master says:

> Conquer anger through gentleness,
> unkindness through kindness,
> greed through generosity,
> and falsehood by truth.[45]

---

[45] Eknath Easwaran, *Essence of the Dhammapada: The Buddha's Call to Nirvana* (Tomales, CA: Nilgiri Press, 2013), 263.

When I first read that, I thought it was strange that the Buddha would instruct us to turn loving-kindness into an instrumentality to conquer others, but that was the wrong way of reading it. On reflection, I realized that *I* am the angry one, the ill-tempered one, the miser, and the liar. My job is to conquer *me.* My tool for doing so is to show warm-heartedness to others, especially when they are not showing it to me.

Your opportunity when treated with contempt is to change at least one heart – yours. You may not be able to control the actions of others, but you can absolutely control your reaction. *You* can break the cycle of contempt. You have the power to do that.

Your opportunity will come sooner than you think, whether on the left or right. Feel that you've been unfairly attacked on social media? Respond with warm-heartedness. Overhear someone make a snide remark about people who vote like you? Respond with kindness. Want to say something insulting about people who disagree with you? Take a breath, and show love instead.

That sounds great, you may be saying, but what if I don't feel it? *It doesn't matter*. It is what we *do* that most often determines how we *feel,* not the other way around. If you wait to feel warm-hearted toward your ideological foes, you may as well have WAITING TO FEEL WARM-HEARTED chiseled on your tombstone. Action doesn't follow attitude except in the rarest of circumstances. Rather, attitude follows action. Don't feel it? Fake it. Soon enough you'll start to feel it.

If we learn how to answer contempt with warm-heartedness, how to choose kindness over contempt, we can be leaders who fight contempt in society and bring more people – no matter how they vote or see the world – to the joy of loving one another.

Don't Dismiss "Safe Spaces"

Michael S. Roth

From "Don't Dismiss 'Safe Spaces.'" *The New York Times*, August 19, 2019.

***Michael S. Roth** (b. 1957) is a professor of history and the humanities and president of Wesleyan University since 2007. His books include* Safe Enough Spaces: A Pragmatist's Approach to Inclusion, Free Speech, and Political Correctness on College Campuses, *published in 2019.*

***Why we are reading this:** Colleges and universities often seem like strange places, particularly to people on the outside looking in. Students arrive, meet new people, learn new things, and then may start to change their minds, their majors, their career plans, their political beliefs, and sometimes their religions. Historically, universities have repeatedly birthed new political and cultural trends. The Protestant Reformation began on a university campus, as have many revolutionary movements. To many people, higher education seems to be a double-edged sword – necessary for a modern society and yet a source of disruption and subversion. It is no surprise that universities are touchstones in today's culture wars, often at the center of arguments about political correctness, trigger warnings, cancel culture, free speech, critical race theory, etc. As a university administrator, Michael Roth is familiar with such questions and has written a book on one much-debated issue – safe spaces. In this opinion piece for a major national newspaper, Roth mounts a defense of "safe enough" spaces. Are you persuaded? Do safe spaces coddle students? Liberate them? What are they for, exactly? What rules would you propose for a "safe enough" space?*

Opinion: Don't Dismiss "Safe Spaces" – *Yes, the concept can be taken too far, but it still underlies the university's primary obligations.*

As a new school year begins and students prepare to head off to college, there will be the usual excitement among family and friends as well as anxiety about the unknowns. Will these young people, especially those first-year students who are essentially entering into a new society, forge friendships? Will they be inspired and supported by their teachers? What will they learn and how will they establish good habits for study and physical and mental health? Will they be happy? Will they be safe?

To those familiar with campus politics, that last question may seem like a loaded one. The idea of a "safe space" – in the broadest terms, the attempt to make sure all students are made to feel welcome in or outside the classroom – has become a favorite target of critics who claim to worry about the preservation of free speech on campus. Easily caricatured or ridiculed, safe spaces can seem like an extreme form of what Jonathan Haidt and Greg Lukianoff call "vindictive protectionism," with social justice border agents policing conversations for possible microaggressions that might inadvertently wound someone.

Is this fair? That depends.

To be sure, there are plenty of examples of sanctimonious "safetyism" – counterproductive coddling of students who feel fragile. Instead of teaching young people to find resources in themselves to deal with chagrin and anxiety, some school officials offer hand-holding, beanbags and puppies. Infantilizing students by overprotecting them, or just treating them as consumers who have to be kept happy at all costs, can be easier and more profitable for institutions than allowing students to learn the hard way that the world is a challenging place and that they have to figure out ways of dealing with it.

On the other hand, the outright dismissal of safe spaces can amount to a harmful disregard for the well-being of students; it can perpetuate environments where the entitled continue to dominate those around them and students never learn how to build a more equitable, inclusive community. With mental health and suicide crises emerging on some campuses, the idea of universities taking conscious steps to protect and nurture students emotionally as well as physically should be welcome.

So what's a university to do?

The first answer is obvious: We should begin by destigmatizing the notion of safe spaces and stop talking about them as if they were part of a zero-sum ideological war.

As a college president for almost 20 years, I am a strong proponent of creating spaces that are "safe enough" on college campuses. (Here, I draw from the psychologist D.W. Winnicott's concept of the "good enough" parent, who enables a child to flourish by letting them experience frustration and failure within the safety of the family, not by coddling or overprotecting.) Like families, campus cultures are different, but each should promote a basic sense of inclusion and respect that enables students to learn and grow – to be open to ideas and perspectives so that the differences they encounter are educative. That basic sense is feeling "safe enough."

Despite the feverish urgency of contemporary debates, the idea of a safe space isn't at all new. The concept can be traced back to Kurt Lewin, a founder of social psychology and of management theory. A Jewish refugee from Nazi Germany, Lewin was asked to work with supervisors and psychologists at the Harwood Manufacturing Company, a family-owned textile company that, having relocated a factory, found itself with a less experienced and more female work force. Lewin wanted to test the impact of participatory decision-making on productivity and absenteeism with small groups of employees, but he had to get honest (and hence useful) answers from workers who might be worried about speaking out in earshot of the boss.

Lewin and his colleagues created "safe spaces" in which groups of employees and managers could speak honestly about working conditions and productivity goals without fear of retaliation or retribution. When members of the group felt they could freely participate in setting factory goals, productivity increased. No puppies there, not even immunity from criticism – only the feeling that one could speak one's mind without being attacked or losing one's job.

As the idea of safe spaces moved from industrial psychology on the manufacturing floor to the private, therapeutic setting, clinicians saw a key benefit in their patients' being able to more easily change their minds, to "unfreeze," if they felt safe enough to entertain criticism and alternative ideas. In group therapy, the psychiatrist Irvin Yalom wrote, one "must experience the group as a safe refuge within which it is possible to entertain new beliefs and experiment with new behavior without fear of reprisal." This wasn't overprotective safetyism – just an environment in which one could speak more freely and encounter different ideas.

In the 1970s, feminist groups created their own "safe spaces" where women could come together and share accounts of life in a sexist society without fear of retaliation. In the gay liberation movement, the concept was equally important. In the face of discrimination, safe spaces allowed for community building. These arenas were not devoid of disagreement, but they were safe enough for the development of a political movement without interference by dominant and hostile groups. Moira Kenney has charted the importance of these spaces for lesbian and feminist groups in Los Angeles 50 years ago, and today the radical feminist bookstore Bluestockings refers to its saf*er* spaces for resistance and critical thinking.

For different people at different times, safety can mean different things, but the baseline is certainly physical security. For most of the past 100 years, students of color were at risk in many campus spaces, as they were in most cities in America. When I was a college student in the 1970s, female students were routinely targeted by male professors who found it easier to get sexual partners among 19-year-olds than among women their own age. Back then, gay students knew that walking near a fraternity house during pledge week might result in getting beaten up as part of a pledging ritual. There were plenty of campus spaces that weren't safe for different segments of the student body. Today, campuses are safer, and it would be hard to find anyone arguing that this isn't a good thing.

Still, college women must continue to take special precautions to ensure their well-being; they pass on the knowledge that at certain parties it's just not safe to drink from a punch bowl because some guys might spike it with knockout pills, or that it is best to stay away from certain professors who have a history of coming on to their students. Students point out that some among them are more vulnerable than others, and they warn that some spaces (and the people who administer them) are more dangerous than others. Does all this mean students are more fragile? Hardly. It means students are protecting themselves.

Critics of "safe spaces" don't, of course, want to return to the days when students from certain demographic groups were at greater risk on some parts of a campus. What they worry about is that the idea of such places encourages the isolation of groups of students from questions that might take them outside their comfort zones. Throughout American culture, groups are enclosing themselves in bubbles that protect them from competing points of view, even from disturbing information; this siloing of perspectives is being exacerbated by social media and economic and cultural segregation.

Universities must push back against this tide; our classrooms should never be so comfortable that intellectual confrontation becomes taboo or assumptions go unchallenged because everyone's emotional well-being is overprotected. Instead, we must promote intellectual diversity in a context in which people can feel safe enough to challenge one another. Vigorous scholarly exchange and academic freedom depend on it.

Acknowledging that campuses need "safe enough" spaces is not saying that students need protection from argument or the discovery that they should change their minds. It is saying that students should be able to participate in argument and inquiry without the threat of harassment or intimidation. Calling for such spaces is to call for schools to promote a basic sense of inclusion and respect that enables all students to thrive – to be open to ideas and perspectives so that the differences they encounter are educative and not destructive. That basic sense is feeling "safe enough" to explore differences without fear and work toward positive outcomes with courage.

Students and their families make great efforts and sacrifices to put themselves on our campuses. Ensuring they have "safe enough spaces" when they get there is our basic obligation. It's the least we can do.

Lost Races of Science Fiction

Octavia E. Butler

Originally published in *Transmission* (Summer 1980): 17-18. Reprinted in *Octavia E. Butler: Kindred, Fledgling, Collected Stories*. Edited by Gerry Canavan. New York: Library of America, 2021, pp. 719-724.

Octavia E. Butler *(1947-2006) was an American science fiction writer, winner of the Hugo, Nebula, and Locus awards, and recipient of a MacArthur "Genius" Fellowship in 1995. Her novels, short stories, essays, and unpublished works often involve a critique of present-day hierarchies (racial, ethnic, gendered, and class-based) and the forms of violence that undergird them. Her heroes are often disenfranchised individuals who create new non-hierarchical communities that include diverse humans and sometimes extraterrestrials as well. For many decades she was the only prominent black female voice in the field of science fiction. Butler is considered a seminal writer in the Afrofuturist school of science fiction. Her first novel,* Patternmaster, *was published in 1976.*

Why we are reading this: *Octavia Butler wrote this essay in 1979. She describes a world (her world!) in which black figures rarely appeared in science fiction stories or films, and then chiefly as minor characters. This was a world where the vast majority of science fiction writers were white and male, and minority voices were rare. Now, more than forty years later, with films like* Black Panther *(2018) and the appearance of the first African American Captain America, it may seem that Butler's essay is a dusty old period piece and not terribly relevant to today's world. But look carefully at her critique. In a few short pages, Butler shows how white racism can creep into all corners of American culture – sometimes deliberately, sometimes unconsciously. She explores the excuses that white authors gave for ignoring blacks and other minorities, these authors' resentment at being asked to diversify their stories, and the phenomenon of what we might call "anti-anti-racist" backlash. She also reflects on some of the recent progress she had seen. Do elements of her critique resonate with you? Are some of the phenomena she describes still with us? Did you learn anything surprising? Did you find yourself agreeing with her analysis? Disagreeing?*

Fourteen years ago, during my first year of college, I sat in a creative writing class and listened as my teacher, an elderly man, told another student not to use black characters in his stories unless those characters' blackness was somehow essential to the plots. The presence of blacks, my teacher felt, changed the focus of a story – drew attention from the intended subject.

This happened in 1965. I would never have expected to hear my teacher's sentiments echoed by a science fiction writer in 1979. Hear them I did, though, at an SF convention where a writer explained that he had decided against using a black character in one of his stories because the presence of the black would change his story somehow. Later, this same writer suggested that in stories that seem to require black characters to make some racial point, it might be possible to substitute extraterrestrials – so as not to dwell on matters of race.

Well, let's do a little dwelling.

Science fiction reaches into the future, the past, the human mind. It reaches out to other worlds and into other dimensions. Is it really so limited, then, that it cannot reach into the lives of ordinary everyday humans who happen not to be white?

Blacks, Asians, Hispanics, Amerindians, minority characters in general have been noticeably absent from most science fiction. Why? As a black and a science fiction writer, I've heard that question often. I've also heard several answers given. And, because most people try to be polite, there have been certain answers I haven't heard. That's all right. They're obvious.

Best, though, and most hopeful from my point of view, I've heard from people who want to write SF, or who've written a few pieces, perhaps, and who would like to include minority characters, but aren't sure how to go about it. Since I've had to solve the same problem in reverse, maybe I can help.

But first some answers to my question: Why have there been so few minority characters in science fiction?

Let's examine my teacher's reason. Are minority characters – black characters in this case – so disruptive a force that the mere presence of one alters a story, focuses it on race rather than whatever the author had in mind? Yes, in fact, black characters can do exactly that if the creators of those characters are too restricted in their thinking to visualize blacks in any other context.

This is the kind of stereotyping, conscious or subconscious, that women have fought for so long. No writer who regards blacks as people, human beings, with the usual variety of human concerns, flaws, skills, hopes, etc., would have trouble creating interesting backgrounds and goals for black characters. No writer who regards blacks as people would get sidetracked into justifying their blackness or their presence unless such justification honestly played a part in the story. It is no more necessary to focus on a character's blackness than it is to focus on a woman's femininity.

Now, what about the possibility of substituting extraterrestrials for blacks – in order to make some race-related point without making anyone... uncomfortable? In fact, why can't blacks be represented by whites who are not too thoroughly described, thus leaving readers free to use their imaginations and visualize whichever color they like?

I usually manage to go on being polite when I hear suggestions like these, but it's not easy.

All right, let's replace blacks with tentacled beings from Capella V. What will readers visualize as we describe relations between the Capellans and the (white) humans? Will they visualize black humans dealing with white humans? I don't think so. This is science fiction, after all. If you tell your readers about tentacled Capellans, they're going to visualize tentacled Capellans. And if your readers are as touchy about human races as you were afraid they might be when you substituted the Capellans, are they really likely to pay attention to any analogy you draw? I don't think so.

And as for whites representing all of humanity – on the theory that people will imagine other races; or better yet, on the theory that all people are alike anyway, so what does it matter? Well, remember when men represented all of humanity? Women didn't care much for it. Still don't. No great mental leap is required to understand why blacks, why any minority, might not care much for it either. And apart from all that, of course, it doesn't work. Whites represent themselves, and that's plenty. Spread the burden.

Back when *Star Wars* was new, a familiar excuse for ignoring minorities went something like this: "SF is escapist literature. Its readers/viewers don't want to be weighted down with real problems." War, okay. Planet-wide destruction, okay. Kidnapping, okay. But the sight of a minority person? Too heavy. Too real. And, of course, there again is the implication that a sprinkling of blacks, Asians, or others could turn the story into some sort of racial statement. The only statement I could imagine being made by such a sprinkling would be that among the white, human people; the tall, furry people; the lumpy, scaly people; the tentacled people, etc., were also brown, human people; black, human people, etc. This isn't a heavy statement – unless it's missing.

From my agent (whose candor I appreciate) I heard what could become an even stronger reason for not using black characters in particular – not using them in film, anyway. It seems that blacks are out of fashion. In an industry that pays a great deal of attention to trends, blacks have had their day for a while. How long a while? Probably until someone decides to take a chance, and winds up making a damn big hit movie about blacks.

All right, forget for a moment the faddishness of the movie industry. Forget that movies about blacks are out. Movies, SF and otherwise, with a sprinkling of minority characters, but no particular minority theme, seem to do well. Yaphet Kotto certainly didn't do *Alien* any harm. In fact, for me, probably for a good many blacks, he gave the movie an extra touch of authenticity. And a monster movie – even a good monster movie – needs all the authenticity it can get.

That brings me to another question I hear often at SF conventions. "Why are there so few black SF writers?" I suspect for the same reason there were once so few women SF writers. Women found a certain lack of authenticity in a genre that postulated a universe largely populated by men, in which all the power was in male hands, and women stayed in their male-defined places.

Blacks find a certain lack of authenticity in a genre which postulates a universe largely populated by whites, in which the power is in white hands, and blacks are occasional oddities.

SF writers come from SF readers, generally. Few readers equal few writers. The situation is improving, however. Blacks are not as likely as whites to spend time and money going to conventions, but there is a growing black readership. Black people I meet now are much more likely to have read at least some science fiction, and are not averse to reading more. My extra copy of *Dreamsnake* (by Vonda McIntyre) has reached its fifth reader, last I heard. Movies like *Alien*, *Star Wars* (in spite of its lack), and *Close Encounters of the Third Kind*, plus the old *Star Trek* TV series, have captured a lot of interest, too. With all this, it's been a pleasantly long time since a friend or acquaintance has muttered to me, "Science fiction! How can you waste your time with anything that unreal?"

Now to those reasons people aren't as likely to give for leaving minorities out of SF: The most obvious one, and the one I feel least inclined to discuss, is conscious racism. It exists. I don't think SF is greatly afflicted with it, but then, racism is unfashionable now, and thus is unlikely to be brought into the open. Instead, it can be concealed behind any of the questions and arguments I've already discussed. To the degree that it is, this whole article is a protest against racism. It's as much of a protest as I intend to make at the moment. I know of too many bright, competent blacks who have had to waste time and energy trying to reason away other people's unreasonable racist attitudes: in effect, trying to prove their humanity. Life is too short.

A more insidious problem than outright racism is simply habit, custom. SF has always been nearly all white, just as until recently, it's been nearly all male. A lot of people had a chance to get comfortable with things as they are. Too comfortable. SF, more than any other genre, deals with change – change in science and technology, social change. But SF itself changes slowly, often under protest. You can still go to conventions and hear deliberately sexist remarks – if the speaker thinks he has a sympathetic audience. People resent being told their established way of doing things is wrong, resent being told they should change, and strongly resent being told they won't be alone any longer in the vast territory – the universe – they've staked out for themselves. I don't think anyone seriously believes the present world is all white. But custom can be strong enough to prevent people from seeing the need for SF to reflect a more realistic view.

Adherence to custom can also cause people to oppose change by becoming even more extreme in their customary behavior. I went back to college for a couple of quarters a few years ago and found one male teacher after another announcing with odd belligerence, "I might as well tell you right now, I'm a male chauvinist!"

A custom attacked is a custom that will be defended. Men who feel defensive about sexist behavior may make sexist bigots of themselves. Whites who feel defensive about racist behavior may make racist bigots of themselves. It's something for people who value open-mindedness and progressive attitudes to beware of.

A second insidious problem is laziness, possibly combined with ignorance. Authors who have always written of all-white universes might not feel particularly threatened by a multicolored one, but might consider the change too much trouble. After all, they already know how to do what they've been doing. Their way works. Why change? Besides, maybe they don't know any minority people. How can they write about people they don't know?

Of course, ignorance may have a category unto itself. I've heard people I don't consider lazy, racist, or bound by custom complain that they did not know enough about minorities and thus hesitated to write about them. Often, these people seem worried about accidentally giving offense.

But what do authors ordinarily do when they decide to write about an unfamiliar subject?

They research. They read – in this case recent biographies and autobiographies of people in the group they want to write about are good. They talk to members of that group – friends, acquaintances, co-workers, fellow students, even strangers on buses or waiting in lines. I've done these things myself in my reverse research, and they help. Also, I people-watch a lot without talking. Any public situation offers opportunities.

Some writers have gotten around the need for research by setting their stories in distant egalitarian futures when cultural differences have dwindled and race has ceased to matter. I created a future like this in my novel, *Patternmaster*, though I did not do it to avoid research. *Patternmaster* takes place in a time when psionic ability is all that counts. People who have enough of that ability are on top whether they're male or female, black, white, or brown. People who have none are slaves. In this culture, a black like the novel's main woman character would, except for her coloring, be indistinguishable from characters of any other race. Using this technique could get a writer accused of writing blacks as though they were whites in Coppertone, and it could be a lazy writer's excuse for doing just that. But for someone who has a legitimate reason for using it, a story that requires it, it can be a perfectly valid technique.

More important than any technique, however, is for authors to remember that they are writing about *people*. Authors who forget this, who do not relax and get comfortable with their racially different characters, can wind up creating unbelievable, self-consciously manipulated puppets; pieces of furniture who exist within a story but contribute nothing to it; or stereotypes guaranteed to be offensive.

There was a time when most of the few minority characters in SF fell into one of these categories. One of the first black characters I ran across when I began reading SF in the fifties was a saintly old "uncle" (I'm not being sarcastic here. The man was described as saintly and portrayed asking to be called "uncle") whom Harriet Beecher Stowe would have felt right at home with. I suspect that like the Sidney Poitier movies of the sixties, Uncle was daring for his time. That didn't help me find him any more believable or feel any less pleased when he and his kind (Charlie Chan, Tonto, that little guy who swiped Fritos…) were given decent burials. Times have changed, thank heavens, and SF has come a long way from Uncle. Clearly, though, it still has a long way to go.

The Attention Merchants

Tim Wu

Introduction to Tim Wu, *The Attention Merchants: The Epic Scramble to Get Inside Our Heads*. New York: Knopf, 2016, pp. 3-7. Slightly edited.

Tim Wu *(b. 1972) is an American attorney, legal scholar, political figure, and the Julius Silver Professor of Law, Science and Technology at the Columbia Law School. He is best known for coining the term "net neutrality" in 2002 and advocating for open and equal access to the Internet. He is a major figure in the revitalization of American antitrust politics and is critical of the growing power of the major tech companies. Wu argues that the concentration of power in the hands of a few large corporations leads to the rise of populism, divisive forms of nationalism, and the growing popularity of extremist politicians.*

Why we are reading this: *Our life experience depends on what we pay attention to and spend our time on. But what, or who, commands our attention? We like to think we are free to apportion our time and attention as we wish, but to what extent is this really true? In his 2016 book* The Attention Merchants, *Tim Wu argues that for over a century powerful corporate and government interests have been working to grab our attention and shape our behavior through things like propaganda campaigns, newspaper ads, TV commercials, website pop-ups, clickbait, and even advertising campaigns inside public schools. Wu is concerned that "we are at risk of being not merely informed but manipulated and even deceived by ads... of living lives that are less fully our own than we imagine." He wrote the book, he explains, with "the basic objective of making apparent the influence of economic ambition and power on how we experience our lives." The excerpt below comes from the introduction to Wu's book and it provides a taste of his argument. Do any of the examples mentioned below bother you, or are you okay with it? Is your attention really being bought and sold without your awareness or consent? Is it worthwhile to try to establish mastery over your own attention? How might one do this?*

In 2011, the Twin Rivers school district in central California faced a tough situation. The district, never wealthy, was hit hard by the housing crisis of the early 2000s and the state government's own financial meltdown. By the 2010s, schools were cutting not only extracurricular activities but even some of the basics, like heat. One day in winter, a student posted a picture of a classroom thermostat reading 44 degrees Fahrenheit.

Such were the circumstances when the Twin Rivers board was approached by a company named "Education Funding Partners." EFP offered a tantalizing new way to help solve the district's financial problems, using what it called "the power of business to transform public education." Acting as broker, the firm promised that it could bring the district as much as $500,000 in private money per year. And, EFP stressed, its services would cost nothing. "EFP is paid solely out of corporate contributions," the pitch explained, "essentially providing a free service to districts."

To gain this free bounty, the board didn't actually have to do anything. It needed only to understand something: that the schools were already holding an asset more lucrative than any bake sale. That asset, simply stated, was their students, who by the very nature of compulsory education were a captive audience. If the schools could seize their attention for the purpose of educating them, why not sell off a bit of it for the sake of improving the educational experience? Specifically, EFP was proposing that Twin Rivers allow corporate advertising within the schools. Moreover, EFP explained, it would bundle students from Twin Rivers with those in other school districts around the nation so as to appeal to bigger brands – the Fortune 500 companies – with deeper pockets.

If EFP was promising the district free money, its pitch to corporate advertisers was no less seductive: "Open the schoolhouse doors," it said, promising "authentic access and deep engagement with audiences in the school environment." Advertisers have long coveted direct access to the young, who are impressionable and easier to influence. Establishing a warm association with Coca-Cola or McDonald's at an early age can yield payoffs that last a lifetime – or, in the lingo, "drive purchase decisions and build brand awareness." That in essence is what EFP offered its clients: "an unparalleled system for engagement in the K-12 market" – a chance to mold the consumers of the future.

Twin Rivers soon began to see the light. "We need to be innovative about the assets we have and learn how to bring in more revenue," said a spokeswoman. In other parts of the country, the prospect of opening schools to commercial advertising had prompted public debate. Not so in Twin Rivers, where the administrators seemed to regard signing the deal, which they did in 2012, as a matter of duty. "In these challenging economic times," said the chief business officer, "our students are counting on us to find ways to make our resources stretch further than ever before." EFP, for its part, promised all messaging would be "responsible" and "educational." With that, the school doors were thrown open.

Twin Rivers is only one of the many school districts in the United States – mostly in poor or middle-class areas – that have begun to rely on selling access to their students as an essential revenue source. Some schools plaster ads across student lockers and hallway floors. One board in Florida cut a deal to put the McDonald's logo on its report cards (good grades qualified you for a free Happy Meal). In recent years, many have installed large screens in their hallways that pair school announcements with commercials. "Take your school to the digital age" is the motto of one screen provider: "everyone benefits."

What is perhaps most shocking about the introduction of advertising into public schools is just how uncontroversial and indeed logical it has seemed to those involved. The deals are seen as a win-win, yielding money that it would be almost irresponsible to refuse. Yet things were not always this way. There was once a time when, whether by convention or technological limitation, many parts of life – home, school, and social interaction among them – were sanctuaries, sheltered from advertising and commerce. Over the last century, however, we have come to accept a very different way of being, whereby nearly every bit of our lives is commercially exploited to the extent it can be. As adults, we are hardly ever unreachable; seldom away from a screen of some kind; rarely not being solicited or sold to. From this perspective, the school administrators are merely giving students a lesson in reality, exposing them to what is, after all, the norm for adults. But where did the norm come from? And how normal is it?

Our current state of affairs is the consequence of the dramatic and impressive rise of an industry that barely existed a century ago: the Attention Merchants. Since its inception, the attention industry, in its many forms, has asked and gained more and more of our waking moments, albeit always, in exchange for new conveniences and diversions, creating a grand bargain that has transformed our lives. In the process, as a society and individually, we have accepted a life experience that is in all of its dimensions – economic, political, social, any way you can think of – mediated as never before in human history. And if each bargain in isolation seems a win-win, in their grand totality they have come to exert a more ambiguous though profound influence on how we live.

Who exactly are the attention merchants? As an industry, they are relatively new. Their lineage can be traced to the nineteenth century, when in New York City the first newspapers fully dependent on advertising were created; and Paris, where a dazzling new kind of commercial art first seized the eyes of the person in the street. But the full potential of the business model by which attention is converted into revenue would not be fully understood until the early twentieth century, when the power of mass attention was discovered not by any commercial entity but by British war propagandists. The disastrous consequences of propaganda in two world wars would taint the subsequent use of such methods by government, at least in the West. Industry, however, took note of what captive attention could accomplish, and since that time has treated it as a precious resource, paying ever larger premiums for it.

If the attention merchants were once primitive, one-man operations, the game of harvesting human attention and reselling it to advertisers has become a major part of our economy. I use the crop metaphor because attention has been widely recognized as a commodity, like wheat, pork bellies, or crude oil. Existing industries have long depended on it to drive sales. And the new industries of the twentieth century turned it into a form of currency they could mint. Beginning with radio, each new medium would attain its commercial viability through the resale of what attention it could capture in exchange for its "free" content.

As we shall see, the winning strategy from the beginning has been to seek out time and spaces previously walled off from commercial exploitation, gathering up chunks and then slivers of our un-harvested awareness. Within living memory it was thought that families would never tolerate the intrusion of broadcasting in the home. An earlier generation would find it astonishing that, without payment or even much outcry, our networks of family, friends, and associates have been recruited via social media to help sell us things. Now, however, most of us carry devices on our bodies that constantly find ways to commercialize the smallest particles of our time and attention. Thus, bit by bit, what was once shocking became normal, until the shape of our lives yielded further and further to the logic of commerce – but gradually enough that we should now find nothing strange about it.

I'd like to pose at the outset the cynic's eternal question: What difference does the rise of the Attention Merchants make to me? Why should I care? Quite simply because this industry, whose very business is the influence of consciousness, can and will radically shape how our lives are lived.

It is no coincidence that ours is a time afflicted by a widespread sense of attentional crisis, at least in the West – one captured by the phrase "homo distractus," a species of ever shorter attention span known for compulsively checking his devices. Who has not sat down to read an email, only to end up on a long flight of ad-laden clickbaited fancy, and emerge, shaking his or her head, wondering where the hours went?

While allowing that many of us are perpetually distracted, spend too much time on social media or watching television, and consequently consume more advertising than could ever serve our own useful purposes, the cynic may still ask: But isn't it simply our choice to live this way? Of course it is – it is we who have voluntarily, or somewhat voluntarily, entered into this grand bargain with the attentional industry, and we enjoy the benefits. But it is essential that we fully understand the deal. Certainly some of our daily attentional barters – for news, good entertainment, or useful services – are good deals. But others are not. My purpose is less to persuade you one way or the other, but to get you to see the terms plainly, and, seeing them plainly, demand bargains that reflect the life you want to live.

For the history also reveals that we are hardly powerless in our dealings with the attention merchants. Individually, we have the power to ignore, tune out, and unplug. At certain times over the last century, the industry has asked too much and offered too little in return, or even been seen to violate the public's trust outright. At such moments, the bargain of the attention merchants is beset with a certain "disenchantment," which, if popular grievance is great enough, can sometimes turn into a full-fledged "revolt." During those revolts – of which there have been several over the last century – the attention merchants and their partners in the advertising industry have been obliged to present a new deal, revise the terms of the arrangement. We may, in fact, be living in such a time today, at least in those segments of the population committed to cord-cutting, ad-avoiding, or unplugging. We are certainly at an appropriate time to think seriously about what it might mean to reclaim our collective consciousness.

Ultimately, it is not our nation or culture but the very nature of our lives that is at stake. For how we spend the brutally limited resource of our attention will determine those lives to a degree most of us may prefer not to think about. As William James observed, we must reflect that, when we reach the end of our days, our life experience will equal what we have paid attention to, whether by choice or default. We are at risk, without quite fully realizing it, of living lives that are less our own than we imagine. We need to understand more clearly how the deal went down and what it means for all of us.

The Apology

Plato

From *Plato: Complete Works*. Translated by G. M. A. Grube and edited by John M. Cooper. Indianapolis: Hackett Publishing Company, 1997.

We have already met **Plato** *(429-347 BCE) as the author of the* Allegory of the Cave. *In the* Apology, *perhaps Plato's most widely read work, he provides an account of what his mentor Socrates said in self-defense when he was on trial in 399 BCE on charges of impiety ("not believing in the gods in whom the city believes, but in other new spiritual things") and corruption of the youth of Athens. The text indicates that Plato attended his teacher's trial.*

Why we are reading this: *First, let's deal with a common misunderstanding about the name of this work. As you will see, Socrates was defiant and did not apologize for his actions; instead, he tries to justify what he had done. In ancient Greek, "apologia" referred to a speech in defense of something, a justification, a well-reasoned reply. This remained true when the word was borrowed into Latin and later English in the early 1400s; this meaning informs the related word "apologetics." The sense of "an expression of regret" did not become the main meaning of "apology" in English until about the 1700s. To avoid confusion, many scholars refer to Socrates' speech as the "Apologia."*

The trial and execution of Socrates (by forced drinking of hemlock) has generated controversy for centuries. Some describe it as the prosecution of an innocent man on trumped-up charges, a travesty of justice perpetrated by Socrates' political enemies, or a case of mob violence. Athens was in crisis in 399 BCE, having recently lost the Peloponnesian War (431-404 BCE) and endured the murderous rule of the Thirty Tyrants (404-403 BCE). The trial of Socrates may have been part of a settling of scores. Others argue that the people of Athens may have had good reasons to convict Socrates, given the beliefs at the time. If the city's recent calamities were believed to be a form of retribution by the gods, then it might seem dangerous to allow people like Socrates to encourage skepticism, freethinking, and disrespect for religious figures and traditional religious practice.

We can read the Apology *as a historical source that provides clues about life in ancient Greece – trial procedures, politics, religious views, ideas about death, and other matters. On another level, the* Apology *is a foundational text dealing with how humans create, evaluate, and critique knowledge. Socrates (or is it really Plato?) outlines the critical importance of inquisitive skepticism and questioning as a path towards knowledge. Socrates was fueled by the conviction that there is always more to understand, that one must begin by admitting one's own ignorance, and that wisdom consists in not pretending to know what one does not know. For Socrates, nothing in human life is more important than the pursuit of wisdom and truth. As he notes in his famous dictum: "the unexamined life is not worth living."*

[*As the text begins, a jury of five hundred men has heard from Socrates' three accusers.*]

SOCRATES: I do not know, men of Athens, how my accusers affected you; as for me, I was almost carried away in spite of myself, so persuasively did they speak. And yet, hardly anything of what they said is true. Of the many lies they told, one in particular surprised me, namely that you should be careful not to be deceived by an accomplished speaker like me. That they were not ashamed to be immediately proved wrong by the facts, when I show myself not to be an accomplished speaker at all, that I thought was most shameless on their part – unless indeed they call an accomplished speaker the man who speaks the truth. If they mean that, I would agree that I am an orator, but not after their manner, for indeed, as I say, practically nothing they said was true. From me you will hear the whole truth, though not, by Zeus, gentlemen, expressed in embroidered and stylized phrases like theirs, but things spoken at random and expressed in the first words that come to mind, for I put my trust in the justice of what I say, and let none of you expect anything else. It would not be fitting at my age, as it might be for a young man, to toy with words when I appear before you.

One thing I do ask and beg of you, gentlemen: if you hear me making my defense in the same kind of language as I am accustomed to use in the market place by the bankers' tables, where many of you have heard me, and elsewhere, do not be surprised or create a disturbance on that account. The position is this: this is my first appearance in a lawcourt, at the age of seventy; I am therefore simply a stranger to the manner of speaking here. Just as if I were really a stranger, you would certainly excuse me if I spoke in that dialect and manner in which I had been brought up, so too my present request seems a just one, for you to pay no attention to my manner of speech – be it better or worse – but to concentrate your attention on whether what I say is just or not, for the excellence of a judge lies in this, as that of a speaker lies in telling the truth.

It is right for me, gentlemen, to defend myself first against the first lying accusations made against me and my first accusers, and then against the later accusations and the later accusers. There have been many who have accused me to you for many years now, and none of their accusations are true. These I fear much more than I fear Anytus and his friends, though they too are formidable. These earlier ones, however, are more so, gentlemen; they got hold of most of you from childhood, persuaded you and accused me quite falsely, saying that there is a man called Socrates, a wise man, a student of all things in the sky and below the earth, who makes the worse argument the stronger. Those who spread that rumor, gentlemen, are my dangerous accusers, for their hearers believe that those who study these things do not even believe in the gods. Moreover, these accusers are numerous, and have been at it a long time; also, they spoke to you at an age when you would most readily believe them, some of you being children and adolescents, and they won their case by default, as there was no defense.

What is most absurd in all this is that one cannot even know or mention their names unless one of them is a writer of comedies.[1] Those who maliciously and slanderously persuaded you – who also, when persuaded themselves then persuaded others – all those are most difficult to deal with: one cannot bring one of them into court or refute him; one must simply fight with shadows, as it were, in making one's defense, and cross-examine when no one answers. I want you to realize too that my accusers are of two kinds: those who have accused me recently, and the old ones I mention; and to think that I must first defend myself against the latter, for you have also heard their accusations first, and to a much greater extent than the more recent.

Very well then, men of Athens. I must surely defend myself and attempt to uproot from your minds in so short a time the slander that has resided there so long. I wish this may happen, if it is in any way better for you and me, and that my defense may be successful, but I think this is very difficult and I am fully aware of how difficult it is. Even so, let the matter proceed as the god may wish, but I must obey the law and make my defense.

Let us then take up the case from its beginning. What is the accusation from which arose the slander in which Meletus trusted when he wrote out the charge against me? What did they say when they slandered me? I must, as if they were my actual prosecutors, read the affidavit they would have sworn. It goes something like this: Socrates is guilty of wrongdoing in that he busies himself studying things in the sky and below the earth; he makes the worse into the stronger argument, and he teaches these same things to others. You have seen this yourself in the comedy of Aristophanes, a

---

[1] This is Aristophanes. Socrates refers later to his character in his *Clouds*, first produced in 423 BC. [note by John M. Cooper, JMC]

Socrates swinging about there, saying he was walking on air and talking a lot of other nonsense about things of which I know nothing at all. I do not speak in contempt of such knowledge, if someone is wise in these things – lest Meletus bring more cases against me – but, gentlemen, I have no part in it, and on this point I call upon the majority of you as witnesses. I think it right that all those of you who have heard me conversing, and many of you have, should tell each other if anyone of you has ever heard me discussing such subjects to any extent at all. From this you will learn that the other things said about me by the majority are of the same kind.

Not one of them is true. And if you have heard from anyone that I undertake to teach people and charge a fee for it, that is not true either. Yet I think it a fine thing to be able to teach people as Gorgias of Leontini does, and Prodicus of Ceos, and Hippias of Elis.[2] Each of these men can go to any city and persuade the young, who can keep company with anyone of their own fellow citizens they want without paying, to leave the company of these, to join with themselves, pay them a fee, and be grateful to them besides. Indeed, I learned that there is another wise man from Paros who is visiting us, for I met a man who has spent more money on Sophists than everybody else put together, Callias, the son of Hipponicus. So I asked him – he has two sons – "Callias," I said, "if your sons were colts or calves, we could find and engage a supervisor for them who would make them excel in their proper qualities, some horse breeder or farmer. Now since they are men, whom do you have in mind to supervise them? Who is an expert in this kind of excellence, the human and social kind? I think you must have given thought to this since you have sons. Is there such a person," I asked, "or is there not?" "Certainly there is," he said. "Who is he?" I asked, "What is his name, where is he from? and what is his fee?" "His name, Socrates, is Evenus, he comes from Paros, and his fee is five minas." I thought Evenus a happy man, if he really possesses this art, and teaches for so moderate a fee. Certainly I would pride and preen myself if I had this knowledge, but I do not have it, gentlemen.

One of you might perhaps interrupt me and say: "But Socrates, what is your occupation? From where have these slanders come? For surely if you did not busy yourself with something out of the common, all these rumors and talk would not have arisen unless you did something other than most people. Tell us what it is, that we may not speak inadvisedly about you." Anyone who says that seems to be right, and I will try to show you what has caused this reputation and slander. Listen then. Perhaps some of

---

[2] These were all well-known Sophists. For Gorgias and Hippias see Plato's dialogues named after them; both Hippias and Prodicus appear in *Protagoras*. [JMC]

you will think I am jesting, but be sure that all that I shall say is true. What has caused my reputation is none other than a certain kind of wisdom. What kind of wisdom? Human wisdom, perhaps. It may be that I really possess this, while those whom I mentioned just now are wise with a wisdom more than human; else I cannot explain it, for I certainly do not possess it, and whoever says I do is lying and speaks to slander me. Do not create a disturbance, gentlemen, even if you think I am boasting, for the story I shall tell does not originate with me, but I will refer you to a trustworthy source. I shall call upon the god at Delphi as witness to the existence and nature of my wisdom, if it be such. You know Chaerephon. He was my friend from youth, and the friend of most of you, as he shared your exile and your return. You surely know the kind of man he was, how impulsive in any course of action. He went to Delphi at one time and ventured to ask the oracle – as I say, gentlemen, do not create a disturbance – he asked if any man was wiser than I, and the Pythian replied that no one was wiser. Chaerephon is dead, but his brother will testify to you about this.

Consider that I tell you this because I would inform you about the origin of the slander. When I heard of this reply I asked myself: "Whatever does the god mean? What is his riddle? I am very conscious that I am not wise at all; what then does he mean by saying that I am the wisest? For surely he does not lie; it is not legitimate for him to do so." For a long time I was at a loss as to his meaning; then I very reluctantly turned to some such investigation as this: I went to one of those reputed wise, thinking that there, if anywhere, I could refute the oracle and say to it: "This man is wiser than I, but you said I was." Then, when I examined this man – there is no need for me to tell you his name, he was one of our public men – my experience was something like this: I thought that he appeared wise to many people and especially to himself, but he was not. I then tried to show him that he thought himself wise, but that he was not. As a result he came to dislike me, and so did many of the bystanders. So I withdrew and thought to myself: "I am wiser than this man; it is likely that neither of us knows anything worthwhile, but he thinks he knows something when he does not, whereas when I do not know, neither do I think I know; so I am likely to be wiser than he to this small extent, that I do not think I know what I do not know." After this I approached another man, one of those thought to be wiser than he, and I thought the same thing, and so I came to be disliked both by him and by many others.

After that I proceeded systematically. I realized, to my sorrow and alarm, that I was getting unpopular, but I thought that I must attach the greatest importance to the god's oracle, so I must go to all those who had any reputation for knowledge to examine its meaning. And by the dog, gentlemen of the jury – for I must tell you the truth – I experienced something like this: in my investigation in the service of the god I found that those who had the highest reputation were nearly the most deficient, while those who were thought to be inferior were more knowledgeable. I must give you an account of my journeyings as if they were labors I had undertaken to prove the oracle irrefutable. After the politicians, I went to the poets, the writers of tragedies and dithyrambs and the others, intending in their case to catch myself being more ignorant than they. So I took up those poems with which they seemed to have taken most trouble and asked them what they meant, in order that I might at the same time learn something from them. I am ashamed to tell you the truth, gentlemen, but I must. Almost all the bystanders might have explained the poems better than their authors could. I soon realized that poets do not compose their poems with knowledge, but by some inborn talent and by inspiration, like seers and prophets who also say many fine things without any understanding of what they say. The poets seemed to me to have had a similar experience. At the same time I saw that, because of their poetry, they thought themselves very wise men in other respects, which they were not. So there again I withdrew, thinking that I had the same advantage over them as I had over the politicians.

Finally I went to the craftsmen, for I was conscious of knowing practically nothing, and I knew that I would find that they had knowledge of many fine things. In this I was not mistaken; they knew things I did not know, and to that extent they were wiser than I. But, gentlemen of the jury, the good craftsmen seemed to me to have the same fault as the poets: each of them, because of his success at his craft, thought himself very wise in other most important pursuits, and this error of theirs overshadowed the wisdom they had, so that I asked myself, on behalf of the oracle, whether I should prefer to be as I am, with neither their wisdom nor their ignorance, or to have both. The answer I gave myself and the oracle was that it was to my advantage to be as I am.

As a result of this investigation, gentlemen of the jury, I acquired much unpopularity, of a kind that is hard to deal with and is a heavy burden; many slanders came from these people and a reputation for wisdom, for in each case the bystanders thought that I myself possessed the wisdom that I proved that my interlocutor did not have. What is probable, gentlemen, is that in fact the god is wise and that his oracular response meant that human wisdom is worth little or nothing, and that when he says this man, Socrates, he is using my name as an example, as if he said: "This man among you, mortals, is wisest who, like Socrates, understands that his wisdom is worthless." So even now I continue this investigation as the god bade me – and I go around seeking out anyone, citizen or stranger, whom

I think wise. Then if I do not think he is, I come to the assistance of the god and show him that he is not wise. Because of this occupation, I do not have the leisure to engage in public affairs to any extent, nor indeed to look after my own, but I live in great poverty because of my service to the god.

Furthermore, the young men who follow me around of their own free will, those who have most leisure, the sons of the very rich, take pleasure in hearing people questioned; they themselves often imitate me and try to question others. I think they find an abundance of men who believe they have some knowledge but know little or nothing. The result is that those whom they question are angry, not with themselves but with me. They say: "That man Socrates is a pestilential fellow who corrupts the young." If one asks them what he does and what he teaches to corrupt them, they are silent, as they do not know, but, so as not to appear at a loss, they mention those accusations that are available against all philosophers, about "things in the sky and things below the earth," about "not believing in the gods" and "making the worse the stronger argument;" they would not want to tell the truth, I'm sure, that they have been proved to lay claim to knowledge when they know nothing. These people are ambitious, violent and numerous; they are continually and convincingly talking about me; they have been filling your ears for a long time with vehement slanders against me. From them Meletus attacked me, and Anytus and Lycon, Meletus being vexed on behalf of the poets, Anytus on behalf of the craftsmen and the politicians, Lycon on behalf of the orators, so that, as I started out by saying, I should be surprised if I could rid you of so much slander in so short a time. That, gentlemen of the jury, is the truth for you. I have hidden or disguised nothing. I know well enough that this very conduct makes me unpopular, and this is proof that what I say is true, that such is the slander against me, and that such are its causes. If you look into this either now or later, this is what you will find.

Let this suffice as a defense against the charges of my earlier accusers. After this I shall try to defend myself against Meletus, that good and patriotic man, as he says he is, and my later accusers. As these are a different lot of accusers, let us again take up their sworn deposition. It goes something like this: Socrates is guilty of corrupting the young and of not believing in the gods in whom the city believes, but in other new spiritual things. Such is their charge. Let us examine it point by point.

He says that I am guilty of corrupting the young, but I say that Meletus is guilty of dealing frivolously with serious matters, of irresponsibly bringing people into court, and of professing to be seriously concerned with things about none of which he has ever cared, and I shall try to prove that this is so. Come here and tell me, Meletus. Surely you consider it of the greatest importance that our young men be as good as possible? – Indeed I do.

Come then, tell the jury who improves them. You obviously know, in view of your concern. You say you have discovered the one who corrupts them, namely me, and you bring me here and accuse me to the jury. Come, inform the jury and tell them who it is. You see, Meletus, that you are silent and know not what to say. Does this not seem shameful to you and a sufficient proof of what I say, that you have not been concerned with any of this? Tell me, my good sir, who improves our young men?

MELETUS: The laws.

SOCRATES: That is not what I am asking, but what person who has knowledge of the laws to begin with?

MELETUS: These jurymen, Socrates.

SOCRATES: How do you mean, Meletus? Are these able to educate the young and improve them?

MELETUS: Certainly.

SOCRATES: All of them, or some but not others?

MELETUS: All of them.

SOCRATES: Very good, by Hera. You mention a great abundance of benefactors. But what about the audience? Do they improve the young or not?

MELETUS: They do, too.

SOCRATES: What about the members of Council?

MELETUS: The Councilors, also.

SOCRATES: But, Meletus, what about the assembly? Do members of the assembly corrupt the young, or do they all improve them?

MELETUS: They improve them.

SOCRATES: All the Athenians, it seems, make the young into fine good men, except me, and I alone corrupt them. Is that what you mean?

MELETUS: That is most definitely what I mean.

SOCRATES: You condemn me to a great misfortune. Tell me: does this also apply to horses do you think? That all men improve them and one individual corrupts them? Or is quite the contrary true, one individual is able to improve them, or very few, namely the horse breeders, whereas the majority, if they have horses and use them, corrupt them? Is that not the case, Meletus, both with horses and all other animals? Of course it is, whether you and Anytus say so or not. It would be a very happy state of affairs if only one person corrupted our youth, while the others improved them.

You have made it sufficiently obvious, Meletus, that you have never had any concern for our youth; you show your indifference clearly; that you have given no thought to the subjects about which you bring me to trial.

And by Zeus, Meletus, tell us also whether it is better for a man to live among good or wicked fellow-citizens. Answer, my good man, for I am not asking a difficult question. Do not the wicked do some harm to those who are ever closest to them, whereas good people benefit them?

MELETUS: Certainly.

SOCRATES: And does the man exist who would rather be harmed than benefited by his associates? Answer, my good sir, for the law orders you to answer. Is there any man who wants to be harmed?

MELETUS: Of course not.

SOCRATES: Come now, do you accuse me here of corrupting the young and making them worse deliberately or unwillingly?

MELETUS: Deliberately.

SOCRATES: What follows, Meletus? Are you so much wiser at your age than I am at mine that you understand that wicked people always do some harm to their closest neighbors while good people do them good, but I have reached such a pitch of ignorance that I do not realize this, namely that if I make one of my associates wicked I run the risk of being harmed by him so that I do such a great evil deliberately, as you say? I do not believe you, Meletus, and I do not think anyone else will. Either I do not corrupt the young or, if I do, it is unwillingly, and you are lying in either case. Now if I corrupt them unwillingly, the law does not require you to bring people to court for such unwilling wrongdoings, but to get hold of them privately, to instruct them and exhort them; for clearly, if I learn better, I shall cease to do what I am doing unwillingly. You, however, have avoided my company and were unwilling to instruct me, but you bring me here, where the law requires one to bring those who are in need of punishment, not of instruction.

And so, gentlemen of the jury, what I said is clearly true: Meletus has never been at all concerned with these matters. Nonetheless tell us, Meletus, how you say that I corrupt the young; or is it obvious from your deposition that it is by teaching them not to believe in the gods in whom the city believes but in other new spiritual things? Is this not what you say I teach and so corrupt them?

MELETUS: That is most certainly what I do say.

SOCRATES: Then by those very gods about whom we are talking, Meletus, make this clearer to me and to the jury: I cannot be sure whether you mean that I teach the belief that there are some gods – and therefore I myself believe that there are gods and am not altogether an atheist, nor am I guilty of that – not, however, the gods in whom the city believes, but others, and that this is the charge against me, that they are others. Or whether you mean that I do not believe in gods at all, and that this is what

I teach to others.

MELETUS: This is what I mean, that you do not believe in gods at all.

SOCRATES: You are a strange fellow, Meletus. Why do you say this? Do I not believe, as other men do, that the sun and the moon are gods?

MELETUS: No, by Zeus, gentlemen of the jury, for he says that the sun is stone, and the moon earth.

SOCRATES: My dear Meletus, do you think you are prosecuting Anaxagoras?[3] Are you so contemptuous of the jury and think them so ignorant of letters as not to know that the books of Anaxagoras of Clazomenae are full of those theories, and further, that the young men learn from me what they can buy from time to time for a drachma, at most, in the bookshops, and ridicule Socrates if he pretends that these theories are his own, especially as they are so absurd? Is that, by Zeus, what you think of me, Meletus, that I do not believe that there are any gods?

MELETUS: That is what I say, that you do not believe in the gods at all.

SOCRATES: You cannot be believed, Meletus, even, I think, by yourself. The man appears to me, gentlemen of the jury, highly insolent and uncontrolled. He seems to have made this deposition out of insolence, violence and youthful zeal. He is like one who composed a riddle and is trying it out: "Will the wise Socrates realize that I am jesting and contradicting myself, or shall I deceive him and others?" I think he contradicts himself in the affidavit, as if he said: "Socrates is guilty ofnot believing in gods but believing in gods," and surely that is the part of a jester!

Examine with me, gentlemen, how he appears to contradict himself, and you, Meletus, answer us. Remember, gentlemen, what I asked you when I began, not to create a disturbance if I proceed in my usual manner.

Does any man, Meletus, believe in human activities who does not believe in humans? Make him answer, and not again and again create a disturbance. Does any man who does not believe in horses believe in horsemen's activities? Or in flute-playing activities but not in flute-players? No, my good sir, no man could. If you are not willing to answer, I will tell you and the jury. Answer the next question, however. Does any man believe in spiritual activities who does not believe in spirits?

MELETUS: No one.

SOCRATES: Thank you for answering, if reluctantly, when these gentlemen made you. Now you say that I believe in spiritual things and

---

[3] Anaxagoras of Clazomenae (c. 510-c. 428) had theorized that heavenly objects like the sun, moon, and stars were not gods but physical objects made of stone or metal. By this point he had been dead almost thirty years. [Ed.]

teach about them, whether new or old, but at any rate spiritual things according to what you say, and to this you have sworn in your deposition. But if I believe in spiritual things I must quite inevitably believe in spirits. Is that not so? It is indeed. I shall assume that you agree, as you do not answer. Do we not believe spirits to be either gods or the children of gods? Yes or no?

MELETUS: Of course.

SOCRATES: Then since I do believe in spirits, as you admit, if spirits are gods, this is what I mean when I say you speak in riddles and in jest, as you state that I do not believe in gods and then again that I do, since I do believe in spirits. If on the other hand the spirits are children of the gods, bastard children of the gods by nymphs or some other mothers, as they are said to be, what man would believe children of the gods to exist, but not gods? That would be just as absurd as to believe the young of horses and asses, namely mules, to exist, but not to believe in the existence of horses and asses. You must have made this deposition, Meletus, either to test us or because you were at a loss to find any true wrongdoing of which to accuse me. There is no way in which you could persuade anyone of even small intelligence that it is possible for one and the same man to believe in spiritual but not also in divine things, and then again for that same man to believe neither in spirits nor in gods nor in heroes.

I do not think, men of Athens, that it requires a prolonged defense to prove that I am not guilty of the charges in Meletus' deposition, but this is sufficient. On the other hand, you know that what I said earlier is true, that I am very unpopular with many people. This will be my undoing, if I am undone, not Meletus or Anytus but the slanders and envy of many people. This has destroyed many other good men and will, I think, continue to do so. There is no danger that it will stop at me.

Someone might say: "Are you not ashamed, Socrates, to have followed the kind of occupation that has led to your being now in danger of death?" However, I should be right to reply to him: "You are wrong, sir, if you think that a man who is any good at all should take into account the risk of life or death; he should look to this only in his actions, whether what he does is right or wrong, whether he is acting like a good or a bad man." According to your view, all the heroes who died at Troy were inferior people, especially the son of Thetis[4] who was so contemptuous of danger compared with disgrace. When he was eager to kill Hector, his goddess mother warned him, as I believe, in some such words as these: "My child, if you avenge the death of your comrade, Patroclus, and you kill Hector, you will die yourself, for your death is to follow immediately after

---

[4] See *Iliad* xviii.94 ff. [JMC]. The "son of Thetis" refers to the hero Achilles. [Ed.]

Hector's." Hearing this, he despised death and danger and was much more afraid to live a coward who did not avenge his friends. "Let me die at once," he said, "when once I have given the wrongdoer his deserts, rather than remain here, a laughing-stock by the curved ships, a burden upon the earth." Do you think he gave thought to death and danger?

This is the truth of the matter, men of Athens: wherever a man has taken a position that he believes to be best, or has been placed by his commander, there he must I think remain and face danger, without a thought for death or anything else, rather than disgrace. It would have been a dreadful way to behave, gentlemen of the jury, if, at Potidaea, Amphipolis and Delium,[5] I had, at the risk of death, like anyone else, remained at my post where those you had elected to command had ordered me, and then, when the god ordered me, as I thought and believed, to live the life of a philosopher, to examine myself and others, I had abandoned my post for fear of death or anything else. That would have been a dreadful thing, and then I might truly have justly been brought here for not believing that there are gods, disobeying the oracle, fearing death, and thinking I was wise when I was not. To fear death, gentlemen, is no other than to think oneself wise when one is not, to think one knows what one does not know. No one knows whether death may not be the greatest of all blessings for a man, yet men fear it as if they knew that it is the greatest of evils. And surely it is the most blameworthy ignorance to believe thatone knows what one does not know. It is perhaps on this point and in this respect, gentlemen, that I differ from the majority of men, and if Iwere to claim that I am wiser than anyone in anything, it would be in this that as I have no adequate knowledge of things in the underworld, so I do not think I have. I do know, however, that it is wicked and shameful to do wrong, to disobey one's superior, be he god or man. I shall never fear or avoid things of which I do not know, whether they may not be good rather than things that I know to be bad. Even if you acquitted me now and did not believe Anytus, who said to you that either I should not have been brought here in the first place, or that now I am here, you cannot avoid executing me, for if I should be acquitted, your sons would practice the teachings of Socrates and all be thoroughly corrupted; if you said to me in this regard: "Socrates, we do not believe Anytus now; we acquit you, but only on condition that you spend no more time on this investigation and do not practice philosophy, and if you are caught doing so you will die;" if, as I say, you were to acquit me on those terms, I would say to you: "Men of Athens, I am grateful and I am your friend, but I will obey the god rather than you,

---

[5] Socrates was a veteran of the Peloponnesian War and had fought at the battles of Potidaea (432 BCE), Amphipolis (422 BCE), and Delium (424 BCE). [Ed.].

and as long as I draw breath and am able, I shall not cease to practice philosophy, to exhort you and in my usual way to point out to anyone of you whom I happen to meet: Good Sir, you are an Athenian, a citizen of the greatest city with the greatest reputation for both wisdom and power; are you not ashamed of your eagerness to possess as much wealth, reputation and honors as possible, while you do not care for nor give thought to wisdom or truth or the best possible state of your soul?" Then, if one of you disputes this and says he does care, I shall not let him go at once or leave him, but I shall question him, examine him and test him, and if I do not think he has attained the goodness that he says he has, I shall reproach him because he attaches little importance to the most important things and greater importance to inferior things. I shall treat in this way anyone I happen to meet, young and old, citizen and stranger, and more so the citizens because you are more kindred to me. Be sure that this is what the god orders me to do, and I think there is no greater blessing for the city than my service to the god. For I go around doing nothing but persuading both young and old among you not to care for your body or your wealth in preference to or as strongly as for the best possible state of your soul, as I say to you: "Wealth does not bring about excellence, but excellence makes wealth and everything else good for men, both individually and collectively."[6]

Now if by saying this I corrupt the young, this advice must be harmful, but if anyone says that I give different advice, he is talking nonsense. On this point I would say to you, gentlemen of the jury: "Whether you believe Anytus or not, whether you acquit me or not, do so on the understanding that this is my course of action, even if I am to face death many times." Do not create a disturbance, gentlemen, but abide by my request not to cry out at what I say but to listen, for I think it will be to your advantage to listen, and I am about to say other things at which you will perhaps cry out. By no means do this. Be sure that if you kill the sort of man I say I am, you will not harm me more than yourselves. Neither Meletus nor Anytus can harm me in any way; he could not harm me, for I do notthink it is permitted that a better man be harmed by a worse; certainly he might kill me, or perhaps banish or disfranchise me, which he and maybe others think to be great harm, but I do not think so. I think he is doing himself much greater harm doing what he is doing now, attempting to have a man executed unjustly. Indeed, gentlemen of the jury, I am far from making a defense now on my own behalf, as might be thought, but on yours, to

[6] Alternatively, this sentence could be translated: "Wealth does not bring about excellence, but excellence brings about wealth and all other public and private blessings for men." [JMC]

prevent you from wrongdoing by mistreating the god's gift to you by condemning me; for if you kill me you will not easily find another like me. I was attached to this city by the god – though it seems a ridiculous thing to say – as upon a great and noble horse which was somewhat sluggish because of its size and needed to be stirred up by a kind of gadfly. It is to fulfill some such function that I believe the god has placed me in the city. I never cease to rouse each and every one of you, to persuade and reproach you all day long and everywhere I find myself in your company.

Another such man will not easily come to be among you, gentlemen, and if you believe me you will spare me. You might easily be annoyed with me as people are when they are aroused from a doze, and strike out at me; if convinced by Anytus you could easily kill me, and then you could sleep on for the rest of your days, unless the god, in his care for you, sent you someone else. That I am the kind of person to be a gift of the god to the city you might realize from the fact that it does not seem like human nature for me to have neglected all my own affairs and to have tolerated this neglect now for so many years while I was always concerned with you, approaching each one of you like a father or an elder brother to persuade you to care for virtue. Now if I profited from this by charging a fee for my advice, there would be some sense to it, but you can see for yourselves that, for all their shameless accusations, my accusers have not been able in their impudence to bring forward a witness to say that I have ever received a fee or ever asked for one. I, on the other hand, have a convincing witness that I speak the truth, my poverty.

It may seem strange that while I go around and give this advice privately and interfere in private affairs, I do not venture to go to the assembly and there advise the city. You have heard me give the reason for this in many places. I have a divine or spiritual sign which Meletus has ridiculed in his deposition. This began when I was a child. It is a voice, and whenever it speaks it turns me away from something I am about to do, but it never encourages me to do anything. This is what has prevented me from taking part in public affairs, and I think it was quite right to prevent me. Be sure, gentlemen of the jury, that if I had long ago attempted to take part in politics, I should have died long ago, and benefited neither you nor myself. Do not be angry with me for speaking the truth; no man will survive who genuinely opposes you or any other crowd and prevents the occurrence of many unjust and illegal happenings in the city. A man who really fights for justice must lead a private, not a public, life if he is to survive for even a short time.

I shall give you great proofs of this, not words but what you esteem, deeds. Listen to what happened to me, that you may know that I will not yield to any man contrary to what is right, for fear of death, even if I should die at once for not yielding. The things I shall tell you are commonplace and smack of the lawcourts, but they are true. I have never held any other office in the city, but I served as a member of the Council, and our tribe Antiochis was presiding at the time when you wanted to try as a body the ten generals who had failed to pick up the survivors of the naval battle.[7] This was illegal, as you all recognized later. I was the only member of the presiding committee to oppose your doing something contrary to the laws, and I voted against it. The orators were ready to prosecute me and take me away; and your shouts were egging them on, but I thought I should run any risk on the side of law and justice rather than join you, for fear of prison or death, when you were engaged in an unjust course.

This happened when the city was still a democracy. When the oligarchy was established, the Thirty[8] summoned me to the Hall, along with four others, and ordered us to bring Leon from Salamis, that he might be executed. They gave many such orders to many people, in order to implicate as many as possible in their guilt. Then I showed again, not in words but in action, that, if it were not rather vulgar to say so, death is something I couldn't care less about, but that my whole concern is not to do anything unjust or impious. That government, powerful as it was, did not frighten me into any wrongdoing. When we left the Hall, the other four went to Salamis and brought in Leon, but I went home. I might have been put to death for this, had not the government fallen shortly afterwards. There are many who will witness to these events.

Do you think I would have survived all these years if I were engaged in public affairs and, acting as a good man must, came to the help of justice and considered this the most important thing? Far from it, gentlemen of the jury, nor would any other man. Throughout my life, in any public activity I may have engaged in, I am the same man as I am in private life. I have never come to an agreement with anyone to act unjustly, neither with anyone else nor with anyone of those who they slanderously say are my pupils. I have never been anyone's teacher. If anyone, young or old, desires to listen to me when I am talking and dealing with my own concerns, I have never begrudged this to anyone, but I do not converse when I receive a fee and not when I do not. I am equally ready to question the rich and the poor if anyone is willing to answer my questions and listen to what I say. And I cannot justly be held responsible for the good or bad

---

[7] This was the battle of Arginusae (south of Lesbos) in 406 BC, the last Athenian victory of the Peloponnesian war. A violent storm prevented the Athenians from rescuing the survivors. [JMC]

[8] This was the harsh oligarchy that was set up after the final defeat of Athens in 404 BC, and that ruled Athens for some nine months in 404-3 before the democracy was restored. [JMC]

conduct of these people, as I never promised to teach them anything and have not done so. If anyone says that he has learned anything from me, or that he heard anything privately that the others did not hear, be assured that he is not telling the truth.

Why then do some people enjoy spending considerable time in my company? You have heard why, men of Athens, I have told you the whole truth. They enjoy hearing those being questioned who think they are wise, but are not. And this is not unpleasant. To do this has, as I say, been enjoined upon me by the god, by means of oracles and dreams, and in every other way that a divine manifestation has ever ordered a man to do anything. This is true, gentlemen, and can easily be established.

If I corrupt some young men and have corrupted others, then surely some of them who have grown older and realized that I gave them bad advice when they were young should now themselves come up here to accuse me and avenge themselves. If they were unwilling to do so themselves, then some of their kindred, their fathers or brothers or other relations should recall it now if their family had been harmed by me. I see many of these present here, first Crito, my contemporary and fellow demesman,[9] the father of Critobulus here; next Lysanias of Sphettus, the father of Aeschines here; also Antiphon the Cephisian, the father of Epigenes; and others whose brothers spent their time in this way; Nicostratus, the son of Theozotides, brother of Theodotus, and Theodotus has died so he could not influence him; Paralius here, son of Demodocus, whose brother was Theages; there is Adeimantus, son of Ariston, brother of Plato here; Aeantodorus, brother of Apollodorus here.

I could mention many others, some one of whom surely Meletus should have brought in as witness in his own speech. If he forgot to do so, then let him do it now; I will yield time if he has anything of the kind to say. You will find quite the contrary, gentlemen. These men are all ready to come to the help of the corruptor, the man who has harmed their kindred, as Meletus and Anytus say. Now those who were corrupted might well have reason to help me, but the uncorrupted, their kindred who are older men, have no reason to help me except the right and proper one, that they know that Meletus is lying and that I am telling the truth.

Very well, gentlemen. This, and maybe other similar things, is what I have to say in my defense. Perhaps one of you might be angry as he recalls that when he himself stood trial on a less dangerous charge, he begged and implored the jury with many tears, that he brought his children and many of his friends and family into court to arouse as much pity as he could, but that I do none of these things, even though I may seem to be running the

[9] Member of the same *deme* or township in ancient Greece. [Ed.]

ultimate risk. Thinking of this, he might feel resentful toward me and, angry about this, cast his vote in anger. If there is such a one among you – I do not deem there is, but if there is – I think it would be right to say in reply: My good sir, I too have a household and, in Homer's phrase, I am not born "from oak or rock" but from men, so that I have a family, indeed three sons, men of Athens, of whom one is an adolescent while two are children. Nevertheless, I will not beg you to acquit me by bringing them here. Why do I do none of these things? Not through arrogance, gentlemen, nor through lack of respect for you. Whether I am brave in the face of death is another matter, but with regard to my reputation and yours and that of the whole city, it does not seem right to me to do these things, especially at my age and with my reputation. For it is generally believed, whether it be true or false, that in certain respects Socrates is superior to the majority of men. Now if those of you who are considered superior, be it in wisdom or courage or whatever other virtue makes them so, are seen behaving like that, it would be a disgrace. Yet I have often seen them do this sort of thing when standing trial, men who are thought to be somebody, doing amazing things as if they thought it a terrible thing to die, and as if they were to be immortal if you did not execute them. I think these men bring shame upon the city so that a stranger, too, would assume that those who are outstanding in virtue among the Athenians, whom they themselves select from themselves to fill offices of state and receive other honors, are in no way better than women. You should not act like that, gentlemen of the jury, those of you who have any reputation at all, and if we do, you should not allow it. You should make it very clear that you will more readily convict a man who performs these pitiful dramatics in court and so makes the city a laughingstock, than a man who keeps quiet.

Quite apart from the question of reputation, gentlemen, I do not think it right to supplicate the jury and to be acquitted because of this but to teach and persuade them. It is not the purpose of a juryman's office to give justice as a favor to whoever seems good to him, but to judge according to law, and this he has sworn to do. We should not accustom you to perjure yourselves, nor should you make a habit of it. This is irreverent conduct for either of us.

Do not deem it right for me, gentlemen of the jury, that I should act towards you in a way that I do not consider to be good or just or pious, especially, by Zeus, as I am being prosecuted by Meletus here for impiety; clearly, if I convinced you by my supplication to do violence to your oath of office, I would be teaching you not to believe that there are gods, and my defense would convict me of not believing in them. This is far from being the case, gentlemen, for I do believe in them as none of my accusers do. I leave it to you and the god to judge me in the way that will be best for me and for you.

[*The jury now gives its verdict of guilty, and Meletus asks for the penalty of death.*]

SOCRATES: There are many other reasons for my not being angry with you for convicting me, men of Athens, and what happened was not unexpected. I am much more surprised at the number of votes cast on each side, for I did not think the decision would be by so few votes but by a great many. As it is, a switch of only thirty votes would have acquitted me. I think myself that I have been cleared on Meletus' charges, and not only this, but it is clear to all that, if Anytus and Lycon had not joined him in accusing me, he would have been fined a thousand drachmas for not receiving a fifth of the votes.

He assesses the penalty at death. So be it. What counter-assessment should I propose to you, men of Athens? Clearly it should be a penalty I deserve, and what do I deserve to suffer or to pay because I have deliberately not led a quiet life but have neglected what occupies most people: wealth, household affairs, the position of general or public orator or the other offices, the political clubs and factions that exist in the city? I thought myself too honest to survive if I occupied myself with those things. I did not follow that path that would have made me of no use either to you or to myself, but I went to each of you privately and conferred upon him what I say is the greatest benefit, by trying to persuade him not to care for any of his belongings before caring that he himself should be as good and as wise as possible, not to care for the city's possessions more than for the city itself, and to care for other things in the same way. What do I deserve for being such a man? Some good, gentlemen of the jury, if I must truly make an assessment according to my deserts, and something suitable. What is suitable for a poor benefactor who needs leisure to exhort you? Nothing is more suitable, gentlemen, than for such a man to be fed in the Prytaneum,[10] much more suitable for him than for anyone of you who has won a victory at Olympia with a pair or a team of horses. The Olympian victor makes you think yourself happy; I make you be happy. Besides, he does not need food, but I do. So if I must make a just assessment of what I deserve, I assess it at this: free meals in the Prytaneum.

When I say this you may think, as when I spoke of appeals to pity and entreaties, that I speak arrogantly, but that is not the case, men of Athens;

---

[10] The Prytaneum was the magistrates' hall or town hall of Athens, in which public entertainments were given, particularly to Olympian victors on their return home. [JMC]

rather it is like this: I am convinced that I never willingly wrong anyone, but I am not convincing you of this, for we have talked together but a short time. If it were the law with us, as it is elsewhere, that a trial for life should not last one but many days, you would be convinced, but now it is not easy to dispel great slanders in a short time. Since I am convinced that I wrong no one, I am not likely to wrong myself, to say that I deserve some evil and to make some such assessment against myself. What should I fear? That I should suffer the penalty Meletus has assessed against me, of which I say I do not know whether it is good or bad? Am I then to choose in preference to this something that I know very well to be an evil and assess the penalty at that? Imprisonment? Why should I live in prison, always subjected to the ruling magistrates, the Eleven? A fine, and imprisonment until I pay it? That would be the same thing for me, as I have no money. Exile? for perhaps you might accept that assessment.

I should have to be inordinately fond of life, gentlemen of the jury, to be so unreasonable as to suppose that other men will easily tolerate my company and conversation when you, my fellow citizens, have been unable to endure them, but found them a burden and resented them so that you are now seeking to get rid of them. Far from it, gentlemen. It would be a fine life at my age to be driven out of one city after another, for I know very well that wherever I go the young men will listen to my talk as they do here. If I drive them away, they will themselves persuade their elders to drive me out; if I do not drive them away, their fathers and relations will drive me out on their behalf.

Perhaps someone might say: But Socrates, if you leave us will you not be able to live quietly, without talking? Now this is the most difficult point on which to convince some of you. If I say that it is impossible for me to keep quiet because that means disobeying the god, you will not believe me and will think I am being ironical. On the other hand, if I say that it is the greatest good for a man to discuss virtue every day and those other things about which you hear me conversing and testing myself and others, for the unexamined life is not worth living for men, you will believe me even less.

What I say is true, gentlemen, but it is not easy to convince you. At the same time, I am not accustomed to think that I deserve any penalty. If I had money, I would assess the penalty at the amount I could pay, for that would not hurt me, but I have none, unless you are willing to set the penalty at the amount I can pay, and perhaps I could pay you one mina of silver.[11] So that is my assessment.

---

[11] One mina was the equivalent of 100 drachmas. In the late fifth century, one drachma was the standard daily wage of a laborer. A mina, then, was a considerable sum. [JMC]

Plato here, gentlemen of the jury, and Crito and Critobulus and Apollodorus bid me put the penalty at thirty minae, and they will stand surety for the money. Well then, that is my assessment, and they will be sufficient guarantee of payment.

[*The jury now votes again and sentences Socrates to death.*]

SOCRATES: It is for the sake of a short time, gentlemen of the jury, that you will acquire the reputation and the guilt, in the eyes of those who want to denigrate the city, of having killed Socrates, a wise man, for they who want to revile you will say that I am wise even if I am not. If you had waited but a little while, this would have happened of its own accord. You see my age, that I am already advanced in years and close to death. I am saying this not to all of you but to those who condemned me to death, and to these same jurors I say: Perhaps you think that I was convicted for lack of such words as might have convinced you, if I thought I should say or do all I could to avoid my sentence. Far from it. I was convicted because I lacked not words but boldness and shamelessness and the willingness to say to you what you would most gladly have heard from me, lamentations and tears and my saying and doing many things that I say are unworthy of me but that you are accustomed to hear from others. I did not think then that the danger I ran should make me do anything mean, nor do I now regret the nature of my defense. I would much rather die after this kind of defense than live after making the other kind. Neither I nor any other man should, on trial or in war, contrive to avoid death at any cost. Indeed it is often obvious in battle that one could escape death by throwing away one's weapons and by turning to supplicate one's pursuers, and there are many ways to avoid death in every kind of danger if one will venture to do or say anything to avoid it. It is not difficult to avoid death, gentlemen; it is much more difficult to avoid wickedness, for it runs faster than death. Slow and elderly as I am, I have been caught by the slower pursuer, whereas my accusers, being clever and sharp, have been caught by the quicker, wickedness. I leave you now, condemned to death by you, but they are condemned by truth to wickedness and injustice. So I maintain my assessment, and they maintain theirs. This perhaps had to happen, and I think it is as it should be.

Now I want to prophesy to those who convicted me, for I am at the point when men prophesy most, when they are about to die. I say gentlemen, to those who voted to kill me, that vengeance will come upon you immediately after my death, a vengeance much harder to bear than that which you took in killing me. You did this in the belief that you would avoid giving an account of your life, but I maintain that quite the opposite will happen to you. There will be more people to test you, whom I now held back, but you did not notice it. They will be more difficult to deal with as they will be younger and you will resent them more. You are wrong if you believe that by killing people you will prevent anyone from reproaching you for not living in the right way. To escape such tests is neither possible nor good, but it is best and easiest not to discredit others but to prepare oneself to be as good as possible. With this prophecy to you who convicted me, I part from you.

I should be glad to discuss what has happened with those who voted for my acquittal during the time that the officers of the court are busy and I do not yet have to depart to my death. So, gentlemen, stay with me awhile, for nothing prevents us from talking to each other while it is allowed. To you, as being my friends, I want to show the meaning of what has occurred. A surprising thing has happened to me, jurymen – you I would rightly call jurymen. At all previous times my familiar prophetic power, my spiritual manifestation, frequently opposed me, even in small matters, when I was about to do something wrong, but now that, as you can see for yourselves, I was faced with what one might think, and what is generally thought to be, the worst of evils, my divine sign has not opposed me, either when I left home at dawn, or when I came into court, or at any time that I was about to say something during my speech. Yet in other talks it often held me back in the middle of my speaking, but now it has opposed no word or deed of mine. What do I think is the reason for this? I will tell you. What has happened to me may well be a good thing, and those of us who believe death to be an evil are certainly mistaken. I have convincing proof of this, for it is impossible that my familiar sign did not oppose me if I was not about to do what was right.

Let us reflect in this way, too, that there is good hope that death is a blessing, for it is one of two things: either the dead are nothing and have no perception of anything, or it is, as we are told, a change and a relocating for the soul from here to another place. If it is complete lack of perception, like a dreamless sleep, then death would be a great advantage. For I think that if one had to pick out that night during which a man slept soundly and did not dream, put beside it the other nights and days of his life, and then see how many days and nights had been better and more pleasant than that night, not only a private person but the great king would find them easy to count compared with the other days and nights. If death is like this I say it is an advantage, for all eternity would then seem to be no more than a single night. If, on the other hand, death is a change from here to another place, and what we are told is true and all who have died are there, what greater blessing could there be, gentlemen of the jury? If anyone arriving in Hades will have escaped from those who call themselves jurymen here, and will find those true jurymen who are said to sit in judgement there, Minos and Radamanthus and Aeacus and Triptolemus and the other demi-gods who have been upright in their own life, would that be a poor kind of change? Again, what would one of you give to keep company with Orpheus and Musaeus, Hesiod and Homer? I am willing to die many times if that is true. It would be a wonderful way for me to spend my time whenever I met Palamedes and Ajax, the son of Telamon, and any other of the men of old who died through an unjust conviction, to compare my experience with theirs. I think it would be pleasant. Most important, I could spend my time testing and examining people there, as I do here, as to who among them is wise, and who thinks he is, but is not.

What would one not give, gentlemen of the jury, for the opportunity to examine the man who led the great expedition against Troy, or Odysseus, or Sisyphus, and innumerable other men and women one could mention? It would be an extraordinary happiness to talk with them, to keep company with them and examine them. In any case, they would certainly not put one to death for doing so. They are happier there than we are here in other respects, and for the rest of time they are deathless, if indeed what we are told is true.

You too must be of good hope as regards death, gentlemen of the jury, and keep this one truth in mind, that a good man cannot be harmed either in life or in death, and that his affairs are not neglected by the gods. What has happened to me now has not happened of itself, but it is clear to me that it was better for me to die now and to escape from trouble. That is why my divine sign did not oppose me at any point. So I am certainly not angry with those who convicted me, or with my accusers. Of course that was not their purpose when they accused and convicted me, but they thought they were hurting me, and for this they deserve blame. This much I ask from them: when my sons grow up, avenge yourselves by causing them the same kind of grief that I caused you, if you think they care for money or anything else more than they care for virtue, or if they think they are somebody when they are nobody. Reproach them as I reproach you, that they do not care for the right things and think they are worthy when they are not worthy of anything. If you do this, I shall have been justly treated by you, and my sons also.

Now the hour to part has come. I go to die, you go to live. Which of us goes to the better lot is known to no one, except the god.

Science and the Paranormal

Donald R. Prothero and Timothy D. Callahan

Chapter 1 in *UFOs, Chemtrails, and Aliens: What Science Says*. Bloomington: Indiana University Press, 2017, pp. 1-15. Slightly shortened.

Donald R. Prothero *(b. 1954) is an American geologist and paleontologist who has authored numerous scientific papers and several geology textbooks. He also writes about science and culture for a general audience, including his recent book* Reality Check: How Science Deniers Threaten Our Future *(2013). His collaborator* **Timothy D. Callahan** *is trained as an artist but also writes about science, mythology, and religion.*

Why we are reading this: *This selection serves as the introduction to the authors' recent book on UFOs and aliens. It explains how scientists evaluate extraordinary and paranormal claims and decide what is most likely to be true. The authors lay out the basic principles of scientific method and critical thinking, show how to distinguish science from pseudoscience, and introduce important concepts such as double-blind testing, peer review, burden of proof, special pleading, and Ockham's razor. Is there anything new or surprising to you about the authors' picture of science? Do you find any of the ideas here useful? Challenging? Off-putting? Inspiring?*

UFO?

> Science is nothing but developed perception, interpreted intent, common sense rounded out and minutely articulated.
>
> – *George Santayana, philosopher*

September 3, 2013: It's the sixth inning of a minor-league baseball game between the Vancouver Canadians and the Everett AquaSox. The game is being played at ScotiaBank Field's Nat Bailey Stadium in Vancouver. A fan is videotaping the game (available on *YouTube*[1]), and you can hear the crowd cheering and clapping and urging the team on the field to play well.

[1] "Did UFO Visit Vancouver Canadians Baseball Game?" *Huffington Post*, September 9, 2013, http://www.huffingtonpost.com/2013/09/09/ufo-canadian-baseball-game-photo-video_ n _3895294.html.

The video clip pans from right to left over a mere 26 seconds, and it zooms in on something in the distance, beyond the trees outside the stadium. For those few brief seconds, it appears that there is some sort of flying saucer, complete with a ring of bright lights flashing in all directions, flying off in the distance. Strangely, however, the videographer doesn't hold the zoom on the mysterious UFO but returns to a wide-angle view of the game, then pans farther to the right. Whatever the videographer sees when he or she zooms in on the UFO, it isn't impressive or startling enough to keep him or her focused on it, because he or she goes right back to filming the game.

Nevertheless, this few seconds of footage is soon all over the Internet, mentioned in the news in Vancouver and elsewhere. The *Vancouver Sun* newspaper jokingly calls the object "divine intervention" that helped the local team win the game.[2] Everyone else seems to think that this startling image is proof that UFOs are alien spacecraft, even though few people in Vancouver seem to have noticed it. The other fans in the stands with the videographer who might have reacted much more strongly if it seemed like an alien spacecraft instead were tweeting as if it were nothing unusual. One tweet mentioned[3] that "it hovered for a while, going up and down then gone… weird, but lucky, C's have tacked on 4 runs since it made appearance." The British Columbia news site *The Province* suggested[4] that the "levitating… shiny blue something" may have been a kite or a remote-controlled helicopter.

But this is not enough to stop the huge community of UFO believers from trumpeting the few seconds of footage as "proof" that UFOs are real – without doing any investigation or digging about what was happening in Vancouver that night. They don't even think about the fact that the videographer didn't find the image startling enough to keep filming it and instead went back to the minor-league baseball game. Marc Dantonio, the chief video analyst for the Mutual UFO Network (MUFON), looks at the footage and testifies[5] that the image is not a camera trick or a computer-generated fake inserted into the video after it was filmed. Still, he finds it suspicious that "there was no reaction at all from anyone, nor the videographer." Rather, he says, "I suspect much more strongly, based on the way it was sideslipping to our right a bit while leaning slightly to that side, that this was likely either a lit up kite or a small drone-type object like we created for a National Geographic show. This object's behavior matches either one of those possibilities in the short video snip of it here that we can see. The stability makes this more likely a flying small hobby-

---

[2] Ibid.

[3] Ibid.

[4] Ibid.

[5] Ibid.

type drone."

After the story has spread around the world through the internet, the culprit finally confesses.[6] The "UFO" was indeed a drone. It is eventually revealed that the H. R. MacMillan Space Centre built the drone, shaped like its new planetarium, as a form of gonzo advertising. Working with a local advertising agent, the drone is part of an "extreme tease campaign" to generate excitement and mystery-and lots of free publicity and increased attendance at its new planetarium.

After the hoax is revealed, it continues circulating on the internet as a legitimate UFO with no explanation, even though the fakery has been exposed. Even sadder, an internet poll on *Huffington Post*[7] shows that almost 34% of the people who clicked on the polling buttons *still* believe it is proof of a Canadian UFO sighting!

This story is typical of most UFO sightings: something is spotted that the observer can't identify, so it becomes an "unidentified flying object," or "UFO." Then the account snowballs into a more exaggerated version as people immediately jump to the conclusion that it is an alien craft. The "unidentified" flying object is then exposed as a hoax or as some other more prosaic natural phenomenon. But even after a satisfactory explanation is given (and even when the hoaxer confesses), people *still* refuse to believe the truth and insist that the object was an alien spacecraft.

But how does a scientist examine the claims about UFOs and aliens?

Science and Pseudoscience

> There are many hypotheses in science which are wrong. That's perfectly all right; they're the aperture to finding out what's right. Science is a self-correcting process. To be accepted, new ideas must survive the most rigorous standards of evidence and scrutiny.
>
> – *Carl Sagan*

Stories such as this one raise important questions: How do we evaluate the claims? How do we decide whether they're credible? How can we tell whether we're being conned and fooled?

In our modern society, critical thinking and science have proven to be the most consistent and effective methods of distinguishing reality from

---

[6] Lee Speigel, "UFO Hoax at Canada Baseball Game Exposed; H.R. MacMillan Space Centre Admits Bizarre Stunt," *Huffington Post*, last updated September 14, 2013, http://www.huffingtonpost.com/2013/09/12/canada-baseball-game-ufo-hoax_n 3908612.html.

[7] "Did UFO Visit Vancouver Canadians Baseball Game?"

illusion. As Carl Sagan put it, "skeptical scrutiny is the means, in both science and religion, by which deep thoughts can be winnowed from deep nonsense." Even though many of us like to imagine that we can have a "lucky streak," and though we might adhere to superstitions such as avoiding walking on sidewalk cracks, when important issues such as money are involved, we all try to be skeptics. As mature adults, we have learned not to be naive about the world. By hard experience, we are all equipped with a certain degree of healthy skepticism. We have learned that politicians and salesmen are often dishonest, deceptive, and untruthful. We see exaggerated advertising claims everywhere, but deep inside we are experienced enough to recognize that they are often false or misleading. We try not to buy products based on a whim but rather look for the best price and the best quality. We try to live by the famous Latin motto *Caveat emptor:* "Let the buyer beware." When we are dealing with important matters, science and critical thinking are the only techniques we can rely on to avoid being fooled. But what are the principles of science and critical thinking? What do they tell us about UFOs and aliens?

A big problem with our conception of science is that it is based on the classic "mad scientist" stereotypes that are so prevalent in the movies, on television, and in other media. Indeed, there are almost no depictions of scientists in the media that don't include the stereotypical white lab coats and bubbling beakers and sparking Van de Graaff generators – and the "scientist" is usually a nerdy old white guy with glasses and wild hair. But that's strictly Hollywood stereotyping, not reality. Unless a scientist is a chemist or biologist working on material that might spill on your clothes, there is no reason to wear a white lab coat. Even though one of us (Prothero) is a professional scientist, I *never* use a lab coat. I haven't needed one since my days in college chemistry class. Most scientists don't need the fancy glassware or sparking apparatuses-or even have a lab!

What makes someone a scientist is not a white lab coat or lab equipment but rather *how he or she asks questions about nature* and what thought processes he or she employs to solve problems. Science is about suggesting an explanation (a hypothesis) to understand some phenomenon, then *testing* that explanation by examining evidence that might show us whether the hypothesis is right or wrong. Contrary to popular myth, most scientists don't try to prove their hypotheses right. As British philosopher of science Karl Popper pointed out long ago, it's almost impossible to prove statements true, but it's much easier to prove them false. For example, you could hypothesize that "all swans are white," but no matter how many white swans you find, you'll never prove that statement true. But if you find just one nonwhite swan (such as the Australian black swan), you've shot down the hypothesis. It's finished –

over – kaput! Time to toss it on the scrap heap and create a new hypothesis) then try to falsify it as well.

Thus science is not about proving things true – it's about proving them false! This is the exact opposite of the popular myths that scientists are looking for "final truth" or that we can prove something "absolutely true." Scientific ideas must *always* remain open to testing, tentative, and capable of being rejected. If they are held up as "truth" and no longer subject to testing or scrutiny, then they are no longer science – they are dogma. This is the feature that distinguishes science from many other beliefs) such as religion or Marxism or any widely accepted belief system. In dogma, you are told what is true, and you must accept it on faith. In science, no one has the right to dictate what is true, and scientists are constantly testing and checking and reexamining ideas to weed out the ones that don't stand up to scrutiny.

Since Popper's time, not all philosophers of science have agreed with the strict criterion of falsifiability, because there are good ideas in science that don't fit this criterion yet that are clearly scientific. Pigliucci[8] proposed a broader definition of science that encompasses scientific topics that might not fit the strict criterion of falsifiability. All science is characterized by the following: (1) *Naturalism:* We can examine only phenomena that happen in the natural world, because we cannot test supernatural hypotheses scientifically. We might want to say about something that "God did it," but there is no way to test that hypothesis. (2) *Empiricism:* Science studies only things that can be observed by our senses – things that are objectively real to not only ourselves but also any other observer. Science does not deal with internal feelings, mystic experiences, or anything else that is in the mind of one person and that no one else can experience. (3) *Theory:* Science works with a set of theories that are well established ideas about the universe and that have survived many tests.

What is a theory? Some ideas in science have been tested over and over again, and instead of being falsified, they are corroborated by more and more evidence. These hypotheses then reach the status of some idea that is well supported and thus widely accepted. In science, that is what is meant by the word *theory*. Sadly, the word *theory* has completely different meanings in general usage. In the pop culture world, a theory is a wild guess, such as the "theories" about why JFK was assassinated. But as we just explained, in science, the word *theory* means something completely different: an extremely well supported and highly tested idea that scientists accept as provisionally true. For example, gravity is "just a theory," and

---

[8] Massimo Pigliucci, *Nonsense on Stilts: How to Tell Science from Bunk* (Chicago: University of Chicago Press, 2010).

we still don't understand every aspect of how it works – but even so, objects don't float up to the ceiling. The germ theory of disease was controversial about 100 years ago, when doctors tried to cure people by bleeding them with leeches – but now people who get sick due to a virus or bacterium will follow modern medical practices if they want to get well. Nevertheless, there are people who don't like what science tells them (such as creationists who reject evolution), and they will deliberately confuse these two different uses of the word *theory* to convey the idea that somehow evolution is not one of the best-tested explanations of the world that we have. Yet these same people do not reject the theory of gravity or the germ theory of disease.

Scientists aren't inherently sourpusses or killjoys who want to rain on everyone else's parades. They are just cautious about and skeptical of any idea until it has survived the gauntlet of repeated testing and possible falsification, then risen to the level of something that is established or acceptable. They have good reason to be skeptical. Humans are capable of all sorts of mistakes and false ideas and self-deception. Scientists cannot afford to blindly accept the ideas of one person, or even a group of people, making a significant claim. They are obligated to criticize and carefully evaluate and test it before accepting it as a scientific idea.

But scientists are human, and we are subject to the same foibles as all mortals. We love to see our ideas confirmed and to believe that we are right. And there are all sorts of ways we can misinterpret or overinterpret data to fit our biases. As the Nobel Prize-winning physicist Richard Feynman put it, "the first principle is that you must not fool yourself and you are the easiest person to fool." That is why many scientific experiments are run by the double-blind method: not only do the subjects of the experiments not know what is in sample A or sample B, but neither do the investigators. Samples are coded so that no one knows what is in each, and only after the experiment is run do they open the key to the code to find out whether the results agree with their expectations.

So if scientists are human and can make mistakes, then why does science work so well? The answer is testability and *peer review.* Individuals might be blinded by their own biases, but once they put their ideas forth in a presentation or publications, their work is subject to intense scrutiny by the scientific community. If the results cannot be replicated by another group of scientists, then they have failed the test. As Feynman put it, "It doesn't matter how beautiful your theory is, it doesn't matter how smart you are. If it doesn't agree with experiment, it's wrong."

The mad scientist stereotype that prevails in nearly all media is completely wrong not only because of the stereotypical dress and behavior and apparatuses that are shown but also because the "mad scientist" is not testing hypotheses about nature or experimenting to find out what is really true. In a famous cartoon widely circulated on the internet, someone interrogating a "mad scientist" asks, "Why did you build a death ray?" The mad scientist says, "To take over the world." "No, I mean what hypothesis are you testing? Are you just making mad observations?" The "mad scientist" responds, "Look, I'm just trying to take over the world. That's all." The interrogator continues, "You at least are going to have some of the world as a mad control group, right?" As the cartoon says, he's really not a scientist at all – he's just a "mad engineer." (Although engineers might understand some science, their goal is not to discover truths about nature but rather to apply science to make inventions or practical devices.)

Sham Science

> The public is happy to admire science as long as they don't have to understand it deeply. Sham inquiry plays to the admiration of science by the public. A lack of familiarity with how science is supposed to work is a major reason why the public has trouble recognizing counterfeit science. Add an '-ology' to the end of whatever you study and it acts like a toupee of credibility – to hide the lack of substance. The public is vulnerable to pseudoscience that resembles real inquiry and genuine knowledge.
>
> – *Sharon Hill*

Because of the prestige and trust that we attach to science, there are lots of con men and zealots out there who try to peddle stuff that looks and even sounds like science but that doesn't actually pass muster through testing) falsification, experimentation, and peer review. Yet it often sounds "science" to most people or imitates the trappings of science, becoming what geologist and skeptic Sharon Hill called "sham science" or "sham inquiry."

A classic case of mistaking the trappings for the real thing are the famous "cargo cults" of the South Pacific islands. During World War II, many of these islands hosted U.S. military bases, and their native peoples came in contact with the advantages of western civilization for the first time. Then the war ended, and the military left. But the natives wanted the airplanes to return and bring their goodies, so they used local materials to build wooden "radio masts," "control towers," and "airplanes" and other replicas of the real things, hoping that they could summon the planes.

A good example of "sham science" is the many paranormal television shows about "ghost hunters" who poke around dark houses with fancy equipment pretending to be "scientific." In other television shows about Bigfoot or other mythical creatures) we see amateur "Bigfoot hunters" blundering around in the bushes in the night with military-style night-vision goggles, completely mystified by each animal noise they hear (which just shows that they are not trained biologists). They set out "camera traps" and other expensive pieces of equipment – which never photograph anything but the common animals of the area. Sure, they are using the trappings of science (expensive machines that look and sound impressive), but are they following the scientific method? No! In these cases, they are violating one of the most important principles that separates science from pseudoscience: *the unexplained is not necessarily unexplainable.* There are many phenomena in nature for which science doesn't yet have an explanation. But scientists know that eventually we'll probably find one. In the meantime, an unexplained mystery is just that: not *yet* explained. Scientists don't jump to the conclusion that it's a ghost or Bigfoot or some other paranormal idea that has never been established to be real by scientific evidence. A UFO is just "unidentified" until further research is done to rule out simple natural causes; it does not automatically become an alien craft.

One common ploy of UFO believers is to bring up a UFO incident that has yet to be explained, assuming that anything not yet explained utterly confounds both science and any possible explanation of the given incident other than its being the work of extraterrestrial aliens. However, just because something hasn't been explained does not mean that we must invoke paranormal causes as a solution for the mystery. In fact, sometimes the most rational approach to a mystery is to accept that it isn't yet, and might never be, solved. A case in point is that of the *Mary Celeste,* an American merchant brigantine that was found adrift and deserted in the Atlantic Ocean, off the Azores Islands, on December 4, 1872, by the Canadian brigantine *Dei Gratia.* She was in a disheveled but seaworthy condition, under partial sail, with no one on board and her lifeboat missing. The last log entry was dated 10 days earlier. She had left New York City for Genoa on November 7 and on discovery was still amply provisioned. Her cargo of denatured alcohol was intact, and the captain and crew's personal belongings were undisturbed. None of those who had been on board – the captain and his wife, their two-year-old daughter, the crew of seven – was ever seen or heard from again. Although there are several theories about what happened to the crew, a number of them quite viable, the simple fact is that we will probably never know what happened to the crew of the *Mary Celeste.* For all that, we needn't invoke either space aliens or the paranormal as the cause of their disappearance. It's quite all right to let a mystery be a mystery. In any case, evidence of extraterrestrial visitation must be positive and testable to be of any worth. The unexplained remains simply the unexplained.

Accordingly, when investigating paranormal claims, we cannot just practice sham science with expensive toys and claim that we're using the "scientific method." No, the first step is to *think* like a scientist, which means testing hypotheses about what the currently mysterious phenomenon might be, then ruling out explanations one by one. If we hear a strange noise on a "ghost hunt" or a "Bigfoot hunt," instead of jumping to the conclusion that it is a ghost or a Bigfoot, first we should rule out the idea that the noise is some common phenomenon, such as the wind blowing through the boards of the "haunted house" or some animal call that we don't happen to recognize. Even if we rule out *every* possible natural explanation for a strange phenomenon, it *still* doesn't give us the right to jump to the conclusion that it must be a paranormal entity. We must still follow the principle that *the unexplained is not necessarily unexplainable.* As scientists, we put the unexplained phenomenon on the back burner, withholding judgment about whether the phenomenon is real until we actually have firm evidence one way or the other. It is not acceptable to jump to a paranormal conclusion without giving science the time to rule out all the normal explanations. Some day we might find out what is really happening, so the paranormal "solution" just gets in the way of doing science properly and distinguishing reality from baloney.

Baloney Detection

> Extraordinary claims require extraordinary evidence.
>
> – *Carl Sagan*

So what are the general principles of science and critical thinking that we need to follow if we wish to separate fact from fiction? How can "deep thoughts... be winnowed from deep nonsense"? Many of these were outlined in Carl Sagan's 1996 book *The Demon-Haunted World* and Michael Shermer's 1997 book *Why People Believe Weird Things.* Some of the most important principles we must use if we are to decipher fact from fiction in UFO claims include the following.

Extraordinary claims require extraordinary evidence: This famous statement by Carl Sagan (or the similar "Extraordinary claims require extraordinary proof" by Marcello Truzzi) is highly relevant to separating garbage from truth in claims about UFOs. As Sagan pointed out, there are hundreds of routine claims and discoveries made by scientists nearly every day, but most are just small extensions of what was already known and don't require extensive testing by the scientific community. By contrast, crackpots, fringe scientists, and pseudoscientists make revolutionary claims about the world and argue strenuously that they are right. For such claims, it is not sufficient to have just one or two suggestive pieces of evidence, such as blurry photographs or ambiguous eyewitness accounts, when most of the evidence goes against their cherished hypothesis. In these cases, we need extraordinary evidence, such as the actual remains of the alien craft or an alien corpse, to overcome the high probability that these things do not exist.

Burden of proof: In a criminal court, the prosecution has the burden of proof. It must prove its case beyond a reasonable doubt, and the defense need do nothing if the prosecution fails to prove its case. In a civil case, the plaintiff needs to prove his or her case based on a preponderance of the evidence, and the respondent need do nothing. In science, extraordinary claims have a higher burden of proof than do routine scientific advances, because they are claiming to overthrow a larger body of knowledge. When evolution by natural selection was first proposed almost 160 years ago, it had the burden of proof, because it overturned the established body of creationist biology. Since then, so much evidence has accumulated to show that evolution has occurred that the burden of proof is now on the shoulders of the creationists who would seek to overthrow evolutionary biology. Similarly, there is so much evidence to show that the Holocaust occurred (not only the accounts of survivors and eyewitnesses but also detailed records kept by the Nazis themselves) that the burden of proof is on the Holocaust deniers to refute this immense body of evidence. Similarly, extraordinary claims about UFOs and aliens require a much higher degree of proof, because so much of what is claimed about them goes against everything we know from biology, astronomy, geology, and other sciences.

Authority, credentials, and expertise: One of the main strategies of pseudoscientists is to cite the authority and credentials of their leading proponents as proof that their claims are credible. But a PhD degree or advanced training is not enough: a true expert has advanced training *in the relevant field.* It's common for people trying to push an argument to point to their advanced degree (usually a PhD) as they make their case. This is a slick strategy to intimidate the audience into believing that the expert's having a PhD makes him or her smarter than the members of the audience-and an expert in everything. But those of us who have earned a PhD know that it qualifies you to talk only about the field of your training-and, moreover, that during the long, hard slog to get your dissertation project finished and written up, you might· actually *lose* some of your breadth of training in other subjects. Most scientists know that anyone who is flaunting his or her PhD in making arguments is "credentialmongering." If a book says "PhD" on the cover, be wary-the arguments between the covers might not be able to stand on their own merits.

Here's a good way to approach it: if you run into someone who flaunts his or her PhD, make sure he or she has some training in a relevant field. Not only did my own training include extensive background in biology and geology (which are relevant to claims about life on other planets), but I have also taught astronomy, meteorology, planetary science, and geophysics at the college level-so I'm familiar with the astronomical issues bearing on the likelihood that life is on other planets. However, most of the "experts" on aliens and UFOs have no training in biology or astronomy, so their "expert opinions" should be taken with a grain of salt. They have no more advanced training in the relevant field than you or I, so their PhD makes no real difference. You wouldn't trust an astronomer to know how to fix your car or write a symphony simply by virtue of his or her having a PhD in astronomy. So why would you trust his or her opinion on biology or some other field in which he or she has no advanced training?

Special pleading and *ad hoc* hypotheses: One of the marks of pseudoscientists is that when the evidence is strongly against them, they do not abandon their cherished hypothesis. Instead, they resort to special pleading to salvage their original idea rather than admitting that it is wrong. These attempts to salvage an idea are known as *ad hoc* (Latin, "for this purpose") hypotheses and are universally regarded as signs of a failed idea. When a psychic conducts a séance and fails to contact the dead, he or she might plead that the skeptic "just didn't believe hard enough" or that the "room wasn't dark enough" or that the "spirits didn't feel like coming out this time." When you demonstrate to a creationist that Noah's ark couldn't possibly have contained the tens of millions of species of animals known, he or she uses evasions such as "only the created kinds were on board" or "fish and insects don't count" or "it was a miracle." If you show a UFO believer the scientific implausibility of his or her claims, he or she usually retreats to some claim that effectively makes the aliens supernatural beings, incapable of being evaluated by any laws of nature or science.

Any time you encounter such special pleading, it is a sure sign that the hypothesis has failed and that the person doing the pleading has abandoned the scientific method and is trying to salvage a favored idea despite the evidence. As the great Victorian naturalist Thomas Henry Huxley said, it is "the great tragedy of science – the slaying of a beautiful hypothesis by an ugly fact."

Ockham's Razor: There is a well-known principle in the philosophy of science known as Ockham's (also spelled "Occam's") Razor, or the Principle of Parsimony. Named after· a famous medieval scholar, William of Ockham (1287-1347) who discussed it many times, it basically says that when there are two or more explanations for something that equally explain the facts, the simplest explanation is likely to be the best. In another formulation, it says that we don't need to create overly complex explanations when simpler ones might do. The metaphorical "razor" shaves away the unnecessarily complicated ideas until only the simplest ones are left. Scientists use this as a basic guide when choosing among hypotheses, although we all know that in the real world, once in a while, the complicated explanation is indeed the real one.

Nonetheless, Ockham's Razor is highly relevant when evaluating two versions or explanations of an event. For example, which seems more likely? Is it more likely that aliens traveled many hundreds of light-years just to make a few crop circles in a farmer's cornfield (and do nothing else, including reveal themselves) or that some prankster made the crop circle in the middle of the night using simple tools such as a long board on a rope staked to the ground? All the difficulties of imagining aliens traveling all that distance just to do something stupid seem positively ridiculous when it's much easier to imagine that it's a prank or a hoax.

In statistics, there is a similar principal: the Null Hypothesis, or the Hypothesis of No Significant Differences. If we want to statistically evaluate whether two things are truly different, we start with the simplifying assumption that there are *no significant differences* ("Null Hypothesis"). Then we must demonstrate that there is a statistically significant difference between the two things before we can make the assertion that they are truly not the same. We can apply this to many other fields in which scientific reasoning is needed. For example, our Null Hypothesis might be that the strange noise in the room is the wind moving the shutters. To prove that it is not something simple and natural such as this but rather a supernatural ghost requires enough evidence to show that the wind could not possibly have caused the noise. Likewise, crop circles or strange lines drawn in the sand can be evaluated this way as well. Our Null Hypothesis is that some simple common phenomenon, such as ordinary pranksters drawing lines in the sand, or dragging a board across the grain field, explains these features. We must prove that these explanations *cannot* explain the feature before we are allowed to embrace the much less parsimonious explanation that aliens came all the way to this planet just to draw lines in the sand or create flattened crops.

Summary

If we wish to scientifically evaluate the claims that UFOs are flying through our skies or aliens landing on this planet, we need to follow the rules of science. In short, we must follow these principles:

- Do not assume that just because we don't have an explanation right now, it cannot be explained by science eventually. The unexplained is not necessarily unexplainable!
- Don't give credence to people who do not have the proper expert training in a field relevant to the claim being examined.
- Don't fall back on special pleading or ad hoc explanations when your favorite explanation falls apart.
- Don't assume a more complicated scenario when a simpler one will do.
- Recognize that for extraordinary claims, the burden of proof lies with the person making that claim to give extraordinary evidence that will overthrow the mountain of evidence against it – not just blurry photos of supposed UFOs or footage of "aliens" that could be hoaxed or just another "eyewitness account" (which are problematic).
- No scientific explanation can veer into the paranormal or the supernatural. If you start talking about aliens and spacecraft that violate the laws of science, you're no longer doing science.
- Most important, be prepared to subject your ideas to critical scrutiny and peer review. If you scorn or ignore the criticisms and corrections of others but persist in your beliefs because they are important to you – despite their rejection by science – then you are no longer acting as a scientist but rather are acting like a true believer or a zealot.

The problem boils down to evidence: how good is it? A with the "evidence" for Bigfoot or the Loch Ness monster or other cryptids, photos and video and footprints and eyewitness accounts are not enough, because all these are easily faked, altered, or hoaxed. A scientist tells the cryptozoologist to "show me the body" (or at least its bones or other convincing piece of tissue). Likewise, a true scientist expects the UFO advocate to "show me the body" of the alien or "show me the spacecraft" before taking these claims seriously and considering them to be valid scientific evidence.

The Selfless Gene

Olivia Judson

From Olivia Judson, "The Selfless Gene." *Atlantic Monthly* (October 2007), pp. 90-98. Slightly edited for formatting purposes.

***Olivia Judson** (b. 1970) teaches evolutionary biology at Imperial College London and writes on science for such publications as* The Economist, The New York Times, *and* Nature. *She is well known for her award-winning book on the sex lives of animals:* Dr. Tatiana's Sex Advice to All Creation *(2003).*

***Why are we reading this?** For centuries there has been a long-running debate about human nature. Are people essentially good, generous, and helpful to one another? Are we instead basically selfish, greedy, self-centered, and hence "evil"? Is human nature somewhere in between? And what is the origin of our basic nature? Religions and philosophical systems answer these questions in various ways, but most have sought to describe and encourage behavior thought to be good or ethical. Several religions, including Christianity, have grounded ethical systems in divine preference or commandment, reinforced by the offer of reward or threat of punishment, often in an afterlife.*

While naturalist and non-religious explanations of human nature have existed for centuries, such approaches gained a new impetus with Charles Darwin's publication of the theory of evolution by natural selection in 1859. In many readings of evolutionary theory, human beings and other animals evolved according to selfish tendencies, or what Herbert Spencer infamously labeled "the survival of the fittest." (Darwin is often misattributed with having coined the phrase.) Yet Darwin did also suggest, against the thinking of many in the biological community, that "group selection" might have some role in the evolution and survival of species. In other words, natural selection might favor traits that improve the survival of the group, not just survival of the individual. Generosity and altruism towards others in one's group could theoretically become encoded in the genes, both of humans and animals. In the current century, biologists are revising their thinking on the subject. This particular essay not only challenges what many have long believed to be conventional wisdom. It also shows how scientists can revise their views over time as new evidence presents itself in their studies. In this sense, it's a prime example of how science operates as a way of knowing, with its capacity to revise and reconsider the evidence.

At 2 a.m. on February 26, 1852, the Royal Navy troopship Birkenhead, which was carrying more than 600 people, including seven women and 13 children, struck a rock near Danger Point, two miles off the coast of South Africa. Almost immediately, the ship began to break up. Just three lifeboats could be launched. The men were ordered to stand on deck, and they did. The women and children (along with a few sailors) were put into the lifeboats and rowed away. Only then were the men told that they could try to save themselves by swimming to shore. Most drowned or were eaten by sharks. The heroism of the troops, standing on deck facing almost certain death while others escaped, became the stuff of legend. But the strange thing is, such heroics are not rare: Humans often risk their lives for strangers – think of the firemen going into the World Trade Center – or for people they know but are not related to.

How does a propensity for self-sacrifice evolve? And what about the myriad lesser acts of daily kindness – helping a little old lady across the street, giving up a seat on the subway, returning a wallet that's been lost? Are these impulses as primal as ferocity, lust, and greed? Or are they just a thin veneer over a savage nature? Answers come from creatures as diverse as amoebas and baboons, but the story starts in the county of Kent, in southern England.

Evolving Generosity

Kent has been home to two great evolutionary biologists. In the 19th century, Charles Darwin lived for many years in the village of Downe. In the 20th, William Donald Hamilton grew up catching beetles and chasing butterflies over the rolling hills near Badgers Mount. Hamilton was a tall man with a craggy face and the tops of a couple of fingers missing from a childhood accident – he blew himself up while making explosives. He died in 2000, at age 63, after an illness contracted while undertaking another risky endeavor: a trip to the Congo to collect chimpanzee feces. When I first met him, in Oxford in 1991, he had a terrific shock of white hair, rode a rickety bicycle at prodigious speed, and was preoccupied with the question of why sex is useful in evolutionary terms. (For my doctorate, I worked with him on this question.) But he began his career studying social behavior, and in the early '60s he published a trio of now-classic papers in which he offered the first rigorous explanation of how generosity can evolve, and under what circumstances it is likely to emerge.

Hamilton didn't call it generosity, though; he called it altruism. And the particular behaviors he sought to explain are acts of extreme self-sacrifice, such as when a bee dies to defend the hive, or when an animal spends its whole life helping others rear their children instead of having some of its own.

To see why these behaviors appear mysterious to biologists, consider how natural selection works. In every generation, some individuals leave more descendants than others. If the reason for their greater "reproductive success" is due to the particular genes they have, then natural selection has been operating.

Here's an example: Suppose you're a mosquito living on the French Mediterranean coast. Tourists don't like mosquitoes, and the French authorities try to keep the tourists happy by spraying insecticide. Which means that on the coast, mosquitoes bearing a gene that confers insecticide resistance tend to leave many more descendants than those lacking it – and so today's coastal mosquitoes are far more resistant to insecticide than those that live inland.

Extreme altruists, by definition, leave no descendants: They're too busy helping others. So at first blush, a gene that promotes extreme altruism should quickly vanish from a population. Hamilton's solution to this problem was simple and elegant. He realized that a gene promoting extreme altruism could spread if the altruist helped its close relations. The reason is that your close relations have some of the same genes as you do. In humans and other mammals, full brothers and sisters have, on average, half the same genes. First cousins have, on average, an eighth of their genes in common. Among insects such as ants and bees, where the underlying genetics work differently, full sisters (but not brothers) typically have three-quarters of their genes in common.

Hamilton derived a formula – now known as Hamilton's rule – for predicting whether the predisposition toward a given altruistic act is likely to evolve: $rB>C$. In plain language, this says that genes that promote the altruistic act will spread if the benefit (B) that the act bestows is high enough, and the genetic relationship (r) between the altruist and the beneficiary is close enough, to outweigh the act's cost (C) to the altruist. Cost and benefit are both measured in nature's currency: children. "Cheap" behaviors – such as when a small bird squawks from the bushes to announce it's seen a cat or a hawk – can, and do, evolve easily, even though they often benefit nonrelatives. "Expensive" behaviors, such as working your whole life to rear someone else's children, evolve only in the context of close kin.

Since Hamilton first proposed the idea, "kin selection" has proved tremendously powerful as a way to understand cooperative and self-sacrificial behavior in a huge menagerie of animals. Look at lions. Lionesses live with their sisters, cousins, and aunts; they hunt together and help each other with child care. Bands of males, meanwhile, are typically brothers and half-brothers. Large bands are better able to keep a pride of lionesses; thus even males who never mate with a female still spread some of their genes by helping their brothers defend the pride. Or take peacocks. Males often stand in groups when they display to females. This is because females are drawn to groups of displaying males; they ogle them, then pick the guy they like best to be their mate. Again, peacocks prefer to display with their brothers rather than with males they are not related to.

Kin selection operates even in mindless creatures such as amoebas. For instance, the soil-dwelling amoeba Dictyostelium purpureum. When times are good, members of this species live as single cells, reproducing asexually and feasting on bacteria. But when times get tough – when there's a bacteria shortage – thousands of individuals join together into a single entity known as a slug. This glides off in search of more suitable conditions. When it finds them, the slug transforms itself into a fruiting body that looks like a tiny mushroom; some of the amoebas become the stalk, others become spores. Those in the stalk will die; only the spores will go on to form the next amoeboid generation. Sure enough, amoebas with the same genes (in other words, clones) tend to join the same slugs: They avoid mixing with genetic strangers and sacrifice themselves only for their clones.

Kin selection also accounts for some of the nastier features of human behavior, such as the tendency stepparents have to favor their own children at the expense of their stepkids. But it's not enough to explain the evolution of all aspects of social behavior, in humans or in other animals.

Living Together

Animals may begin to live together for a variety of reasons – most obviously, safety in numbers. In one of his most engaging papers, Hamilton observed that a tight flock, herd, or shoal will readily appear if every animal tries to make itself safer by moving into the middle of the group – a phenomenon he termed the "selfish herd." But protection from predators isn't the only benefit of bunching together. A bird in a flock spends more time eating and less time looking about for danger than it does when on its own. Indeed, eating well is another common reason for group living. Some predatory animals – chimpanzees, spotted hyenas, and wild dogs, for example – have evolved to hunt together.

Many social animals thus live in huge flocks or herds, and not in family groups – or even if the nexus of social life is the family, the family group is itself part of a larger community. In species such as these, social behavior must extend beyond a simple "Be friendly and helpful to your family and hostile to everybody else" approach to the world. At the least, the evolution of social living requires limiting aggression so that neighbors can tolerate each other. And often, the evolution of larger social groupings is accompanied by an increase in the subtlety and complexity of the ways animals get along together.

Consider baboons. Baboons are monkeys, not apes, and are thus not nearly as closely related to us as chimpanzees are. Nonetheless, baboons have evolved complex social lives. They live in troops that can number from as few as eight to as many as 200. Females live with their sisters, mothers, aunts, and infants; males head off to find a new troop at adolescence (around age 4). Big troops typically contain several female family groups, along with some adult males. The relationships between members of a troop are varied and complex. Sometimes two or more males team up to defeat a dominant male in combat. Females often have a number of male "friends" that they associate with (friends may or may not also be sex partners). If a female is attacked or harassed, her friends will come bounding to the rescue; they will also protect her children, play with them, groom them, carry them, and sometimes share food with them. If the mother dies, they may even look after an infant in her place.

Yet friendliness and the associated small acts of affection and kindness – a bout of grooming here, a shared bite to eat there – seem like evolutionary curiosities. Small gestures like these don't affect how many children you have. Or do they?

Among social animals, one potentially important cause of premature death is murder. Infanticide can be a problem for social mammals, from baboons and chimpanzees to lions and even squirrels. During one four-year study of Belding's ground squirrels, for example, the main cause of death for juveniles was other Belding's ground squirrels; at least 8 percent of the young were murdered before being weaned. Similarly, fighting between adults – particularly in species where animals are well armed with horns, tusks, or teeth – can be lethal, and even if it is not, it may result in severe injuries, loss of status, or eviction from the group.

The possibility of death by murder creates natural selection for traits that reduce this risk. For example, any animal that can appease an aggressor, or that knows when to advance and when to retreat, is more likely to leave descendants than an animal that leaps wildly into any fray. Which explains why, in many social-mammal species, you don't see many murders, though you do see males engaging in elaborate rituals to see who's bigger and stronger. Serious physical fights tend to break out only when both animals think they can win (that is, when they are about the same size).

Thus, among animals such as baboons, friendships mean more than a bit of mutual scratching; they play a fundamental role in an animal's ability to survive and reproduce within the group. Friendships between males can be important in overcoming a dominant male – which may in turn lead to an improvement in how attractive the animals are to females. Similarly, females that have a couple of good male friends will be more protected from bullying – and their infants less likely to be killed. Why do the males do it? Males that are friends with a particular female are more likely to become her sex partners later on, if indeed they are not already. In other words, friendship may be as primal an urge as ferocity.

Becoming Human

The lineage that became modern humans split off from the lineage that became chimpanzees around 6 million years ago. Eventually this new lineage produced the most socially versatile animal the planet has ever seen: us. How did we get to be this way?

One clue comes from chimpanzees. Chimpanzee society is the mirror image of baboon society, in that it's the females that leave home at adolescence, and the males that stay where they were born. Chimpanzee communities can also be fairly large, comprising several different subcommunities and family groups. Males prefer to associate with their brothers and half-brothers on their mother's side, but they also have friendships with unrelated males. Friends hang out together and hunt together and – gang up on other males.

However, unlike baboon troops, which roam around the savannah freely intermingling, chimpanzee communities are territorial. Bands of males patrol the edges of their community's territory looking for strangers – and sometimes make deep incursions into neighboring terrain. Males on patrol move together in silence, often stopping to listen. If they run into a neighboring patrol, there may be some sort of skirmish, which may or may not be violent. But woe betide a lone animal that runs into the patrolling males. If they encounter a strange male on his own, they may well kill him. And sometimes, repeated and violent attacks by one community lead to the annihilation of another, usually smaller, one. Indeed, two of the three most-studied groups of chimpanzees have wiped out a neighboring community.

Chimpanzees have two important sources of premature death at the hands of other chimpanzees: They may be murdered by members of their own community, or they may be killed during encounters with organized bands of hostile neighbors.

Just like humans. Except that humans aren't armed with big teeth and strong limbs. Humans carry weapons, and have done so for thousands of years.

On Love and War

Darwin wondered whether lethal warring between neighboring groups might have caused humans to evolve to be more helpful and kind to each other. At first, the idea seems paradoxical. But Darwin thought this could have happened if the more cohesive, unified, caring groups had been better able to triumph over their more disunited rivals. If so, the members of those cohesive, yet warlike, groups would have left more descendants.

For a long time, the idea languished. Why? A couple of reasons. First, it appears to depend on "group selection." This is the idea that some groups evolve characteristics that allow them to outcompete other groups, and it's long been out of favor with evolutionary biologists. In general, natural selection works much more effectively on individuals than it does on groups, unless the groups are composed of close kin. That's because group selection can be effective only when the competing groups are genetically distinct. Members of a kin group tend to be genetically similar to each other, and different from members of other kin groups. In contrast, groups composed of non-kin tend to contain considerable genetic variation, and differences between such groups are generally much smaller. Moreover, contact between the groups – individuals migrating from one to another, say – will reduce any genetic differences that have started to accumulate. So unless natural selection within the groups is different – such that what it takes to survive and reproduce in one group is different from what it takes in another – migration quickly homogenizes the genetics of the whole population.

A second reason Darwin's idea has been ignored is that it seems to have a distasteful corollary. The idea implies, perhaps, that some unpleasant human characteristics such as xenophobia or even racism, evolved in tandem with generosity and kindness. Why? Because banding together to fight means that people must be able to tell the difference between friends (who belong in the group) and foes (who must be fought). In the mid-1970s, in a paper that speculated about how humans might have evolved, Hamilton suggested that xenophobia might be innate. He was pilloried.

But times have changed. Last year, the science journal *Nature* published a paper that tested the idea of "parochial altruism," the notion that people might prefer to help strangers from their own ethnic group over strangers from a different group; the experiment found that indeed they do. In addition, the idea that natural selection might work on groups – at least in particular and narrow circumstances – has become fashionable again. And so Darwin's idea about the evolution of human kindness as a result of war has been dusted off and scrutinized.

Sam Bowles, an economist turned evolutionary biologist who splits his time between the Santa Fe Institute, in New Mexico, and the University of Siena, in Italy, notes that during the last 90,000 years of the Pleistocene Epoch (from about 100,000 years ago until about 10,000 years ago, when agriculture emerged), the human population hardly grew. One reason for this was the extraordinary climactic volatility of the period. But another, Bowles suggests, was that our ancestors were busy killing each other in wars. Working from archaeological records and ethnographic studies, he estimates that wars between different groups could have accounted for a substantial fraction of human deaths – perhaps as much as 15 percent, on average, of those born in any given year – and as such, represented a significant source of natural selection.

Bowles shows that groups of supercooperative, altruistic humans could indeed have wiped out groups of less-united folk. However, his argument works only if the cooperative groups also had practices – such as monogamy and the sharing of food with other group members – that reduced the ability of their selfish members to out-reproduce their more generous members. (Monogamy helps the spread of altruism because it reduces the differences in the number of children that different people have. If, instead, one or two males monopolized all the females in the group, any genes involved in altruism would quickly disappear.) In other words, Bowles argues that a genetic predisposition for altruism would have been far more likely to evolve in groups where disparities and discord inside the group – whether over mates or food – would have been relatively low. Cultural differences between groups would then allow genetic differences to accumulate.

"That's Not the Way You Do It"

If Bowles's analysis is right, it suggests that individuals who could not conform, or who were disruptive, would have weakened the whole group; any group that failed to drive out such people, or kill them, would have been more likely to be overwhelmed in battle. Conversely, people who fit in – sharing the food they found, joining in hunting, helping to defend the group, and so on – would have given their group a collective advantage, and thus themselves an individual evolutionary advantage.

This suggests two hypotheses. First, that one of the traits that may have evolved in humans is conformity, an ability to fit in with a group and adopt its norms and customs. Second, that enforcement of those norms and customs could have been essential for group cohesion and harmony, especially as groups got bigger (bigness is important in battles against other groups).

Let's start with conformity. This hasn't been studied much in other animals, but male baboons do appear to conform to the social regimens of the groups they join. For example, in one baboon troop in Kenya in the 1980s, all the aggressive males died of tuberculosis. The aggressives were the ones to snuff it because they'd eaten meat infected with bovine TB that had been thrown into a garbage dump; only the more-aggressive males ate at the dump.

After their deaths, the dynamics of the troop shifted to a more laid-back way of life. Ten years later – by which time all the original resident males had either died or moved on – the troop was still notable for its mellow attitude. The new males who'd arrived had adopted the local customs.

What about humans? According to Michael Tomasello – a psychologist at the Max Planck Institute, in Leipzig, Germany, who studies the behavior of human children and of chimpanzees – children as young as 3 will quickly deduce and conform to rules. If an adult demonstrates a game, and then a puppet comes in and plays it differently, the children will clamor to correct the puppet with shouts of "No, that's not the way you do it – you do it this way!" In other words, it's not just that they infer and obey rules; they try to enforce them, too. Which brings me to the question of punishment.

Punishment Games

I'll be dictator. Here's how we play: An economist puts some money on the table – let's say $1,000. Since I'm dictator, I get to decide how you and I are going to split the cash; you have no say in the matter. How much do you think I'll give you? Now, let's play the ultimatum game. We've still got $1,000 to play with, and I still get to make you an offer. But the game has a wrinkle: If you don't like the offer I make, you can refuse it. If you refuse it, we both get nothing. What do you think I'll do here?

As you've probably guessed, people tend to play the two games differently. In the dictator game, the most common offer is nothing, and the average offer is around 20 percent. In the ultimatum game, the most common offer is half the cash, while the average is around 45 percent. Offers of less than 25 percent are routinely refused – so both players go home empty-handed.

Economists scratch their heads at this. In the first place, they are surprised that some people are nice enough to share with someone they don't know, even in the dictator game, where there's nothing to lose by not sharing. Second, economists predict that people will accept any offer in the ultimatum game, no matter how low, because getting something is better than getting nothing. But that's not what happens. Instead, some people forgo getting anything themselves in order to punish someone who made an ungenerous offer. Money, it seems, is not the only currency people are dealing in.

Bring in the neuroscientists, and the other currency gets clearer. If you measure brain activity while such games are being played (and there are many variants, for the fun doesn't stop with dictators and ultimatums), you find that the reward centers of the brain – the bits that give you warm, fuzzy feelings – light up when people are cooperating. But they also light up if you punish someone who wasn't generous, or watch the punishment of someone who wasn't. Whether these responses are universal isn't clear: The genetic basis is obscure, and the number of people who've had their brain activity measured is tiny. Moreover, most economic game playing has been done with college students; the extent to which the results hold among people from different cultures and backgrounds is relatively unknown. But the results suggest an intriguing possibility: that humans have evolved both to be good at conforming to the prevailing cultural norms and to enjoy making sure that those norms are enforced. (Perhaps this explains why schemes such as zero-tolerance policing work so well: They play into our desire to conform to the prevailing norms.)

Bringing Out the Best

If the evolutionary scenario I've outlined is even half right, then we should expect to find that there are genes involved in mediating friendly behavior. And there are. Consider Williams syndrome.

People who have Williams syndrome tend to have poor cardiovascular function and a small, pointed, "elfin" face. They are typically terrible with numbers but good with words. And they are weirdly, incautiously friendly and nice – and unafraid of strangers.

They are also missing a small segment of chromosome 7. Chromosomes are long strings of DNA. Most people have 46 chromosomes in 23 pairs; you get one set of 23 from your mother, and the other from your father. In Williams syndrome, one copy of chromosome 7 is normal; the other is missing a small piece. The missing piece contains about 20 genes, some of which make proteins that are important in the workings of the brain. Since one chromosome is intact, the problem isn't a complete absence of the proteins that the genes encode, but an insufficiency. Somehow, this insufficiency results in people who are too nice. What's more, they can't learn not to be nice. Which is to say, someone with Williams syndrome can learn the phrase "Don't talk to strangers" but can't translate it into action. Much about Williams syndrome remains mysterious.

How the missing genes normally influence behavior is unclear; moreover, the environment has a role to play, too. But despite these complexities, Williams syndrome shows that friendliness has a genetic underpinning – that it is indeed as primal as ferocity. Indirectly, it shows something else as well. Most of us are able to apply brakes to friendly behavior, picking and choosing the people we are friendly to; those with Williams syndrome aren't. They cannot modulate their behavior. This is even odder than being too friendly. And it throws into sharp relief one of the chief features of ordinary human nature: its flexibility.

One of the most important, and least remarked upon, consequences of social living is that individual behavior must be highly flexible and tailored to circumstance: An individual who does not know whom to be aggressive toward, or whom to help, is unlikely to survive for long within the group. This is true for baboons and chimpanzees. It is also true for us.

Indeed, the ability to adjust our behavior to fit a given social environment is one of our main characteristics, yet it's so instinctive we don't even notice it, let alone consider it worthy of remark. But its implications are profound – and hopeful. It suggests that we can, in principle, organize society so as to bring out the best facets of our complex, evolved natures.

The Dialectic of Theology and Life Speaking the Truth

James H. Cone

From *Union Seminary Quarterly Review* 29.2 (1974): 75-89.

***James H. Cone** (1938-2018) was an American theologian and one of the primary advocates of what is known as Black Liberation Theology. His books,* Black Theology and Black Power (1969) *and* A Black Theology of Liberation (1970) *were pivotal moments in contemporary theology, as they moved theological consideration from abstract concerns to those in line with the lived experiences of people, particularly oppressed people – with the conclusion that God was not the God of oppressors, but of the oppressed. Cone received his PhD from Northwestern University, authored eleven books, and taught for most of his career at Union Theological Seminary in New York City.*

***Why we are reading this:** Christian theologians tend to rely on several kinds of sources as they work out their ideas about God, Jesus Christ, and the Christian life. The primary source is always Holy Scripture – the Christian Bible, comprising the Hebrew scriptures (Old Testament) and the Christian New Testament. Another source of ideas is the wisdom and writing of theologians, philosophers, and church leaders through the ages, beginning with the so-called "Church Fathers" in the first few centuries of the Christian era and stretching down to the recent past. For many theologians, a third source is religious experience, which might be rooted in their individual life-story or in the life of a worshipful community.*

Cone's approach falls in this tradition, but with some critical differences. Cone seeks to outline how "Black Theology" arises from Scripture understood in the light of the black experience in the United States. In the article below he describes and analyzes African American folklore, song, and sermons, drawing out religious and theological implications and showing how and why black and white Christians in the United States may experience and think about their Christianity in very different ways. This raises interesting questions about whether there is a single "true" Christianity, and how one might identify it. Modern Christians don't much like to accuse one another of "heresy," but at the end of his essay, Cone argues that distinguishing valid theology from heresy is a useful and important exercise. "Not every theology that claims to be Christian is Christian," he writes. Do you agree? What else strikes you as interesting in Cone's article?

Speak the truth to the people
Talk sense to the people
Free them with reason
Free them with honesty
Free the people with Love and Courage and Care for their being[1]

Black theologians are living in a period in which we must investigate anew "the problem of the color line," as that problem is reflected in the social existence of African peoples. We cannot afford to do theology unrelated to human existence. We cannot be "objective," but must recognize with Imamu Baraka, that "there is no objective anything"[2] – least of all, theology. Our theology must emerge consciously from an investigation of the socio-religious experience of black people, as that experience is reflected in *black* stories of God's dealings with black people in the struggle of freedom. Tertullian's question, "What . . . has Athens to do with Jerusalem?"[3] is not our central question. His concern was to state the primacy of faith in relation to reason on matters of theological discourse. We have another concern, and thus, we must rephrase that question in the light of our cultural history, asking: "What has *Africa* to do with Jerusalem, and what difference does Jesus make for African people oppressed in North America?" As Gerard Bissainthe puts it:

From the despair of our cry,
The heart's intensity,
Out of death and dereliction
In the land of our uprootedness,
We shall one day give birth to our Christ,
A Christ made flesh of our flesh,
Our dark flesh of the black people.[4]

---

[1] Marie Evans, *I Am a Black Woman* (New York: William Morrow & Co., 1970), p. 91.
[2] Cited in Don L. Lee, *Dynamite Voices* (Detroit: Broadside Press, 1971), p. 14. Baraka's concern was to give a critique of the so-called "objectivity" in poetry and other art forms. The same critique applies to other human expressions, especially theology.
[3] "On Prescription Against Heretics" in *The Ante-Nicene Fathers,* ed. A. Roberts and J. Donaldson, Vol. III, Chap. 7 (Grand Rapids, Michigan: William B. Eerdman's, 1951), p. 246.
[4] Cited in John V. Taylor, *The Primal Vision* (London: SCM Press, 1963), pp. 16-17.

If our theological vocation emerges out of the matrix of that vision, then we will not be limited to Euro-American definitions of theology. The ecstasy of the poet's vision and the concreteness of the historical reality from which the vision is created bestow upon us a new perspective, a *black* perspective that grants free thinking in relation to our cultural history and thus enables us to hear the urgent call to speak the truth. In this context, truth is not an intellectual datum that is entrusted to academic guilds. Truth cannot be separated from the people's struggle and the hopes and dreams that arise from that struggle. Truth is that transcendent reality, disclosed in the people's historical struggle for liberation, which enables them to know that their fight for freedom is not futile. The affirmation of truth means that the freedom hoped for will be realized. Indeed, the freedom hoped for is already partly realized in our present history, because the realization of hope is the very ground of our present struggle. We do not struggle in despair but in hope, not from doubt but from faith, not out of hate but out of love for ourselves and for humanity. And as black theologians, who have been grasped by the truth, we are accountable to black people.

What does it mean to speak the truth from a black theological perspective; that is, what are the sources and the content of theology? To examine this question we must begin by exploring the theological function of the black experience.

The Black Experience as a Source of Theology

There is no truth for and about black people that does not emerge out of the context of their experience. Truth in this sense is Black Truth, a truth disclosed in the history and culture of black people. This means that there can be no Black Theology which does not take the black experience as a source for its starting point. Black Theology is a theology of and for black people, an examination of their stories, tales, and sayings. It is an investigation of the mind into the raw materials of our pilgrimage, telling the story of "how we got over." For theology to be black, it must reflect upon what it means to be black. Black Theology must uncover the structures and forms of the black experience, because the categories of interpretation must arise out of the thought forms of the black experience itself.

What are we to make of the moan and the shout and the call to get on board the gospel train? What must we say about the song, the sermon, the prayer, and the feeling of the Spirit when the people gather for worship and praise to the One they say is "a rock in the weary land, a shelter in a mighty storm, and a stronghold in the day of trouble"?[5]

The Sermon. When dealing with the sermon, we must listen to the proclamation of the gospel as disclosed in the Black Word. Sometimes the Word is expressed with apocalyptic imagination:

And now I leave dis thought wid you,
Standing out on de eaves of ether
Breathing from out of his nostrils.
Blowing storms from 'tween his lips
I can see!!
Him seize de mighty axe of his proving power
And smite the stubborn-standing space,
And laid it wide open in a mighty gash—
Making a place to hold the world I can see him—
Molding de world out of thought and power
And whirling it out on its eternal track,
Ah hah, my strong-armed God![6]

This sermon makes clear that the Word and its proclamation in the black church is more than the conceptualization of theological doctrine. The Word is more than *words* about God. God's Word is a poetic happening,

---

[5] Cited in J. Mason Brewer, *American Negro Folklore* (Chicago: Quadrangle Books, 1968), p. 140.

[6] Cited in Langston Hughes and Ara Bontemps, *Book of Negro Folklore* (New York: Dodd, Mead & Co., 1958), pp. 234-35. This is an excellent collection of sermons, prayers, songs and other folkloric material. Perhaps the earliest and the best study of old-time black preaching is William H. Pipes, *Say Amen, Brothers!* (Westport, Connecticut: Negro Universities Press, 1970), originally published in 1951. See also James W. Johnson's excellent book, *God's Trombones* (New York: The Viking Press, 1927). Another excellent study and collection of folkloric material in general and sermons in particular is Brewer, *op. cit.* See also Bruce A. Rosenberg, *The Art of the American Folk Preacher* (New York: Oxford University Press, 1970); Henry H. Mitchell, *Black Preaching* (New York: Lippincott, 1970). But the best introduction to the black sermon is through the black preacher himself at a black church on any given Sunday morning. Failing that possibility, I would recommend the recordings of the Reverend C. L. Franklin, who perhaps represents in his tradition what his daughter, Aretha, represents in hers. The Rev. C. L. Franklin has recorded more than fifty sermons at New Bethel Baptist Church in Detroit, and they are available on Chess long-playing records. For a listing of these sermons, see his album, "The Inner Conflict," sermon No. 43, Chess Producing Corporation, 320 East 21st St., Chicago, Illinois. For other black sermons, see The Rev. Clay Evans' albums.

an evocation of an indescribable reality in the lives of the people. This is the meaning behind the occasion when a black preacher "who after reading a rather cryptic passage took off his spectacles, closed the Bible with a bang and by way of preface said, 'Brothers and sisters, this morning – I intend to explain the inexplainable – find out the undefinable – ponder over the imponderable – and unscrew the inscrutable.'"[7] Here the preacher is affirming not only his freedom in relation to the text; he is also making a sharp distinction between the *words* of the text and the *Word* disclosed in the text.

The black theologian must also make similar distinctions in his use of the sermon as a source of theology. He must not be bound to white, academic conceptualizations of the Christian gospel. If the gospel means freedom, then the freedom disclosed in that gospel must also be revealed in the event of proclamation. The preaching of the Word must itself be the embodiment of freedom. When freedom is a constituent of the language itself, then that language refuses to be bound to the limitations of categories not indigenous to its being. Possibilities are thus given for the communication of the Word that transcends intellectual concepts. In black preaching, the Word becomes embodied in the rhythm and the emotions of language as the people respond bodily to the Spirit in their midst. The black sermon arises out of the totality of the people's existence – their pain and joy, trouble and ecstasy.[8]

The Prayer. What was said about the freedom inherent in the sermon can also be said about the prayers of black people. Black prayers are not the same as white prayers. In the black perspective, white folks prayed like this:

> O Lahd, the first thing I want you to understand is that it is a white man talking to you. This ain't no nigger whooping and hollering for something and then don't know what to do with it after he gets it. This is a white man talking to you, and I want you to pay some attention. Now, in the first place, Lahd, we would like a little rain. It's been powerful dry around here, and we needs rain mighty bad. But don't

[7] James W. Johnson, *op. cit.,* pp. 4-5.

[8] Some interpreters have misunderstood the black preacher because of the limitations of their conceptual tools of evaluation. See especially Bruce Rosenberg's *The Art of the American Folk Preacher*. The importance of this book is perhaps limited to its inclusion of valuable texts of sermons. From my viewpoint and concern, the chief defect of this work was his failure to take seriously, as an *interpretative tool,* the socio-religious consciousness of the preachers under investigation.

come in no storm like you did last year. Come ca'm and gentle and water our crops.

And now another thing, Lahd – don't let these niggers be as sassy this coming year as they have been in the past. That's all, Lahd, Amen.[9]

When the black man prayed, he did not accept the religious outlook of the white master. To be sure, the historical situation of slavery may have forced the black person to worship with and "like" the white master, but in many subtle ways the slave transcended the limitations of servitude and affirmed a religious value-system that differed from his master's. In response to a white minister, conducting a revival at a black church, "the brother in black" offered this prayer for "his brother in white":

> Oh Lawd, gib him de eye de eagle, dat he may spy out sin afar off, weave his hands to the gospel plow, tie his tongue to de limbs ob truth, nail his ear to de South Pole. Bow his head away down between his knees, and his knees way down in some lonesome dark and narrow valley where prayer is much wanted to be made. 'Noint him wid de kerosene oil of salvation and set him on fire.[10]

Sometimes black people in their praying were more direct in their rejection of white people's value-system. On one occasion, the white preacher, in his sermon to a black congregation, suggested that "in heaven there must be some Jim Crow partition, with the white saints on one side and the black saints on the other. And after the sermon, when one of the black deacons was called on to pray, he got his chance to reply to this white preacher; for like many praying people, the old black man knew how to talk *to* the Lord and talk *at* other people, in the same phrases." This is what he said:

> And, O Lord, we thank thee fer the brother preacher who has spoke to us, – we thank thee for heaven, – we thank thee that we kin all go to heaven, – but as to that partition, O Lord, we thank thee that we'se a shoutin' people, – we thank thee that we kin shout so hard in heaven that we will break down that partition an' spread all over heaven, – an'

---

[9] Cited in Brewer, *op. cit.*, p. 139.

[10] *Ibid.*, quoted on p. 140. Like the sermon, the best source for black prayers is the black church on a given Sunday morning or a Wednesday night prayer service. The next best source would be recordings contained on many sermon albums. See The Reverend C. L. Franklin, "Rev. C. L. Franklin Sings," LP-3, Chess Producing Corporation. Written prayers are found in Hughes and Bontemps, *op. cit.*, Johnson, *op. cit.*, Brewer, *op. cit.*, and Pipes, *op. cit.*

we thank thee that if the white fokes can't stand it, they can get on out of heaven an' go to elsewhere![11]

Here the black theologian should reflect not only upon humor as an artistic expression of black survival but also upon the Word of prayer as disclosed in the affirmation of black identity. God is the Spirit of Jesus that guides and moves the people in their struggle to be what they were created to be. He is their "Captain who never lost a battle." In prayer, sometimes, he is called the "mighty good leader," the "dying-bed maker," and the "soul's emancipator." All these phrases point to God as the living and ever-present One who grants freedom for the humiliated and stands in judgment upon oppressors who attempt to destroy black dignity.

The Song. A similar emphasis is found in the song – the spirituals, gospels, and other melodious expressions of the people's struggle for freedom.[12] The function of the song is to sing the truth as it is lived by the people.

Who found me when I was lost?
Who helped me to bear my heavy cross?
Who fixed me up, turned me 'round,
Left my feet on solid ground?

---

[11] Cited in Hughes and Bontemps, *op. cit.,* pp. 156-57.

[12] Sources and texts of the spirituals are numerous. For an interpretation of the theological significance of the spirituals, see my *The Spirituals and the Blues* (New York: Seabury Press, 1972); see also Howard Thurman, *The Negro Spiritual Speaks* of *Life and Death* (New York: Harper and Row, 1947), and *Deep River* (Port Washington, New York: Kennikat Press, 1969), originally published in 1945. The best collection of the text and music of the spirituals is James W. Johnson and J. Rosamond Johnson, *The Books of American Negro Spirituals* (New Viking Press, 1925). See also John W. Work, *American Negro Songs and Spirituals,* (New York: Bonanza Books, 1940). The earliest book collection of slave songs is William F. Allen, Charles P. Ware, and Lucy McKim Garrison, *Slave Songs of the United States* (New York: A. Simpson & Co., 1867). One of the best and most comprehensive studies on the spirituals is John Lovell, Jr., *Black Song: The Forge and the Flame* (New York: Macmillan Co., 1972). Unfortunately, the gospel songs have not been studied as seriously as the spirituals. The best volume I know of is *The Gospel Sound* by Tony Heilbut (New York: Simon and Schuster, 1971). For the lyrics, see Hughes and Bontemps, op. cit., Chapter XII.

Again, the best introduction to the black song is the black church. Failing that, I would suggest the recordings by Mahalia Jackson, James Cleveland, Clara Ward, and Paul Robeson. I would strongly suggest Aretha Franklin's recent album entitled "Amazing Grace," with James Cleveland and The Southern California Community Choir, Atlantic Recording Corporation, New York, 1972.

I know it was Jesus!
I **know** it was the Lord!
Who do you think gave sight to the blind?
Made the lame to walk
And dead men rise?
Who took the fishes and the loaves of bread
And made 500 so all could be fed?
Oh, Jesus, Oh Lord, Jesus! My Lord!
I know it was Jesus! I know it was the Lord!

As with the sermon and prayer, the spirituals and gospel songs reveal that the truth of black religion is not limited to the literal meaning of the words. Truth is also disclosed in the movement of the language and the passion created when a song is sung in the right pitch and tonal quality. Truth is found in the shout, hum, and moan as these expressions move the people closer to the source of their being.

In these "churchly expressions," among others, the divine One informs and discloses himself in black reality and is best defined in terms of black people's response in body and spirit to that divine source believed to be greater than themselves. If asked the theological question, "Who is God?" one black person might say: "I don't know much about him. All I know is that I was weak and he gave me strength. I was lost and he found me. I was crying and he wiped away the tears from my eyes." Another might testify in this manner: "God is a heart fixer and a mind regulator. He is the One who binds the broken heart and eases the pain of the afflicted. He rescued me from the gates of Hell and restored my soul to his bosom." The key to the theological affirmation here is not only the verbal assent to the power of God to grant identity and liberation to an oppressed and humiliated people. Equally important is the verbal passion with which these affirmations are asserted and the physical responses they elicit in the community in which the testimony is given. Some will shout, moan, and cry; others will walk, run, and clap their hands. Then there are those who will keep still, using silence as a sign of the presence of God in their midst. This is part of the matrix of Black Theology and the source out of which truth is given.

Other Black Expressions. The black experience as a source of theology is more than the so-called "church experience," more than singing, praying, and preaching about Jesus, God, and the Holy Spirit. The other side of the black experience should not be rigidly defined as "secular," if by that term one means the classical western distinction between secular and sacred, for it is not anti-religious nor even non-religious. This side of the black experience is secular only to the extent that it is earthy and seldom uses "God" or "Christianity" as the chief symbols of its hopes and dreams. It is sacred because it is created out of the *same* historical community as the church experience and thus represents the people's attempt to shape life and to live it according to their dreams and aspirations. Included in these black expressions are animal tales, tales of folk figures, slave seculars, blues, and accounts of personal experiences.

In the animal and folk figure tales, the emphasis is often on the wit and cleverness of the weak in triumph over the strong. Brer Rabbit is the central hero of the animal tales. J. Mason Brewer writes:

> The role of the Rabbit in the tales of the American Negro is similar to that of the hare in African folk narratives – that of the trickster who shrewdly outwits and gains a victory over some physically stronger or more powerful adversary. The animal tales told by Negro slaves with Brer Rabbit as the hero had a meaning far deeper than mere entertainment. The rabbit actually symbolized the slave himself. Whenever the rabbit succeeded in proving himself smarter than another animal the slave rejoiced secretly, imaging himself smarter than his master.[13]

With this perspective on the lore about the rabbit, it is understandable why folktales have been described as "hitting a straight lick with a crooked stick."[14] The slave was "putting one over on the white man, in a subtle, and partially disguised way," often singing to himself:[15]

> Got one mind for white folks to see
> 'Nother for what I know is me;
> He don't know, he don't know my mind,
> When he see me laughing
> Just laughing to keep from crying.

A similar theme is found in tales about the folk hero, High John the Conqueror.[16] He was the "hopebringer," an expression of the slaves' desire

---

[13] Brewer, *op. cit.,* pp. 3-4. For authenticity, most scholars still regard Joel Chandler Harris' *Uncle Remus: His Songs and His Sayings* (New York: Houghton, Mifflin and Co., 1881) as the most significant. On Brer Rabbit and other animal tales, see also Hughes and Bontemps, *op. cit.,* Chapters I and II.

[14] Cited in William F. Cheek, *Black Resistance Before the Civil War* (Beverly Hills, California: Glencoe Press, 1970), p. 51.

[15] *Ibid.*

[16] For an account of the tales about High John the Conqueror, see Zora Neal

to transcend the historical limitations of servitude and the attempt to affirm the "otherness" of existence not defined by the auction block and slave codes. High John, though not identical with Jesus Christ in the spirituals, serves a similar function. He symbolizes the slaves' desire for freedom and the recognition that they are not alone in the world. That was why High John was described as "a whisper, a will to hope, a wish to find something worthy of laughter and song." But the "whisper was put into flesh" and was "sure to be heard when and where the work was the hardest and the lot the most cruel."[17] High John was the slaves' incarnation of hope, that unbeatable reality deep in the souls of the slaves, enabling them to endure the harsh realities of servitude without losing their dignity. "So they pulled the covers up over their soul and kept them from all hurt, harm and danger ...."[18]

Unlike Jesus, who came from Nazareth and taught in Galilee, High John the Conqueror came from Africa, "walking on the waves of sound,"[19] and took flesh in America. Just as Jesus' birth in Bethlehem took place without the Romans and Jewish religious leaders recognizing Jesus' significance, so John came without slavemasters knowing the meaning of his appearance. The "Messianic secret" so dominant in Mark's portrayal of Jesus is also present in the tales about John. While the slaves knew who he was, the white masters did not perceive that they were not dealing with an ordinary slave. And perhaps the significance of John was best described by Aunt Sutton when she said John meant power,[20] the power of the slaves to hold themselves together in struggle.

In the slave, seculars and blues are revealed another black expression in song.[21] In contrast to the spirituals and gospels, God is not the subject of these songs. The seculars and blues deal with the concreteness of life's

---

Hurston, "High John De Conquer," in Hughes and Bontemps, *op. cit.,* pp. 93-102; see also her excellent work, *Mules and Men* (New York: Harper and Row, 1970), originally published in 1935. See also Brewer, *op. cit.,* and Julius Lester, *Black Folktales* (New York: Grove Press, 1969).

[17] Hurston, "High John De Conquer," in Hughes and Bontemps, *op. cit.,* pp. 93,94.

[18] *Ibid.*

[19] *Ibid.*

[20] See *Ibid.*, p. 96.

[21] The blues have been given much study. For an introduction to the theological implications of the blues, see my *The Spiritual and the Blues,* Chapter VI. The best one volume work on the blues and jazz is LeRoi Jones, *Blues People* (New York: William Morrow and Co., 1963); see also Charles Keil, *Urban Blues* (Chicago: University of Chicago Press, 1966); Paul Oliver, *The Meaning of the Blues* (New York: Collier Books, 1963); and *The Story of the Blues* (Philadelphia: Chilton Book Co., 1969).

contradictions without reference to a divine reality as a source of strength. What are we to make of this expression of truth?

> I'll eat when I'm hungry An' I' drink when I'se dry;
> An' if de whitefolks don't kill me,
> I'll live till I die.

The seculars deal with the absurdity of existence without using Jesus Christ as their central focal point. There is hope and transcendence, but only as the vision is created from life itself.

The same this-worldly emphasis is found in the blues. The theme is endurance and transcendence in the face of despair, and that is what the black folk experience is about.

> House catch on fire
> And ain't no water around.

The blues deal with all those sensitive areas of bodily expression and desire that were only indirectly touched in church music. They deal openly with sex, love, and the agony of life when a woman cannot find her man.

> The man I'll marry ain't born yet,
> An' his mammy's dead.

In the blues, there is revealed black people's ability to express the tragic side of life and use the artistic expression of tragedy as the means for transcending it.

> Ef you ever been down, you know jes how I feel—
> Lak a broken-down engine got no drivin' wheel,
> Lak a po' sojer boy lef' on de battle-fiel.

Another important theological source of the black experience is the narratives of slaves and ex-slaves, the personal accounts of black people's triumphs and defeats.[22] Here are found many dimensions of the black

---

[22] For an introduction to slave and ex-slave narratives, see Arna Bontemps, *Great Slave Narratives* (Boston: Beacon Press, 1969); W. L. Katz, ed., *Five Slave Narratives* (New York: Arno Press, 1969); B. A. Botkin, *Lay My Burden Down* (Chicago: University of Chicago Press, 1945); Norman R. Yetman, *Life Under the "Peculiar Institution"* (New York: Holt, Rinehart and Winston, 1970). See also Frederick Douglass' autobiography, *Life and Times of Frederick Douglass* (New York: Collier Books, 1962), reprinted from the revised edition of 1892. See

experience as told by those who lived it in the midst of servitude and oppression. There are those who might be described as "religious" and there are others who are indifferent toward "religion." There are slaves who praise their masters for "kind" treatment; and there are those who said, "I had much rather starve in England, a free woman, than be a slave for the best man that ever breathed upon the American continent."[23] This is the stuff of the black experience which makes Black Theology possible and necessary.

More recent black literature is another expression of the black experience. Particularly notable are the poets of the Harlem Renaissance and their successors. In the midst of the destruction of black dignity, Claude McKay articulated a poetic vision of black people's strivings for freedom.

> If we must die, let it not be like hogs,
> Hunted and penned in an inglorious spot,
> While all around us bark the mad and hungry dogs,
> Making their mock at our accursed lot.[24]

Like many black artists of that period, he recognized that art is never for its own sake but for people's sake. Black art is black people creating values based on their own experience and affirming the willingness to invent new definitions and lifestyles commensurate with their struggle to be free. That was why Claude, McKay said: "If we must die, O let us nobly die."[25]

The affirmation of *blackness* as an essential ingredient in the definition of humanity has never been easy in *white* America. But to believe in the *divine* in the context of black suffering can often bring a curious burden to bear upon a poet. As Countee Cullen puts it:

> Yet do I marvel at this curious thing:

---

also the very important *God Struck Me Dead,* Clifton H. Johnson, ed. (Boston: Pilgrim Press, 1969).

[23] This comment was made by the celebrated ex-slave, Ellen Craft; see her letter in Carter G. Woodson, *The Mind of the Negro as Reflected in Letters During the Crisis 1800-1860* (New York: Russell and Russell, 1969), p. 265, originally published in 1926.

[24] McKay, *op. cit.,* Abraham Chapman, ed. (New York: New American Library, 1968), pp. 372-73. For a critical evaluation of the Harlem Renaissance of the 1920's and early 1930's, see Nathan I. Huggins, *Harlem Renaissance* (New York: Oxford University Press, 1971). See also Alain Locke, *The New Negro* (New York: Atheneum, 1969), originally published in 1925.

[25] *Ibid.,* p. 273.

> To make a poet black and bid him sing![26]

What shall a black poet sing? In a society where black people sing,

> I wish I knew how it would feel to be free
> I wish I could break all the chains holdin' me.[27]

What is the role of the black thinker? The artists of the Harlem Renaissance did not plumb the fullest depths of that question. The black artists of the 1960's and 1970's, who are influenced by the new black consciousness as defined in the context of the Black Power Revolution, usually take their cue from Imamu Amiri Baraka:

> The Black Artist's role in America is to aid in the destruction of America as he knows it. His role is to report and reflect so precisely the nature of the society, and of himself in that society, that other men will be moved by the exactness of his rendering and, if they are black men, grow strong through this moving, having seen their own strength, and weakness; and if they are white men, tremble, curse, and go mad, because they will be drenched with the filth of their evil.[28]

To summarize: The folklore of black people centers on the ability of the weak to survive through cunning, trickery, and sheer deception in an environment of the strong and powerful. Brer Rabbit tricks Brer Fox into throwing him into the briar patch and then hollers out: "Bred en bawn in a brier-patch, Brer Fox – bred en bawn in a brier-patch!"[29] High John the Conqueror outwits the master, and another slave survives. This same theme of survival and liberation is found in the sermon, prayer, and song – including seculars, spirituals, and blues. On the one hand, there is the theological emphasis that God will liberate the weak from the injustice of the strong:

> When Israel was in Egypt's land,

---

[26] Countee Cullen, "Yet Do I Marvel," in *Black Voices,* p. 383.

[27] Billy Taylor and Dick Dallas, "I Wish I Knew How It Would Feel to Be Free," in *The Poetry of Soul,* A. X. Nicholas, ed. (New York: Bantam Books, 1971), p. 57.

[28] LeRoi Jones (Imamu Amiri Baraka), *Home* (New York: William Morrow & Co., 1966), p. 251. For an analysis of the black poets of the 1960's, see Lee, *op. cit.,* Vol. I. See also Abraham Chapman, ed., *New Black Voices* (New York: New American Library, 1972).

[29] Brewer, *op. cit., American Negro Folklore,* p. 6.

Let my people go;
Oppressed so hard they could not stand,
Let my people go;
Go down, Moses, 'way down in Egypt's land.
Tell ole Pharaoh,
Let my people go.

On the other hand, transcendence over historical negations was affirmed through the recognition that

De big bee flies high
  De little bee makes the honey
De black man raised the cotton,
  An' de white man gets de money.

But in both cases, black people expressed the contradictions of existence, while affirming the need to live in history without being conquered by it. The whole of black expression, Christian and non-Christian, that of preachers and that of poets, deals with the theme of liberation and the transcendence that happens in struggle.

Black Experience, Scripture, and Jesus Christ

The question inevitably arises, what is the relation of the black experience as a source of Black Theology to the Bible, which is traditionally identified as the source of Christian theology? The connection is simply this: when black people sing, preach, and tell stories about their struggle, one fact is clear, they are not dealing simply with themselves. They are talking about another reality – "so high you can't get over him, so low you can't get under him, so wide you can't get around him." It is this affirmation of transcendence that prevents Black Theology from being reduced merely to the cultural history of black people. For black people the transcendent reality is none other than Jesus Christ, of whom Scripture speaks. The Bible is the witness to God's self-disclosure in Jesus Christ. Thus the black experience requires that Scripture be a source of Black Theology. For it was Scripture that enabled slaves to affirm a view of God that differed radically from that of the slave masters. The slave masters' intention was to present a "Jesus" who would make the slave obedient and docile. Jesus was supposed to make black people better slaves, that is, faithful servants of white masters. But many blacks rejected that view of Jesus not only because it contradicted their African heritage, but because it contradicted the witness of Scripture. That was why Richard Allen and his companions walked out of St. George Methodist Episcopal Church in 1787 as a prophetic protest against segregated worship.[30] The same was true for Henry Highland Garnett. Through the reading of Scripture, he concluded that liberty was a gift from God, and that therefore black slaves ought to use any available means that promised success in the attainment of freedom.[31] Throughout black history Scripture was used for a definition of God and Jesus that was consistent with the black struggle for liberation. Further examples are found in Henry M. Turner's affirmation that "God is a Negro," Howard Thurman's association of Jesus with the disinherited, and Martin Luther King's view that political struggle was consistent with the gospel of Jesus.[32] Scripture established limits to white people's use of Jesus Christ as a confirmation of black oppression.

The importance of Scripture as the witness to Jesus Christ does not mean that Black Theology can therefore ignore the tradition and history of Western Christianity. It only means that our study of that tradition must be done in the light of the Word disclosed in Scripture as interpreted by black people. Although we recognize the inter-relationship of Scripture and tradition, especially in the early centuries of the church, yet the full meaning of the Scripture is not limited to the interpretation of it as given in that particular tradition. Indeed, Scripture and tradition often contradict each other. As the meaning of Jesus Christ is not to be identified with the *words* of Scripture, so the meaning of Scripture as the witness to the Word is not defined exclusively by Cyprian, Anselm, and Thomas. As theologians, we must interpret the latter in the light of the former.

On the one hand, we must evaluate a given interpreter of Scripture in the light of the *particularity* of his history, refusing to use the relativity of our present as the norm for the investigation of the past. We cannot criticize the early church fathers for their failure to address the critical questions of our contemporary situation. They are accountable only for dealing with the historical issues in their time as they relate to Jesus' presence among them. On the other hand, there are common elements in human experience that enable us to evaluate past interpreters of the faith. Since oppression of the weak by the powerful is one of these elements, we can put the critical question to Athanasius, Augustine, or Luther: What has

---

[30] See Richard Allen, *The Life Experience and Gospel Labors of the Rt. Rev. Richard Allen* (Nashville: Abingdon Press, 1960).

[31] See H.H. Garnett, *Walker's Appeal and An Address to the Slaves of the United States of America* (New York: Arno Press, 1969).

[32] See H. M. Turner, "God is A Negro," in J. H. Bracey, Jr., A. Meier, and E. Rudwick, eds., *Black Nationalism in America* (New York: Bobbs-Merrill, 1970), pp. 154-55; Howard Thurman, *Jesus and the Disinherited* (Nashville: Abingdon Press, 1949); M. L. King, Jr., *Why We Can't Wait* (New York: Signet Book, 1963).

the gospel of Jesus, as witnessed in Scripture, to do with the humiliated and the abused? If they failed to ask that question or only made it secondary in their interpretation of the gospel, then it is our task to make clear how their approach to the gospel differs from Scripture. This creates the possibility of distinguishing valid theology from heresy, a matter to be discussed later in this essay.

Jesus Christ. Having described the two sources of Black Theology (black experience and Scripture), it is now important to distinguish both of those sources from their subject or essence, which is Jesus Christ. The subject of theology is that which creates the precise character of theological language, thereby distinguishing it from other ways of speaking. By contrast, the sources of theology are the materials that make possible a valid articulation of theology's subject.

Jesus Christ is the subject of Black Theology because he is the content of the hopes and dreams of black people. He was chosen by our grandparents, who saw in his liberating presence that he had chosen them and had become the foundation of their struggle for freedom.[33] He was their Truth, enabling them to know that white definitions of black humanity were lies. When their way became twisted and senseless, they told Jesus about it. He lifted their burdens and eased their pain, thereby bestowing upon them a vision of freedom that transcended historical limitations. That was why they sang:

> Sometimes I hangs my head an' cries,
> But Jesus goin' to wipe my weepin' eyes.

Of course, for some people who live in this modern, scientific age with its emphasis on unlimited human possibilities, such a faith sounds simplistic and childish. But that is because their consciousness is defined by masters and rulers who really believe that they know what is best for everybody. However, the victims of such attitudes have only two alternatives: 1) to accept the oppressor's value system and thus be contented with the place set for them by others, or 2) to find a completely new way of looking at reality that enables them to fight against oppression. Many black slaves chose the latter, using Jesus Christ as the basis of their struggle. Through Jesus Christ they could know that they were *somebody,* when so much in their experience said they were *nobody.* Through him they could know that they were *people,* even though they were bought and sold like cattle. Jesus

---

[33] Paul makes a similar point in I Cor. l:26f: "To shame the wise, God has chosen what the world counts folly, and to shame what is strong, God has chosen what the world counts weakness. He has chosen things low and contemptible, mere nothings, to overthrow the existing order."

Christ was that reality who invaded their history from beyond and bestowed upon them a definition of humanity that could not be destroyed by the whip and the pistol.

The emphasis on Jesus Christ and Scripture as the subject and source of the presence of transcendence in black experience raises the question of the precise relationship between them. To paraphrase, some of my critics have stated the issue in this manner: "On page thirty-two of *Black Theology and Black Power,* quoting Ron Karenga, you said that 'The fact that I am Black is my ultimate reality.' But then on page thirty-four of the same book, you wrote that 'Christianity begins and ends with the man Jesus – his life, death, and resurrection.' Which do you *really* mean? Blackness or Jesus Christ? You cannot have it both ways."

This is an important matter, and perhaps the way to initiate understanding is to state emphatically that, like Scripture, the black experience is a *source* of the Truth but not the Truth itself. Jesus Christ is the Truth and thus stands in judgment over all statements about truth. But having said that, we must immediately balance it with another statement, without which the first statement falsifies what it intends to affirm. We must state the other side of the paradox emphatically: There is no truth in Jesus Christ independent of the oppressed of the land – their history and culture. And in America, the oppressed are the people of color – Black, Red, and Brown. Indeed it can be said that to know Jesus is to know him as revealed in the struggle of the oppressed for freedom. Their struggle is Jesus' struggle, and he is thus revealed in the particularity of their cultural history – their hopes and dreams of freedom.

The difficulty some people have in understanding the relation between Jesus and the black experience in Black Theology is due partly to their inability to appreciate the dialectical character of theological speech, especially when related to the black struggle for liberation. They use a dialectical model when dealing with such things as divinity and humanity in Jesus Christ or justification in St. Paul or John Wesley. But there is a failure of nerve when their abstractions about Jesus are applied to the historical present. Jesus Christ is not a proposition, not a theological concept that exists merely in our heads. He is an event of liberation, a happening in the lives of oppressed people struggling for political freedom. Therefore, to know him is to encounter him in the history of the weak and the helpless. That is why it can be rightly said that there can be no knowledge of Jesus independent of the history and culture of the oppressed. It is impossible to interpret Scripture correctly and thus understand Jesus rightly unless the interpretation is done in the light of the consciousness of the oppressed in their Struggle for liberation.

A similar convergence occurs when it is asked whether the black experience exists independently of Jesus Christ. If by "Jesus Christ" is meant the formal preaching and teachings of white missionaries, at a particular point in time, then the answer is an unqualified Yes. As we must say that Jesus' existence in himself is not a product of culture, so the black experience existed before black people were introduced to Christianity. That is such an obvious historical fact that we need not debate it further. But if by "Jesus Christ" is meant "the image of the invisible God, the firstborn of all creation, for in him all things were created in heaven and on earth, visible and invisible" (Col. 1:15-16), then the answer is an unqualified No. In this context, Jesus is not simply a doctrine or even a particular event limited by time. He is the eternal event of liberation in the divine person who makes freedom a constituent of human existence. There is no existence apart from him, because he is the ground of existence without whom nothing is. Therefore, where human beings struggle for freedom and refuse to be defined by unauthorized earthly authorities, there Jesus Christ is present among them. His presence is the sustaining and liberating event in the lives of the oppressed that makes possible the continued struggle for freedom.

From the context of the eternal presence of Christ the Liberator emerges the interdependence of Jesus and the black experience as expressed in the lives of many black people. This interdependence is expressed so forcibly and concretely that to speak truly of the black experience is to speak of Jesus. He is the Word in their lives, and thus to speak of their experience as it is manifested in the joys and sorrows of black life is to speak of the One they say is the Comforter in time of trouble, "the lily of the valley," and "the bright and morning star."

He's King of Kings, and Lord of Lords,
Jesus Christ, the first and the last
No man works like him.

Others have testified that he is a "bridge over trouble waters," the "One who has been better to us than we have been to ourselves." In *God Struck Me Dead,* a collection of conversion experiences and autobiographies of ex-slaves, one called him a "time-God"! "He don't come before time; he don't come after time. He comes just on time."[34] And he comes as the preserver of the weak in time of trouble and as the sustaining Spirit of freedom in wretched places. This encounter of Jesus as the Christ of God makes his reality an eternal presence of liberation before and after the

[34] Clifton H. Johnson, ed., *op. cit.,* p. 170.

slave ships and Middle Passage.

Theologically, the convergence of Jesus Christ and the black experience is the meaning of the Incarnation. Because God became man in Jesus Christ, He disclosed the divine will to be with humanity in our wretchedness. And because we blacks accept his presence in Jesus as the true definition of our humanity, blackness and divinity are dialectically bound together as one reality. This is the theological meaning of the paradoxical assertion about the primacy of the black experience and Jesus Christ as witnessed in Scripture.

Heresy. This brings us to the issue of heresy, which is an important matter if the church intends to be clear about its message and its vocation in the world. Heresy here refers to any activity or teaching that contradicts the liberating truth of Jesus Christ. It is an action that denies the Lordship of Christ or a word that refuses to acknowledge his liberating presence in the struggle for freedom. In short, heresy is the refusal to speak the truth or to live the truth in the light of the One who is the Truth.

The early church was correct in identifying problems of heresy as a critical theological issue, although the church itself was often the heretic. But every community that is serious about the gospel of Jesus Christ must ask, When does the church cease to be the Church of Jesus Christ? When do the church's actions deny the faith that it verbalizes? These questions must be answered for every given situation, if the people of God are to remain relatively clear-headed about the relation between their existence as God's people and Jesus' existence as their Lord. Not every church that claims to be the Church is the Church, because being the Church requires concrete commitments to the One who is the essence of the Church. Not every theology that claims to be Christian is Christian, because the doing of Christian theology requires specific commitments to the One who is the content of that reality to which the word "Christian" points.

The question of heresy must be reopened in our time, *not* for the purpose of witch-hunting, but for the sake of the Church's life. We need to be clear about the Subject to which our proclamation points and the relation of our words about that Subject to our *actions* in the world. Here it must be emphasized that we are not simply concerned with our theological conceptualizations of Jesus Christ, although that is included. Theological concepts have meaning only as they are translated into theological praxis, that is, the Church living in the world on the basis of what it proclaims. This means that theology and ethics, though not identical, are closely interrelated: the mission of the Church is defined by its proclamation, and the proclamation is authenticated by the mission. For the sake of the mission of the Church in the world, we must continually ask, What actions deny the truth disclosed in Jesus Christ? Where should the line be drawn? Can the Church of Jesus Christ be racist and Christian at the same time? Can the Church of Jesus Christ be politically, socially, and economically identified with the structures of oppression and also be a servant of Christ? Can the Church of Jesus Christ fail to make the liberation of the poor the center of its message and work and still remain faithful to its Lord?

On the level of theory, these questions are easy to answer. Yet they are very difficult to answer in the day-to-day life of the Church. This difficulty is increased because we live in a society of many denominations under an ethos of the "freedom" of religion. But difficulties do not make the questions less important. Indeed their importance is grounded in the integrity of our faith and the obedience that is inherent in the reality of Jesus Christ. The answer to the question of heresy as it relates both to our past and to our present situation begins and ends with the centrality of Jesus Christ as the Liberator of the oppressed. Any interpretation of the gospel in any historical period that fails to see Jesus as the Liberator of the oppressed is heretical. Any view of the gospel that fails to understand the Church as that community whose work and consciousness are defined by the community of the oppressed is not Christian and is thus heretical. It is within this context that the issue of heresy must be debated.

It is true that identifying the liberation of the oppressed as crucial to the authenticity of the gospel could be interpreted as accidental to my historical situation. I admit readily that the social context of my existence plays an important role in my understanding of the gospel message. However, it would be ridiculous to claim that there is some secret language by which Africans could be persuaded by what I say, while non-Africans could never understand it. Clearly there is a basis for speaking across cultural lines, namely the Bible. Looking at the message of Scripture exegetically, we ask, Does the Bible in fact center upon the proclamation of the liberation of the oppressed? I have shown on other occasions that the message of Scripture is the proclamation and record of God's liberation. If it is not this, it is nothing. Indeed, it is the encounter of this truth of Scripture that enables us black theologians to know that we must

> Speak the Truth to the people
> To identify the enemy is to free the mind
> Free the mind of the people
> Speak to the mind of the people
> Speak Truth.[35]

---

[35] Cited in J. Mason Brewer, *American Negro Folklore* (Chicago: Quadrangle Books, 1968), p. 140.

Veil

Rafia Zakaria

Chapters 1 and 2 in *Veil (Object Lessons)*. London: Bloomsbury Academic Press, 2017, pp. 11-43.

***Rafia Zakaria** is a human rights attorney, political philosopher, and columnist for both* Dawn *(a newspaper in Pakistan) and* Al Jazeera America. *She is a frequent contributor to the* Los Angeles Review of Books, The Nation, Aeon, Guernica, The New York Times *and other periodicals. Her book* The Upstairs Wife: An Intimate History of Pakistan *(2015) received positive reviews in* The New York Times, NPR, Ms. Magazine, Christian Science Monitor, The Boston Globe, The Toronto Star, Bustle, Hindustan Times, DNA India, Indian Express, Calcutta Statesman, Dissent *and* The Nation. *Zakaria is an alumna of Belmont University, where she studied philosophy.*

***Why we are reading this**: In the previous essay, James Cone invites his reader into the African American religious experience. Here, Zakaria uses an exploration of veiling practices to introduce us to her own world as a Pakistani Muslim woman with a transnational life-story. The wearing of the veil, in its varying degrees, styles, and practices (chador, burqa, niqab, hijab, etc.) is among the most controversial and misunderstood practices both within and outside of Muslim-populated countries. In some quarters in the United States, the veil invites suspicion or incites anger and fear. Some Western nations (e.g., France) have gone so far as to ban veiling. In many nations, veiling is an option for women or a strong cultural norm. In a few countries it is legally required. As this selection shows, the extent to which moral, social, cultural, and religious pressures determine whether or not one wears a veil, or whether one is free to choose to wear one or not, is exceedingly complex. What can you learn from Zakaria's account about when and why Muslim women veil themselves? Does veiling seem to be a religious practice, a cultural tradition, a bit of both, or something else entirely? What associations do different people have with veiling? Why do some people experience fear or anger about a piece of clothing? What does the object suggest about femininity and masculinity in different cultural worlds? What can you learn about the interactions between the identities that individuals create for themselves and the identities that are imposed upon them by others?*

Submission

I wore the full-face veil for the first time on my wedding day. I was eighteen years old and I had never worn it before. In Pakistani Muslim tradition, this was the day of the ceremonial giving away of the bride, the day I was to say goodbye to my family (theatrically and before an audience of a few hundred) and go off to be with my husband and his family. The fabric I had chosen over a year before for my wedding dress had been selected for hue and sheen – a fiery red-orange – and it was utterly opaque. I could see nothing. For navigation, I had the assistance of two younger cousins, unveiled and full of giggles. It was September in Karachi; I was pouring sweat and also blind.

The story of how I ended up fully veiled and a bride did not begin that day. The skein connecting it to incidents past could be reeled back to an event a few years earlier, one that had led me to begin wearing the half-veil or the headscarf. Fifteen then, I was a student at an all-girls school that prided itself on being almost entirely free of the contaminating male presence, whose very existence made veils necessary in the first place. The hundreds of girls that were students there were instructed almost entirely by women. From the time we were six years old and began first grade to the time we were seventeen and graduated eleventh, it was women, women and all women. At five past eight every morning, the gates of the school would be locked and the man-free day would begin. The only men left inside were the very poor ones that the school employed, who mopped the halls, set up the nets for games of volleyball behind our high walls, or guarded the gates. The fact that they were poor seemed to cancel out their masculinity.

There were no men at school and so within its walls there were no veils, the walls and seclusion functioning as its own sort of full veil. This changed when school hours ended; when the gates were opened in the afternoon many girls were quick to put on a head scarf, and some, notably fewer, even a full-face veil. The rest of us took the small distance from our school, where we were kept from the male presence, to the cars that took us home, to attract as much male attention as we could. Meaningful glances, wordless flirting, and eventually telephone numbers were all exchanged surreptitiously. A boys' school was not far away, and the boys came in droves – to see and, if they were more ambitious, to seduce. It was a window of opportunity for young love.

It was that December that our tenth-grade class, of 35 sixteen-year-old girls, decided to plan a picnic. Central to the excursion was the hefty battalion of chaperones who would accompany us, six or seven matronly teachers who had taught us Physics or Chemistry or Mathematics and could be convinced to add another day to their workweek for the promise of a bit of sun and sea. To insure that the all-girl environment of the school could be replicated on the picnic, we would be headed to a private beach, where we would spend the day at a private beach house, all of it guarded by armed private guards at the entrance and exit. Because of this, we could be unveiled if fully clothed, out in the open but still unseen, still out of the reach of men.

The day of the picnic came, spirits were high and laughter was everywhere. There was no one at all on the empty stretch of private beach except our group of girls and chaperones. They sat in a line watching us, their own heads covered against the sun or by habit while we giggled and squealed at the shoreline – December is the only month in which Karachi's heavy heat abates but the breeze, the sun, and the ocean, despite their proximity, were not usually available to us. Our school building, dating all the way back to 1905, sat in the fetid heart of a polluted downtown, the air we breathed choked up with the fumes of buses and cars. In studies it was cited as the most polluted point of a very polluted city. Freed from this miasma, we drank fitfully of the freedom, the lack of walls, and gates, the veils that stood between us, the natural and unnatural barriers that made up our lives.

It was in the midst of this that the boys came. They had been unable to come from the land, its single route blocked off by the guards, and so they came from the sea. There they were in a speedboat that appeared on the horizon, four or five of them dark haired and excited against a blue sun-drenched horizon. As we watched, the boat they were in came closer and closer, until their faces and their voices and their maleness was visible to all. Then, they began to call out my name. They did it once, and then again after they brought the boat to the shore, after they dragged it to an adjoining house, and after they took up spots in its front porch. They could see everything.

The chaperones were terrified. It was their worst nightmare: exposed girls on an exposed beach beset by unknown men. They called out to us to come back up the beach, to come closer to them, to hide ourselves. With the appearance of men, even boys, our visibility was a problem. Once we had been evacuated from the beach, new instructions were issued; we had to stay close as possible to the chaperones, as far away as possible from the boys. There was an air of doom to it all; a terrible thing had happened, the fun was over. Many promises had been made to the parents that had permitted their daughters to go and now those promises had been broken.

We did not leave immediately. We stayed long enough for the boys to call out my name a few more times, for several of my classmates to hear it and for them to tell others. We were raised to be good girls and most were better girls and eager to prove it by emphasizing my complicity. By the time we all packed up for the long morose ride back to school, there were also accusing glances from the teachers. Glib and meaningful, they all said the same thing: "I know you had a part in this." I was in trouble. The coastal road connected us back to the highway, which led us back into the city, to the safety of the walled school that veiled us from the outside. My crime was clear: I had somehow inspired a collective, non-consensual unveiling of those that did not wish it.

Not long after the picnic, I began to wear the headscarf. There had been much fallout in its aftermath; my mother was summoned to school for solemn discussions. The smug and indignant chaperones, spinsters all, had hinted at expulsion, fueled by the certainty of my immorality, the horror of what had happened.

I was not expelled, since there was no proof and I refused to supply it. To save myself, I stolidly stuck to denial. I did not know who the boys were; I had no idea why or how they screamed my name. I was certain that some of the girls were inflating their stories.

It was a lie, but a self-preserving one. I could not admit that I knew the boys, or at least the one of them that had slipped me his phone number as I walked out from school one day. Nor could I say that I had talked to him several times on the phone and that he had asked to meet every one of those times. Every time, I had told him it was impossible, that I was kept behind wall and key, never alone or unwatched. Then, one day I had mentioned the picnic, half-knowingly but assured of the fact that he would not be able to penetrate the defenses of guards and cordons. I had underestimated his persistence, his belief in the possibility of a rendezvous.

Even though I was not expelled or suspended, I faced banishment of another sort. In the delicate moral ecosystem of our classroom of sixteen-year-old girls, I had ceded space to a premature male invasion, an impermissible one. We inhabited a climate in which the precariousness of our condition, our veiled yet unveiled state behind the sheltering walls of our school, was constantly and consistently underscored. There were threats and warnings and prognostications of how awful that world, that world where men dominated, where their gaze was omnipresent was a harsh one. We were to relish this time of sequestered freedom. I had disrespected it and I deserved no mercy.

To survive that last year of school, I needed a visible act of contrition – and so I chose the headscarf. There was a redundancy to it that could have been comical: I was choosing to be additionally veiled in an environment that was, owing to its sequestration, already veiled and hidden away. But I was suffering the long and deep pangs of teenage exclusion; there was no humor in it for me. Luckily and eventually there was also some respite. My one-and-a-half-times veiled (once by the sequestered school and another half by the headscarf), newly pious self appeared sufficiently recalcitrant. My betrayal, if not forgotten, was forgiven. I was slowly and again included in conversations, in potlucks arranged for recess, in all the little joys of our sequestered world.

I had been a rebel, and then I became a conformist – and I discovered that it was lovely and even addictive. There were fewer secrets and less intrigue. All suffering, particularly the sort of imposed by men, was shared suffering; there were loads of camaraderie and a sense of shared identity. We were all girls in it together against a male world that wanted to claim us. Being walled-in at school, to December picnic, to the half veil and then, a year or so later, the full veil were all steps on a path, I can see it now-but the ultimate destination of course was unknown to me then. I knew, however, that it implicated connections between all of this: dots drawn between veiling, sequestering, men, submission and rebellion. There was strategy in it and manipulation, some instinctual and not quite explicit understanding of what it meant to belong and how belonging could be accomplished, in this case via an object, a headscarf and then a veil.

Veiled Meanings

The full-veiled self that arrived at my wedding that September in Karachi was in some part high on the same drug of approval and approbation. The issue of choice, Muslim women's choices as a collective, their choices surrounding arranged marriages, and of course and centrally the choices concerning veiling and unveiling, are the matter of much and heated debate. Entire legislative sessions in several countries have been devoted to the issue, not to mention hundreds of pages of precedent-twisting judicial decisions that come down on either side of this vexing issue. It is a difficult project, however, and one so heavy with the weight of its political implications. Separating the threads of any dense woven fabric is a daunting task and so of course is the case here, even when the decision and its dimensions were my very own.

I was not forced to marry, or even persuaded to marry; but I was, at a very young age, whose significance was emphasized by all those who posed the choice to me, presented with the opportunity. I was sixteen and I said yes to the proposal and to marrying the man I had been introduced to at my grandmother's house six months earlier. We had not spoken for longer than a few minutes, and even then I had known that there was something momentous about the occasion. In the nearly all-female environment (save young male cousins) of my grandmother's house, there had been the sudden and inexplicable presence of a man. Accustomed to being sent upstairs or away when such visitors appeared, the very arrangement of the event was indicative. The proposal itself came months later, after many more relatives had been involved, many fervent discussions held as my mother grilled her sisters who knew his mother. Visits by his parents, discussions about him all generally proceeding and persisting like a growing chorus in the background of my life. That life, however, also continued – school and its incipient dramatics, the stress of this or that test, the inequities of teachers I didn't like, the coveting of freedoms I didn't have.

Unlike so much else in Pakistan that relies centrally on ritual, the moment I was asked whether I agreed to the marriage was simple and unassuming. We, my parents, my brother, and I, had just returned from a wedding. I was still in the finery I had been permitted for the occasion. A long burgundy velvet tunic, the gold thread embroidery at its neck cut carefully from an old one that had belonged to my mother, tradition and beauty given new life via a talented and temperamental tailor. I was sitting on the edge of my bed, the glass-topped table in front of me covered with schoolbooks, behind me the three-mirrored dressing table that had belonged to an aunt. The two side mirrors were hinged to the larger one and could be turned so that you could get a good look at the back of your head. It was useful for French braids or if you wanted to be surrounded by endless, infinitely regressing images of yourself.

I said yes. I was asked if I was sure and I insisted I was. That was the extent of the conversation. My parents seemed surprised and perhaps they really were. Apart from the very recent turn toward the headscarf, a fad that had flummoxed rather than flattered them, I had been the most predictably rebellious and argumentative of their offspring. I had, in the past and as a young child, defied the idea of marriage, castigated my mother's domesticity and insisted I would not marry at all. Riding the initial, heady waves of pubescent hormones I had denounced all that was part of my mother's life: the raising of children, the cooking of meals, the waiting for the husband. In retrospect, it seems of course both predictable and banal, the parameters of what I thought wrong, the kitchen chores I skirted, the entirely usual ways in which I sought to convince myself that my life would not be my mother's life.

Scary Veils and Pretty Veils

The ceremonial wedding gown, often accompanied by the veil, is a centerpiece of nuptials in many cultures. Even in the United States and other Western countries, the drama surrounding the selection of the dress, its price and particulars, its cut and crease, who pays for it and who gets to veto it are milestones in the run-up to a couple's nuptials. The popularity of the television show *Say Yes to the Dress*, now in its fourteenth season, can be considered a rough testament that even in cultures where ritual and tradition are never usually enough to alter decisions to dictate the denouement of events or selections of spouses, they retain a level of importance. The amalgamated drama of the bride's big day, the relatives varying opinions and expectations, tight budgets and amorphous ones, first-time brides versus grandmothers marrying later in life all make for good television. Even the arguably un-feminist obsession with how the bride as the centerpiece of the day is cast to the side, the veritable obsession with female physicality, too-big or too-small hips and bosoms, the blessedness of camouflage accomplished by the architecture of fabrics, all deemed permissible within this particular context. The American wedding is also the only place that the full-face veil makes an appearance without its usual attachments of sinister suspicions; the veiled bride is considered neither repressed nor suffering, not a terrorist in hiding nor a woman marking her resistance against visibility by pursuit of its dogged opposite. Rather, this veiled bride is sweet and pure, not only permissible but ideal.

The comparison is necessary because it captures the benign lack of consideration I attached to the full-face veil or that I was to wear it for a time at the wedding reception. And while I may have been like an American bride in that I spent little time considering the veil or my wearing of it, I was dramatically different in other ways. Selecting an extremely expensive dress at sixteen felt not like the siren of freedom abridged but rather more like an achievement of empowered personhood. Suddenly, I had a say in serious details involving large expenditures; a rather intoxicating feeling for one used at best to considering selections of books or friends or ice-cream flavors. What I remember from those days leading up to the wedding was the sheer variety of the choices and (in retrospect) the somewhat arbitrary basis on which I made them. My husband-to-be (we were now permitted phone conversations in light of our fast-approaching coupledom) asked whether I would deign to live in the apartment he already lived in. The other option was to move to a new apartment closer to his work and the city and not quite so suburban (which I would later learn also means desolate). I hedged; I had lived in the same house and in the same city all of my life, but I was a teenager very committed to appearing worldly. So I hedged and hedged and when pressed said that we could decide together once I got there. I did not know about leases, the requirements to fulfill their terms. It seemed like a very clever solution.

The choices others put before me were at least seemingly of less import: what sort of luggage did I want? (!) I had never been on a plane or purchased anything more than my school backpack. Clever as I was, I insisted upon green suitcases, tough plastic ones since they don't lose their shape. From my mother-in-law-to-be there were inquiries about my favorite perfume, my brand of cosmetics, what color bedding, what sort of towels, what brand of china. I perused a few dated issues of *Vogue* and came up with responses to all that, too. I felt like I was proceeding at a successful clip to becoming a wife.

Overwhelmed by these choices, I did not notice the choices that were not offered. My husband-to-be, who was so graciously asking my opinion of various apartments or suburbs I had never seen, did not ask where I would like to go to college. My parents, arranging the details of the wedding, the extensive menus for three days of celebrations, did not ask if I wanted a smaller wedding, something fewer than the five hundred people. Like most brides in Pakistan then, I knew only some of the people at my wedding and had less of an idea of what sort of college, apartment, or husband awaited me at the other side of the wedding. Too young to be really worried and too overwhelmed to inquire after details, I dressed up in my wedding gown, was primped and coiffed by friends and family, was laden with the ceremonial gifts of jewelry from his parents and mine and waited. The bride must arrive last.

Unveiling and Tradition

The veiling did not take place until I had arrived at the venue. To get there, I had to be wrapped in a large white piece of cloth. This was not due to tradition but an effort at crime prevention and the reality that in increasingly lawless Karachi, a bride meant jewelry and jewelry signified an opportunity for robbery. For my father, at least, this was a pressing concern and hence the huge white cloth. It felt already late when my father's cousin, entrusted with the task of transporting the bride to the groom, finally arrived. And so, in a terrible hurry to get to my wedding, I was wrapped up and planted in the front passenger seat of a Toyota hatchback. I had never been in a car driven by this relative before. He braked suddenly and often, and each time I – wearing several yards of silk wrapped in complicated layers all around me, laden with several pounds of gold – lurched forward nearly into the dashboard.

My mother was waiting when I got there, as were the cousins who would be escorting me down the long red carpet, at the end of which and on a dais, my groom awaited. The veil was necessary for the ritual that would be performed once the groom and I were seated. My aunt, the common relative – his aunt by marriage, mine by blood – would raise the veil. In her hand she would hold a mirror, an antique piece that belonged to my maternal grandmother. On our wedding day, the groom and I would first see each other in this mirror, in reflection, such that all the evil eyes directed at us would be warded off.

When I look at pictures of the moment now, the veil seems terribly long, made even longer in the photograph by the fact that my head is bowing downward. It could not but have been so; the fabric was heavy, bordered with huge pieces of gold lacework weighing several pounds. I wanted to, but I could not lift my head up. I also learned that when I looked down I could at least in some small way, see the ground that I was walking on. It was better to see a little than to be completely blind.

There is a picture also of the unveiling. In it you can see my aunt's arm as it holds the mirror; she had worn pink silk that dayand she holds the mirror as best as she can between our faces. My veil has been lifted and I can be seen. My husband peers into the mirror following the instruction. I do not remember looking into it or finding him there, but as traditions go, I am sure I pretended to look. I knew that the bride is not supposed to say anything at all at that moment. The groom duly exclaimed at the beauty of the bride, hidden from others, so that he would be the very first to see.

The Veil as Object

I trace the moment of my veiled entrance at my wedding to the ostracism I faced at that school picnic at the beach to provoke the literal question that has been at the center of my own grappling with the veil in particular, and the nature of choices in general. Are our choices, represented by the literal actions we take, the physical picking up of an object such as the veil and its putting on, or are these snapshots of decisions culminations of ever larger and more involved webs of considerations – a previous experience, a parent's love, a lover's command, a friend's insistence whose collective congruence is sometimes reflected in what we wear or how we choose to appear? Decisions in this sense have a genealogy that, like all genealogies, has a complexity of content, an innate and obstinate resistance to being synthesized to just one thing. As with all things, we see only the visible, but what we see is not the sum total of what is.

Similarly, moments of submission and rebellion cannot be distilled into the embrace or disavowal of objects. Coercion and constraints, force and rebellion, can undoubtedly use objects to exact their ends, but the simple attachment of these to the absence or presence of choice is not simply reductive; it is destructive, unconcerned with an object's inherent possibility, its multidimensionality. The moral architecture of our decisions is complicated, and I present this investigation of my own here to reveal not its universality but to suggest the necessity of a sort of structure that reveals the complexity of the decisions themselves.

Many of my friends who had been present at the picnic attended my wedding. They were, like many of my teachers, surprised that I would be the first among us to be married. My instances of past rebellion had suggested to them that I would choose a different path from that of the veiled and jeweled teenage bride. The conversations with our younger selves are too weighted in favor of our present selves to bear many truths. I look back at the pictures, at the veil, at the mirror in whose reflection I never saw what I was supposed to see. I can remember only a feverish and forceful wish to show everyone that I was good and bold, obedient and independent. Unveiled for the rest of the reception, I talked loudly, laughed openly, and flung off all semblances of the demure. I was done with the good and obedient, I thought; I now had license to be bold and independent.

Purity, Necessity, Unity

My grandmother liked to visit a market that was very far from our house and near where she and my grandfather lived before I was born. The market was not like the brightly lit shops that I visited with my mother. Its lanes and corridors were open to the sky even though little light shone through the cloth canopies that stretched from the roofs of one stall to another. The stalls themselves were narrow and cavernous and most times one did not go inside but lingered near the mouth. A man usually sat there. There was no browsing; instead an assistant, always a boy and usually not much older than my four or five years at the time, would disappear into the recesses of the store and bring out whatever it was we were in the market for. Sometimes, if we were going to make a more substantial purchase, he would fetch us glass bottle of Coca-Cola with neat white straws standing at attention. I would look at my grandmother and if she nodded yes, I would drink it.

I have another memory of those trips to the bazaar. My grandmother, who still wore a sari, would on her visits to this bazar drape a long white chador around herself. Even if the sun sat high in the sky and my hand sweaty in hers, she would wear this large white cloth, her entire body enveloped within it. Sometimes, when the crowds were particularly heavy and men jostled close to us, she would drape the cloth around her face, not just her head and body. She held it in place by holding its edge in her mouth.

It was on one of these crowded days when I was walking beside her, my sweaty hand in hers, looking closely at the ground when I felt something I had never felt before. Suddenly, I felt a hand creep around my waist and pull me in the opposite direction. I resisted and the hand slipped and grabbed my behind. I think I made a small scream but I do not remember my grandmother stopping or even noticing. I never saw who it was that touched me. I remember looking up at my grandmother, all enveloped in white, all covered up, and wished I could crawl insider her veil. I do not know if I told my mother what happened, but I never went to that market with my grandmother again.

Karachi is not a very green city. Water is scarce and almost never comes in through the government water pipes. Parks, sometimes green when they are inaugurated or if they happen to be within eyeshot of powerful politicians, usually whither to dusty brown as the mostly hot months exact their lushness from them. It is perhaps for just this reason that green spaces, when they exist, are so notable, spots of verdant respite amid the dust and smog of a city of too many thirsty people. One such spot, an island really in the midst of a busy boulevard, is located near a major intersection. No larger than perhaps a thousand square feet, it features green grass, a protuberance of pink and red bougainvillea and hibiscus, terracotta pots of other flowers, and a few fledgling palm trees. Among the nonliving inhabitants of this spot, around which traffic in large choking torrents and spurting fumes of fury stops and starts constantly, are a stone bench and a small windowless room with a door. This is the pump room, which holds the means by which the city's main water line supposedly pumps water into the neighboring areas.

The little green island is circled by buildings of greater height, six and ten story structures housing stuffy offices and at least in one case, a privately run dental clinic. It was from a window in one of these clinics that one of my cousins reported seeing the following incident. At around three in the afternoon, when the heat of the city lulls people into a sort of heat-bred catatonia and traffic thins by a hair or two, a woman appeared clad in a black burka and a full veil. By herself, she sat on the bench, an oddity enjoying the grass and the flowers. Not long after, a man appeared and sat down next to her, leaving just a bit of distance between them.

From the third floor where my cousin watched them, a conversation was taking place. What was said and told and considered, could not of course be heard. What could be seen was that after a time, the man moved a bitcloser to the woman. They continued to talk, albeit sporadically and then while staring straight ahead, the man put an arm around the woman. More minutes passed and a few more words appeared to have been said. Then the woman, who was even until then fully veiled, removed the portion of the veil that covered her nose and mouth. Her face could now be seen.

It was what happened next that shocked my cousin. The woman got up by herself and walked across the tiny grassy patch to where the yellow-painted pump room stood. From her purse she removed a key and undid the padlock to the pump room and went inside. The man stayed seated on the bench for a bit, shooting the heavy breeze, consuming fitful breaths of the smog-laden spot. Then he too got up, walked to the pump room and went inside. About twenty minutes later, he reappeared, taking quick steps and crossing the island into the throng on the streets surrounding the boulevard. He seemed no longer interested in or arrested by the verdant greenery. Another five minutes passed and she emerged, fully veiled again and similarly hurried. Both were lost to the crowds of Karachi.

Prostitutes are often fully veiled in Karachi. Many such burka-clad women are known to frequent busy bus stops where they can whisper to clients and quickly clasp a strange man's hand from underneath the all-covering burka, their intention and proposition clear to all parties. In a Muslim country (and fully veiled prostitutes are said to be common in many) the equation of being fully veiled with being morally pure is the sort of reductionism that begs to be co-opted. As varying oppressive regimes, from supposedly democratic Iran to the profligate monarchy of Saudi Arabia, impose the veil as a requirement, insisting that good and pure women are the ones that are completely covered, responses such as these call their bluff. The veil then serves as an armor of unassailable moral goodness that shockingly provides cover to women to make independent moral choices that may not otherwise be culturally or religiously acceptable.

The anonymity of the veil also has a role in the equation. One afternoon in Karachi, some family members and I were in the lobby of a famous five-star hotel, one of the most elite destinations in the city. In the marble lobby lit with chandeliers we sat down at the only sofa that was unoccupied. We were waiting for someone and the air-conditioned lobby of the hotel provided the sort of cool reprieve for which we had been longing. Grateful to have found a place to sit at all, we did not notice the couple that was seated at an adjacent sofa. In their early twenties, they sat next to each other and seemed perturbed that we had chosen to sit so close to them. The woman was again wearing a full burka, her veil lifted to show only her face. The man was dressed casually in khakis and a button-down shirt. They spoke in awkward bursts of sentences, all of which suggested that this was a date, likely one arranged (as in not uncommon in Pakistan) after a long flirtation via texts or social media.

In the enforced proximity of urban life, we all sat there, brought together by our desire to enjoy free air-conditioning in Karachi. The girl kept furtively scanning the room, toying with the edge of her veil. If someone she knew were to enter the lobby, she could and likely would cover up her face in an instant, retreating into the anonymity that would leave this encounter with the man who was not her husband null and void, incurring no cost at all on the unforgiving moral calculations by which Pakistan measures the moral worth of women. No one she knew ever did show up, but our proximity (even though we were both women) seemed to have added too much risk to this already risky rendezvous. Fifteen minutes or so after we arrived, the girl pulled the veil back over her face, got up and left, her heeled shoes clacking on the marble floor under the hem of her burka. Her beau, smiling and giddy, left not long after. In-person meetings are always awkward; they probably resumed and returned to the more comfortable medium of Skype and texts. Yet functioning somewhat like the easily assumed anonymity of those mediums, the veil allowed her to appear and disappear whenever she wished and wherever she was.

Not Muslim Enough

The first man to tell me that I was an incomplete or inadequate Muslim because I did not veil myself was not himself a Muslim. It happened in the first several days of a class I took at the Southern Baptist college where I had been enrolled by my husband, as my continuing education was a part of the arrangement of our marriage. I was new to the United States, newer still to my understanding of the spectrum of religious denominations that constitute the American religious landscape. It was spring and as homage to the season the instructor was holding class outside on the lawns that had once been part of a large plantation. We were spliced into little groups, meant probably to encourage exchange and conversation. I cannot remember now whether the particular subject of religion was allotted or whether it intruded, but it came up and instigated the sort of memorable small and destructive fires that such discussions have the capacity to do.

Our conversation was simple enough: I told him I was Muslim and from Pakistan. He smiled and told me this was not possible because Muslim women are required to wear a veil and I was unveiled. I remember being shocked, and as is the unfortunate curse of unforeseen moments, speechless. There were good reasons for my particular surprise. The college was almost entirely white and in the sea of whiteness were the two of us, this man and I, having an unpleasant exchange. He was Native American, and an older student; I was Pakistani and a married woman. We were both not the usual students, but this did not provide any kind of camaraderie or filial feeling. I remember telling him that he had no idea what he was talking about, that veiling was not a requirement of faith, that

I had never veiled and that most women in Pakistan did not wear full-face veils and that all of them were indeed Muslim.

He smiled glibly through the whole thing – or at least that is what I remember of the incident. The slight had been sudden and sharp and expertly delivered and my defensiveness was gratifying. Here was a man telling me that I was inadequately Muslim simply because I did not fulfill his idea, his very visual idea of what a Muslim woman was supposed to be. The material of that conversation would constitute "What I could have said" and "What I should have said" for many years to come – sharp retorts whose razor edges would have wiped the smile off the man's face, freeing me of the weight of being a less than adequate Muslim, and one who was merely visibly so.

The truth regarding Muslim women and veils, non-Muslims (and many Muslims) assume, must be written up in divine doctrine, availed by an index search or a chat with a scholar then taken borne to be digested, and for the truly devoted practiced. This is not so. True to the nature of all truths, rather than the particularity of this one, the reality is far more vexing. Yet the valuation or prescription of the veil as a verifiable object has continued to be rooted in its supposed religious necessity, its "requiredness" as an article of faith. For this very reason, and based perhaps on the novelty of feminist historiography within Islam (and in general), the veil debate continues to be fought with the implements of contesting verses and Hadith, or sayings of the Prophet Muhammad.[1] The two – verses of the Holy Quran and the Hadith – make up the divine sources of Islamic law.

There are no verses in the Holy Quran itself that specifically prescribe the veil for all women. As can be expected, for those that believe in the centrality of the veil as a tenet of religious practice, even the above statement is a contentious one – since the literal absence of a prescription must not be molded, in their opinion, into its invalidity. So goes the battle regarding the veil, with soldiers on either side prodded into greater, more vehement hostility which in turn is capitalized on by both repressive governments that enforce its wearing and supposedly liberal ones that ban its use.

Instead of focusing on whether Chapter 24, Verse 30-31 of the Holy Quran – which instructs both men and women to lower their gazes and guard their private parts, and whose translation and interpretation is challenged by feminists – I would like instead to consider the rift that the

---

[1] See Amina Wadud, *Quran and Women* (New York: Oxford University Press, 1993); Jonathan Brown, *Misquoting Muhammad: The Challenges of Interpreting the Prophet's Legacy* (London: Oneworld Publications, 2014).

debate itself has birthed among Muslim feminists. The iterations of this rift has divided friends and created enemies, not to mention imposing a measuring scale of piety whose gradations make collective unity an increasingly elusive possibility for Muslim feminists.

Nor is it a hidden divide; its ugly ramparts and the whizzing grenades each side lobs at the other are in plain view (perhaps problematically so) for those who may not have a stake in the debate. One recent moment when these came into view occurred around the commemoration of World Hijab Day, held annually on February 1.[2] This is an occasion where non-Muslim women could wear the veil to show solidarity with the many veiled and Muslim women. The website for World Hijab Day states "Better Awareness, Greater Understanding, Peaceful World" as its motto.[3] Offering stories of headscarf-wearing women, the general effort is to humanize these women, and hence end harassment that so many of them experience. When I last looked, there were no stories of women who choose to wear a full-face veil. The ones available feature Muslim women who have chosen to wear the hijab, their testimonies shaking up the stereotype that all women who veil are oppressed. Also provided are testimonials of non-Muslim women, participants in previous hijab days who gush over its many unexpected lessons ranging from an awareness of their own ignorance to a better understanding of Islam.

The assumption of World Hijab Day is of course that the headscarf and its stricter cousin the full-face veil are synonymous with Islam, required for its practice. Undoubtedly anti-headscarf proponents in places like France are complicit in this development – at least in contemporary terms, having forced a confrontation where an argument for not banning the headscarf relied for its strength on the false premise that it was in fact essential for Muslim practice. Preserving the *option* for some women who wished to wear the headscarf or the veil only resulted in entrenching its position as an incontrovertible prerogative of Muslim religious practice. This is not to say that conservative Muslims and Muslim eschatology in general have not promoted the picture of veiled woman as a true and best representative of the faith, routinely choosing women who wear the headscarf for public speaking events as visible spokespersons. At one time the Islamic Society of North America, the largest umbrella organization for American Muslims, required all female employees regardless of their faith to wear the headscarf on their premises.

The unveiled are expectedly perturbed by the construction of the truly pious Muslim woman as duly veiled; in the shadow of World Hijab Day

---

[2] See http://worldhijabday.com/about-us (last accessed April 17, 2017).

[3] Ibid.

2016 Sara Yasin, a self-described hijab alum, wrote a post called "World Hijab Day has Got it All Wrong." In her piece Yasin takes issue both with the premise that the hijab protects women from the male gaze but also a series of pro-hijab cartoons that present a woman that is not wearing the hijab as an unwrapped lollipop or as rotting fruit. None of it, she rightly concludes, encourages an environment where the choice of wearing or not wearing a veil can be safely availed by women and recognized as a human right.

Unveiled and Muslim

In my own experience the issue of the veil, its wearing and non-wearing, is a festering and still-bleeding gash in the body of Muslim women as a collective. While many veiled and unveiled Muslim women including myself have pointed to their frustration with the West's preoccupation with the veil, the fact remains that it exists not simply as an object but as a moral delineator. As such, it will continue to preclude the organization of Muslim women as a collective that can take on male dominance within the faith. The political cost of wearing the veil in Western countries, where it increasingly exposes the wearers to harassment and religious profiling, forces the equation that these women – brave enough to declare a much maligned religious identity in public – are willing to take on the cost of being Muslim in a way that unveiled women are not. The sorts of appropriations that Muslim women have made of the "veil = pure" equation in Muslim countries are not really available in Western nations where the veil signifies something sinister and marginal and, if only partially, anonymous.

In the summer of 2009 I visited Egypt. I went as part of a delegation made up mostly of South Asian Muslims (some of whom lived in the United States) and American academics. This was still Mubarak's Egypt; the Arab Spring had not yet dawned nor been quashed by the military with its consequent bloodletting. In his speech, President Obama had sought "a new beginning between the United States and the Muslims of the world, one based on mutual interest and mutual respect." No one could have known what was coming then, but the divisions were still obvious. The academics and students that we met from the American University in Cairo were fluent in English and Westernized. Most were dressed in Western clothes and indeed seemed eager to underscore, particularly to the white Americans among our group, just how cosmopolitan and West-friendly they were.

At Cairo University, the very venue where President Obama gave his speech, there was more skepticism – particularly toward me. I was the only woman who was Muslim and who was not wearing a headscarf. Two of the three faculty members that we met were similarly Muslim women and both were wearing their headscarves. They asked me several times if I was Muslim and several times I said yes. They did not respond but they also did not engage; they seemed to imply that if I was Muslim, I should be dressed like they were, should choose to wear my Islam visibly. It was as if our sense of common experience and history, our opposition of imperialism and hegemony, was now irrelevant – a sideshow to my lack of a veil. In choosing not to wear it, my allegiances were suspect; I had chosen a team and it was not their team. I had also refused to wear the headscarf when we briefly visited Al-Azhar University, the oldest and most highly revered center for Islamic learning in the world. There had, however, been no other women present and so no stated objections to my omission.

Unspoken censure changed to loudly articulated disagreement toward the end of the trip. On this occasion we went to a large center devoted to the propagation of Islamic studies, located outside Cairo in one of the suburbs then named after various dates important to the then rulers of Egypt. The building was funded by a Qatari foundation and scholar and was large and imposing, a white swan among the suburban dunes of Cairo. Inside, over fifty young people, all employees of the foundation, awaited us. The topic was not only a mutual exchange of ideas but also to learn more about what they were doing to proliferate a moderate and inclusive Islam via the internet.

Inside, the arrangement was an unusual one: we the guests were lined up on chairs along one wall, foreign specimens of whom all must have a good view. Our audience sat opposite us in a similar line, the principals from the place in the first row with assumedly less important others behind them. The idea was to have a discussion, with questions posed by either side and then discussed among the group. So we began with the usual silence that inaugurates such plans – the reticence to speak first a common habit. Then, after a bit, things got going and we had the usual back and forth about the differences in forms of government, what mosques are like in the United States and so on. Ten or fifteen minutes into it, we got to the heart of the matter. One among them asked: "Given that the veil (the headscarf at least) is required in Islam, how could I stand or give answers about Muslim women, even really consider myself a good Muslim?" Behind her, silhouettes of heads nodded in appreciation and agreement; unveiled women were not to be called Muslim. This was an important topic.

With flaming, feverish cheeks I responded that I did not think I had to wear a veil, a headscarf like some in the audience or a face veil like others. My own interpretation of my faith did not see the practice as necessary, I said. I found it much more crucial and pressing, for instance, to work for social justice. I was working as a lawyer representing Muslim victims of domestic violence, and that, I believed, was the core of living my faith. No one heard the second portion of my answer; at that point a chorus of voices rose-exclamations against my obviously uninformed and incorrect perspective regarding the veil. Many objectors were men, who duly addressed me as sister, before proceeding to disdain my views.

In this cacophony, one of the Muslim men in our delegation gave a command for order. Its very tone foretold the authoritative and conclusive summation he was going to deliver to pacify the crowd, mend the tears that the catty women in the congregation had just made in the otherwise pristine fabric of cross-cultural exchange. "We understand that the dominant view in Islamic scholarship is that women must be modest and that modesty is interpreted variously as the covering of the hair and the face." Having delivered the mollifying morsel, he continued "of course not all of us on this side agree with each other" – suggesting clearly that the immorality of my unveiled state must not be attached to him – "and of course you may disagree with some of the people on this side of the room" – me. "But of course, we have all come here in the spirit of exchange, to listen and understand the other."

I had already lost him; I spent the rest of the day in an inflamed fury. On the bus back to Cairo many in the group, including, much to my utter disappointment, a white female academic, lauded our great male peacemaker for his efforts. If my female questioner had insisted that I was not a Muslim, this man, who lived and worked with unveiled Muslim women in the West (and would never have challenged their choice), had grasped the opportunity to do something in this climate more amenable to his perspective. Moral disciplining is done in a variety of ways, and that evening as I lay awake, replaying the morning in my mind with shame and anger and disappointment, I knew that this was one of them.

Veiled Contexts

As an unveiled woman, there is a danger in recounting incidents such as these. The current construction of the veil both within Islam and beyond it is interested primarily and perhaps singularly in a yes-and-no vote, one that is reflected in whether the veil as object forms a part of one's daily attire. If this book, or chapter or paragraph or sentence is in any way a no, it is also a refusal of this very formulation. The raw recounting of these incidents, repeated numerous times in various other contexts, the times I have capitulated and veiled myself for the sake of belonging, for the sake of delivering some more important message in mosques or Islamic Centers that would not admit me otherwise, is presented for one purpose. That purpose is not to reveal or explicate the doctrinal truth or falsity of the veil, its necessity or optionality, not even its connection to context or history – but rather the emotional rancor, the unsoothed rawness with which it rends women, particularly Muslim women, apart.

The fissure created by the veil, by the moral scale attached to its avowal and disavowal, is the core obstacle that confronts Muslim feminism, while scholars like Fatima Mernissi and more recently Saher Amer have discussed at length the male centric interpretations of religious doctrine that have led to the elevation of veiling as a requirement. There is, however, still a need to explore the consequences the disagreement over the veil has had to the relationships between Muslim women – and the extent to which this disagreement has permitted and promoted male interlopers, such as the man in Cairo, to intercede and impose their pronouncement. The questions then are not simply whether or not the veil is required, mandated, an essential tenet, but also what it accomplishes in the path of realizing a religious community that is not dictated by one or another interpretation, but rather inculcating respecting and maintaining a unity that has been elusive.

In a world framed in the crude language of "us and them," the veil has been marked and graded, and then attached to a constant and unforgiving moral judgment that is deemed to be a woman's unshakable burden. What is judged *by means* of an object is also reduced to an object and so it is with the veil. When there is no need to inquire further, to question or know, to go beyond the physical, the easily avowed and the visibly apprehended, the two entities, object and wearer, become synonymous, losing the possibility of subjectivity and becoming together one object. This single object is then judged permissible or impermissible and is always the signifier of one or another truth: either the rightness of Western opposition to the veil, or the correctness of the Islamist insistence on it.

The Learning Curve

Atul Gawande

From *The New Yorker*, January 28, 2002, pp. 52-55.

Atul Gawande *(b. 1965) is a winner of the MacArthur "Genius" Fellowship and many other accolades for his work on modern surgical practices and medical ethics. A practicing surgeon, he is professor in both the Department of Health Policy and Management at the Harvard School of Public Health and the Department of Surgery at Harvard Medical School. His four books have all been* New York Times *bestsellers; his fourth,* Being Mortal: Medicine and What Matters in the End, *was released in 2014.*

Why we are reading this: *This essay reminds us that there are forms of knowledge other than the discursive knowledge and "book learning" typically associated with higher education. As Gawande shows us, to learn a difficult physical skill like surgery, it is not enough to read and understand a medical manual. Like learning to play the violin or sink a free throw, mastery of surgery requires practice – a lot of practice. Gawande suggests that the best predictor of who will become a great surgeon is not raw talent but instead the raw tenacity to keep practicing until things finally begin to click.*

Unlike music and sports, the big difference with learning medical procedures is that most of the practice must be done on living human beings, sometimes in life-or-death situations. This is true not only for residents beginning their careers, but also for experienced and mid-career physicians who need to learn the latest "new and improved" medical techniques. Despite the care and precautions taken during training, medical outcomes for beginners are simply not as reliably excellent as with highly-experienced physicians. For a number of reasons, some of which Gawande explains, medical "practice" is more likely to be done on patients who are poor, less educated, or less familiar with the medical profession. Gawande prompts us to explore the moral and ethical dilemmas that arise because of these facts. How can we balance the need to train health care workers and the moral requirement to provide each patient with the best possible care available? Is it right for the best medical care to be a privilege of the wealthy and well-connected in our society? Is this a systemic inequality built into our health care system? Are there others?

The patient needed a central line. "Here's your chance," S., the chief resident, said. I had never done one before. "Get set up and then page me when you're ready to start."

It was my fourth week in surgical training. The pockets of my short white coat bulged with patient printouts, laminated cards with instructions for doing CPR and reading EKGs and using the dictation system, two surgical handbooks, a stethoscope, wound-dressing supplies, meal tickets, a penlight, scissors, and about a dollar in loose change. As I headed up the stairs to the patient's floor, I rattled.

This will be good, I tried to tell myself: my first real procedure. The patient – fiftyish, stout, taciturn – was recovering from abdominal surgery he'd had about a week earlier. His bowel function hadn't yet returned, and he was unable to eat. I explained to him that he needed intravenous nutrition and that this required a "special line" that would go into his chest. I said that I would put the line in him while he was in his bed, and that it would involve my numbing a spot on his chest with a local anesthetic, and then threading the line in. I did not say that the line was eight inches long and would go into his vena cava, the main blood vessel to his heart. Nor did I say how tricky the procedure could be. There were "slight risks" involved, I said, such as bleeding and lung collapse; in experienced hands, complications of this sort occur in fewer than one case in a hundred.

But, of course, mine were not experienced hands. And the disasters I knew about weighed on my mind: the woman who had died within minutes from massive bleeding when a resident lacerated her vena cava; the man whose chest had to be opened because a resident lost hold of a wire inside the line, which then floated down to the patient's heart; the man who had a cardiac arrest when the procedure put him into ventricular fibrillation. I said nothing of such things, naturally, when I asked the patient's permission to do his line. He said, "O.K."

I had seen S. do two central lines; one was the day before, and I'd attended to every step. I watched how she set out her instruments and laid her patient down and put a rolled towel between his shoulder blades to make his chest arch out. I watched how she swabbed his chest with antiseptic, injected lidocaine, which is a local anesthetic, and then, in full sterile garb, punctured his chest near his clavicle with a fat three-inch needle on a syringe. The patient hadn't even flinched. She told me how to avoid hitting the lung ("Go in at a steep angle," she'd said. "Stay right under the clavicle"), and how to find the subclavian vein, a branch to the vena cava lying atop the lung near its apex ("Go in at a steep angle. Stay right under the clavicle"). She pushed the needle in almost all the way. She drew back on the syringe. And she was in. You knew because the syringe filled with maroon blood. ("If it's bright red, you've hit an artery," she said. "That's not good.") Once you have the tip of this needle poking in the vein, you somehow have to widen the hole in the vein wall, fit the catheter in, and snake it in the right direction – down to the heart, rather than up to the brain – all without tearing through vessels, lung, or anything else.

To do this, S. explained, you start by getting a guide wire in place. She pulled the syringe off, leaving the needle in. Blood flowed out. She picked up a two-foot-long twenty-gauge wire that looked like the steel D string of an electric guitar, and passed nearly its full length through the needle's bore, into the vein, and onward toward the vena cava. "Never force it in," she warned, "and never, ever let go of it." A string of rapid heartbeats fired off on the cardiac monitor, and she quickly pulled the wire back an inch. It had poked into the heart, causing momentary fibrillation. "Guess we're in the right place," she said to me quietly. Then to the patient: "You're doing great. Only a few minutes now." She pulled the needle out over the wire and replaced it with a bullet of thick, stiff plastic, which she pushed in tight to widen the vein opening. She then removed this dilator and threaded the central line – a spaghetti-thick, flexible yellow plastic tube – over the wire until it was all the way in. Now she could remove the wire. She flushed the line with a heparin solution and sutured it to the patient's chest. And that was it.

Today, it was my turn to try. First, I had to gather supplies – a central-line kit, gloves, gown, cap, mask, lidocaine – which took me forever. When I finally had the stuff together, I stopped for a minute outside the patient's door, trying to recall the steps. They remained frustratingly hazy. But I couldn't put it off any longer. I had a page-long list of other things to get done: Mrs. A needed to be discharged; Mr. B needed an abdominal ultrasound arranged; Mrs. C needed her skin staples removed. And every fifteen minutes or so I was getting paged with more tasks: Mr. X was nauseated and needed to be seen; Miss Y's family was here and needed "someone" to talk to them; Mr. Z needed a laxative. I took a deep breath, put on my best don't-worry-I-know-what-I'm-doing look, and went in.

I placed the supplies on a bedside table, untied the patient's gown, and laid him down flat on the mattress, with his chest bare and his arms at his sides. I flipped on a fluorescent overhead light and raised his bed to my height. I paged S. I put on my gown and gloves and, on a sterile tray, laid out the central line, the guide wire, and other materials from the kit. I drew up five cc's of lidocaine in a syringe, soaked two sponge sticks in the yellow-brown Betadine, and opened up the suture packaging.

S. arrived. "What's his platelet count?"

My stomach knotted. I hadn't checked. That was bad: too low and he could have a serious bleed from the procedure. She went to check a computer. The count was acceptable.

Chastened, I started swabbing his chest with the sponge sticks. "Got the shoulder roll underneath him?" S. asked. Well, no, I had forgotten that, too. The patient gave me a look. S., saying nothing, got a towel, rolled it up, and slipped it under his back for me. I finished applying the antiseptic and then draped him so that only his right upper chest was exposed. He squirmed a bit beneath the drapes. S. now inspected my tray. I girded myself.

"Where's the extra syringe for flushing the line when it's in?" Damn. She went out and got it.

I felt for my landmarks. Here? I asked with my eyes, not wanting to undermine the patient's confidence any further. She nodded. I numbed the spot with lidocaine. ("You'll feel a stick and a burn now, sir.") Next, I took the three-inch needle in hand and poked it through the skin. I advanced it slowly and uncertainly, a few millimetres at a time. This is a big goddam needle, I kept thinking. I couldn't believe I was sticking it into someone's chest. I concentrated on maintaining a steep angle of entry, but kept spearing his clavicle instead of slipping beneath it.

"Ow!" he shouted.

"Sorry," I said. S. signaled with a kind of surfing hand gesture to go underneath the clavicle. This time, it went in. I drew back on the syringe. Nothing. She pointed deeper. I went in deeper. Nothing. I withdrew the needle, flushed out some bits of tissue clogging it, and tried again.

"Ow!"

Too steep again. I found my way underneath the clavicle once more. I drew the syringe back. Still nothing. He's too obese, I thought. S. slipped on gloves and a gown. "How about I have a look?" she said. I handed her the needle and stepped aside. She plunged the needle in, drew back on the syringe, and, just like that, she was in. "We'll be done shortly," she told the patient.

She let me continue with the next steps, which I bumbled through. I didn't realize how long and floppy the guide wire was until I pulled the coil out of its plastic sleeve, and, putting one end of it into the patient, I very nearly contaminated the other. I forgot about the dilating step until she reminded me. Then, when I put in the dilator, I didn't push quite hard enough, and it was really S. who pushed it all the way in. Finally, we got the line in, flushed it, and sutured it in place.

Outside the room, S. said that I could be less tentative the next time, but that I shouldn't worry too much about how things had gone. "You'll get it," she said. "It just takes practice." I wasn't so sure. The procedure remained wholly mysterious to me. And I could not get over the idea of jabbing a needle into someone's chest so deeply and so blindly. I awaited the X-ray afterward with trepidation. But it came back fine: I had not injured the lung and the line was in the right place.

Not everyone appreciates the attractions of surgery. When you are a medical student in the operating room for the first time, and you see the surgeon press the scalpel to someone's body and open it like a piece of fruit, you either shudder in horror or gape in awe. I gaped. It was not just the blood and guts that enthralled me. It was also the idea that a person, a mere mortal, would have the confidence to wield that scalpel in the first place.

There is a saying about surgeons: "Sometimes wrong; never in doubt." This is meant as a reproof, but to me it seemed their strength. Every day, surgeons are faced with uncertainties. Information is inadequate; the science is ambiguous; one's knowledge and abilities are never perfect. Even with the simplest operation, it cannot be taken for granted that a patient will come through better off – or even alive. Standing at the operating table, I wondered how the surgeon knew that all the steps would go as planned, that bleeding would be controlled and infection would not set in and organs would not be injured. He didn't, of course. But he cut anyway.

Later, while still a student, I was allowed to make an incision myself. The surgeon drew a six-inch dotted line with a marking pen across an anesthetized patient's abdomen and then, to my surprise, had the nurse hand me the knife. It was still warm from the autoclave. The surgeon had me stretch the skin taut with the thumb and forefinger of my free hand. He told me to make one smooth slice down to the fat. I put the belly of the blade to the skin and cut. The experience was odd and addictive, mixing exhilaration from the calculated violence of the act, anxiety about getting it right, and a righteous faith that it was somehow for the person's good. There was also the slightly nauseating feeling of finding that it took more force than I'd realized. (Skin is thick and springy, and on my first pass I did not go nearly deep enough; I had to cut twice to get through.) The moment made me want to be a surgeon – not an amateur handed the knife for a brief moment but someone with the confidence and ability to proceed as if it were routine.

A resident begins, however, with none of this air of mastery – only an overpowering instinct against doing anything like pressing a knife against flesh or jabbing a needle into someone's chest. On my first day as a surgical resident, I was assigned to the emergency room. Among my first patients was a skinny, dark-haired woman in her late twenties who hobbled in, teeth gritted, with a two-foot-long wooden chair leg somehow nailed to the bottom of her foot. She explained that a kitchen chair had collapsed under her and, as she leaped up to keep from falling, her bare foot had stomped down on a three-inch screw sticking out of one of the chair legs. I tried very hard to look like someone who had not got his medical diploma just the week before. Instead, I was determined to be nonchalant, the kind of guy who had seen this sort of thing a hundred times before. I inspected her foot, and could see that the screw was embedded in the bone at the base of her big toe. There was no bleeding and, as far as I could feel, no fracture.

"Wow, that must hurt," I blurted out, idiotically.

The obvious thing to do was give her a tetanus shot and pull out the screw. I ordered the tetanus shot, but I began to have doubts about pulling out the screw. Suppose she bled? Or suppose I fractured her foot? Or something worse? I excused myself and tracked down Dr. W., the senior surgeon on duty. I found him tending to a car-crash victim. The patient was a mess, and the floor was covered with blood. People were shouting. It was not a good time to ask questions.

I ordered an X-ray. I figured it would buy time and let me check my amateur impression that she didn't have a fracture. Sure enough, getting the X-ray took about an hour, and it showed no fracture – just a common screw embedded, the radiologist said, "in the head of the first metatarsal." I showed the patient the X-ray. "You see, the screw's embedded in the head of the first metatarsal," I said. And the plan? she wanted to know. Ah, yes, the plan.

I went to find Dr. W. He was still busy with the crash victim, but I was able to interrupt to show him the X-ray. He chuckled at the sight of it and asked me what I wanted to do. "Pull the screw out?" I ventured. "Yes," he said, by which he meant "Duh." He made sure I'd given the patient a tetanus shot and then shooed me away.

Back in the examining room, I told her that I would pull the screw out, prepared for her to say something like "You?" Instead she said, "O.K., Doctor." At first, I had her sitting on the exam table, dangling her leg off the side. But that didn't look as if it would work. Eventually, I had her lie with her foot jutting off the table end, the board poking out into the air. With every move, her pain increased. I injected a local anesthetic where the screw had gone in and that helped a little. Now I grabbed her foot in one hand, the board in the other, and for a moment I froze. Could I really do this? Who was I to presume?

Finally, I gave her a one-two-three and pulled, gingerly at first and then hard. She groaned. The screw wasn't budging. I twisted, and abruptly it came free. There was no bleeding. I washed the wound out, and she found she could walk. I warned her of the risks of infection and the signs to look for. Her gratitude was immense and flattering, like the lion's for the mouse – and that night I went home elated.

In surgery, as in anything else, skill, judgment, and confidence are learned through experience, haltingly and humiliatingly. Like the tennis player and the oboist and the guy who fixes hard drives, we need practice to get good at what we do. There is one difference in medicine, though: we practice on people.

My second try at placing a central line went no better than the first. The patient was in intensive care, mortally ill, on a ventilator, and needed the line so that powerful cardiac drugs could be delivered directly to her heart. She was also heavily sedated, and for this I was grateful. She'd be oblivious of my fumbling.

My preparation was better this time. I got the towel roll in place and the syringes of heparin on the tray. I checked her lab results, which were fine. I also made a point of draping more widely, so that if I flopped the guide wire around by mistake again, it wouldn't hit anything unsterile.

For all that, the procedure was a bust. I stabbed the needle in too shallow and then too deep. Frustration overcame tentativeness and I tried one angle after another. Nothing worked. Then, for one brief moment, I got a flash of blood in the syringe, indicating that I was in the vein. I anchored the needle with one hand and went to pull the syringe off with the other. But the syringe was jammed on too tightly, so that when I pulled it free I dislodged the needle from the vein. The patient began bleeding into her chest wall. I held pressure the best I could for a solid five minutes, but still her chest turned black and blue around the site. The hematoma made it impossible to put a line through there anymore. I wanted to give up. But she needed a line and the resident supervising me – a second-year this time – was determined that I succeed. After an X-ray showed that I had not injured her lung, he had me try on the other side, with a whole new kit. I missed again, and he took over. It took him several minutes and two or three sticks to find the vein himself and that made me feel better. Maybe she was an unusually tough case.

When I failed with a third patient a few days later, though, the doubts really set in. Again, it was stick, stick, stick, and nothing. I stepped aside. The resident watching me got it on the next try.

Surgeons, as a group, adhere to a curious egalitarianism. They believe in practice, not talent. People often assume that you have to have great hands to become a surgeon, but it's not true. When I interviewed to get into surgery programs, no one made me sew or take a dexterity test or checked to see if my hands were steady. You do not even need all ten fingers to be accepted. To be sure, talent helps. Professors say that every two or three years they'll see someone truly gifted come through a program – someone who picks up complex manual skills unusually quickly, sees tissue planes before others do, anticipates trouble before it happens. Nonetheless, attending surgeons say that what's most important to them is finding people who are conscientious, industrious, and boneheaded enough to keep at practicing this one difficult thing day and night for years on end. As a former residency director put it to me, given a choice between a Ph.D. who had cloned a gene and a sculptor, he'd pick the Ph.D. every time. Sure, he said, he'd bet on the sculptor's being more physically talented; but he'd bet on the Ph.D.'s being less "flaky." And in the end that matters more. Skill, surgeons believe, can be taught; tenacity cannot. It's an odd approach to recruitment, but it continues all the way up the ranks, even in top surgery departments. They start with minions with no experience in surgery, spend years training them, and then take most of their faculty from these same homegrown ranks.

And it works. There have now been many studies of elite performers – concert violinists, chess grand masters, professional ice-skaters, mathematicians, and so forth – and the biggest difference researchers find between them and lesser performers is the amount of deliberate practice they've accumulated. Indeed, the most important talent may be the talent for practice itself. K. Anders Ericsson, a cognitive psychologist and an expert on performance, notes that the most important role that innate factors play may be in a person's willingness to engage in sustained training. He has found, for example, that top performers dislike practicing just as much as others do. (That's why, for example, athletes and musicians usually quit practicing when they retire.) But, more than others, they have the will to keep at it anyway.

I wasn't sure I did. What good was it, I wondered, to keep doing central lines when I wasn't coming close to hitting them? If I had a clear idea of what I was doing wrong, then maybe I'd have something to focus on. But I didn't. Everyone, of course, had suggestions. Go in with the bevel of the needle up. No, go in with the bevel down. Put a bend in the middle of the needle. No, curve the needle. For a while, I tried to avoid doing another line. Soon enough, however, a new case arose.

The circumstances were miserable. It was late in the day, and I'd had to work through the previous night. The patient weighed more than three hundred pounds. He couldn't tolerate lying flat because the weight of his chest and abdomen made it hard for him to breathe. Yet he had a badly infected wound, needed intravenous antibiotics, and no one could find veins in his arms for a peripheral I.V. I had little hope of succeeding. But a resident does what he is told, and I was told to try the line.

I went to his room. He looked scared and said he didn't think he'd last more than a minute on his back. But he said he understood the situation and was willing to make his best effort. He and I decided that he'd be left sitting propped up in bed until the last possible minute. We'd see how far we got after that.

I went through my preparations: checking his blood counts from the lab, putting out the kit, placing the towel roll, and so on. I swabbed and draped his chest while he was still sitting up. S., the chief resident, was watching me this time, and when everything was ready I had her tip him back, an oxygen mask on his face. His flesh rolled up his chest like a wave. I couldn't find his clavicle with my fingertips to line up the right point of entry. And already he was looking short of breath, his face red. I gave S. a "Do you want to take over?" look. Keep going, she signalled. I made a rough guess about where the right spot was, numbed it with lidocaine, and pushed the big needle in. For a second, I thought it wouldn't be long enough to reach through, but then I felt the tip slip underneath his clavicle. I pushed a little deeper and drew back on the syringe. Unbelievably, it filled with blood. I was in. I concentrated on anchoring the needle firmly in place, not moving it a millimetre as I pulled the syringe off and threaded the guide wire in. The wire fed in smoothly. The patient was struggling hard for air now. We sat him up and let him catch his breath. And then, laying him down one more time, I got the entry dilated and slid the central line in. "Nice job" was all S. said, and then she left.

I still have no idea what I did differently that day. But from then on my lines went in. That's the funny thing about practice. For days and days, you make out only the fragments of what to do. And then one day you've got the thing whole. Conscious learning becomes unconscious knowledge, and you cannot say precisely how.

I have now put in more than a hundred central lines. I am by no means infallible. Certainly, I have had my fair share of complications. I punctured a patient's lung, for example – the right lung of a chief of surgery from another hospital, no less – and, given the odds, I'm sure such things will happen again. I still have the occasional case that should go easily but doesn't, no matter what I do. (We have a term for this. "How'd it go?" a colleague asks. "It was a total flog," I reply. I don't have to say anything more.)

But other times everything unfolds effortlessly. You take the needle. You stick the chest. You feel the needle travel – a distinct glide through the fat, a slight catch in the dense muscle, then the subtle pop through the vein wall – and you're in. At such moments, it is more than easy; it is beautiful.

Surgical training is the recapitulation of this process – floundering followed by fragments followed by knowledge and, occasionally, a moment of elegance – over and over again, for ever harder tasks with ever greater risks. At first, you work on the basics: how to glove and gown, how to drape patients, how to hold the knife, how to tie a square knot in a length of silk suture (not to mention how to dictate, work the computers, order drugs). But then the tasks become more daunting: how to cut through skin, handle the electrocautery, open the breast, tie off a bleeder, excise a tumor, close up a wound. At the end of six months, I had done lines, lumpectomies, appendectomies, skin grafts, hernia repairs, and mastectomies. At the end of a year, I was doing limb amputations, hemorrhoidectomies, and laparoscopic gallbladder operations. At the end of two years, I was beginning to do tracheotomies, small-bowel operations, and leg-artery bypasses.

I am in my seventh year of training, of which three years have been spent doing research. Only now has a simple slice through skin begun to seem like the mere start of a case. These days, I'm trying to learn how to fix an abdominal aortic aneurysm, remove a pancreatic cancer, open blocked carotid arteries. I am, I have found, neither gifted nor maladroit. With practice and more practice, I get the hang of it.

Doctors find it hard to talk about this with patients. The moral burden of practicing on people is always with us, but for the most part it is unspoken. Before each operation, I go over to the holding area in my scrubs and introduce myself to the patient. I do it the same way every time. "Hello, I'm Dr. Gawande. I'm one of the surgical residents, and I'll be assisting your surgeon." That is pretty much all I say on the subject. I extend my hand and smile. I ask the patient if everything is going O.K. so far. We chat. I answer questions. Very occasionally, patients are taken aback. "No resident is doing my surgery," they say. I try to be reassuring. "Not to worry – I just assist," I say. "The attending surgeon is always in charge."

None of this is exactly a lie. The attending is in charge, and a resident knows better than to forget that. Consider the operation I did recently to remove a seventy-five-year-old woman's colon cancer. The attending stood across from me from the start. And it was he, not I, who decided where to cut, how to position the opened abdomen, how to isolate the cancer, and how much colon to take.

Yet I'm the one who held the knife. I'm the one who stood on the operator's side of the table, and it was raised to my six-foot-plus height. I was there to help, yes, but I was there to practice, too. This was clear when it came time to reconnect the colon. There are two ways of putting the ends together – handsewing and stapling. Stapling is swifter and easier, but the attending suggested I handsew the ends – not because it was better for the patient but because I had had much less experience doing it. When it's performed correctly, the results are similar, but he needed to watch me like a hawk. My stitching was slow and imprecise. At one point, he caught me putting the stitches too far apart and made me go back and put extras in between so the connection would not leak. At another point, he found I wasn't taking deep enough bites of tissue with the needle to insure a strong closure. "Turn your wrist more," he told me. "Like this?" I asked. "Uh, sort of," he said.

In medicine, there has long been a conflict between the imperative to give patients the best possible care and the need to provide novices with experience. Residencies attempt to mitigate potential harm through supervision and graduated responsibility. And there is reason to think that patients actually benefit from teaching. Studies commonly find that teaching hospitals have better outcomes than non-teaching hospitals. Residents may be amateurs, but having them around checking on patients, asking questions, and keeping faculty on their toes seems to help. But there is still no avoiding those first few unsteady times a young physician tries to put in a central line, remove a breast cancer, or sew together two segments of colon. No matter how many protections are in place, on average these cases go less well with the novice than with someone experienced.

Doctors have no illusions about this. When an attending physician brings a sick family member in for surgery, people at the hospital think twice about letting trainees participate. Even when the attending insists that they participate as usual, the residents scrubbing in know that it will be far from a teaching case. And if a central line must be put in, a first-timer is certainly not going to do it. Conversely, the ward services and clinics where residents have the most responsibility are populated by the poor, the uninsured, the drunk, and the demented. Residents have few opportunities nowadays to operate independently, without the attending docs scrubbed in, but when we do – as we must before graduating and going out to operate on our own – it is generally with these, the humblest of patients.

And this is the uncomfortable truth about teaching. By traditional ethics and public insistence (not to mention court rulings), a patient's right to the best care possible must trump the objective of training novices. We want perfection without practice. Yet everyone is harmed if no one is trained for the future. So learning is hidden, behind drapes and anesthesia and the elisions of language. And the dilemma doesn't apply just to residents, physicians in training. The process of learning goes on longer than most people know.

I grew up in the small Appalachian town of Athens, Ohio, where my parents are both doctors. My mother is a pediatrician and my father is a urologist. Long ago, my mother chose to practice part time, which she could afford to do because my father's practice became so busy and successful. He has now been at it for more than twenty-five years, and his office is cluttered with the evidence of this. There is an overflowing wall of medical files, gifts from patients displayed everywhere (books, paintings, ceramics with Biblical sayings, hand-painted paperweights, blown glass, carved boxes, a figurine of a boy who, when you pull down his pants, pees on you), and, in an acrylic case behind his oak desk, a few dozen of the thousands of kidney stones he has removed.

Only now, as I get glimpses of the end of my training, have I begun to think hard about my father's success. For most of my residency, I thought of surgery as a more or less fixed body of knowledge and skill which is acquired in training and perfected in practice. There was, I thought, a smooth, upward-sloping arc of proficiency at some rarefied set of tasks (for me, taking out gallbladders, colon cancers, bullets, and appendixes; for him, taking out kidney stones, testicular cancers, and swollen prostates). The arc would peak at, say, ten or fifteen years, plateau for a long time, and perhaps tail off a little in the final five years before retirement. The reality, however, turns out to be far messier. You do get good at certain things, my father tells me, but no sooner do you master something than you find that what you know is outmoded. New technologies and operations emerge to supplant the old, and the learning curve starts all over again. "Three-quarters of what I do today I never learned in residency," he says. On his own, fifty miles from his nearest colleague – let alone a doctor who could tell him anything like "You need to turn your wrist more" – he has had to learn to put in penile prostheses, to perform microsurgery, to reverse vasectomies, to do nerve-sparing prostatectomies, to implant artificial urinary sphincters. He's had to learn to use shock-wave lithotripters, electrohydraulic lithotripters, and laser lithotripters (all instruments for breaking up kidney stones); to deploy Double J ureteral stents and Silicone Figure Four Coil stents and Retro-Inject Multi-Length stents (don't even ask); and to maneuver fibre-optic ureteroscopes. All these technologies and techniques were introduced after he finished training. Some of the procedures built on skills he already had. Many did not.

This is the experience that all surgeons have. The pace of medical innovation has been unceasing, and surgeons have no choice but to give the new thing a try. To fail to adopt new techniques would mean denying patients meaningful medical advances. Yet the perils of the learning curve are inescapable – no less in practice than in residency.

For the established surgeon, inevitably, the opportunities for learning are far less structured than for a resident. When an important new device or procedure comes along, as happens every year, surgeons start by taking a course about it – typically a day or two of lectures by some surgical grandees with a few film clips and step-by-step handouts. You take home a video to watch. Perhaps you pay a visit to observe a colleague perform the operation – my father often goes up to the Cleveland Clinic for this. But there's not much by way of hands-on training. Unlike a resident, a visitor cannot scrub in on cases, and opportunities to practice on animals or cadavers are few and far between. (Britain, being Britain, actually bans surgeons from practicing on animals.) When the pulse-dye laser came out, the manufacturer set up a lab in Columbus where urologists from the area could gain experience. But when my father went there the main experience provided was destroying kidney stones in test tubes filled with a urinelike liquid and trying to penetrate the shell of an egg without hitting the membrane underneath. My surgery department recently bought a robotic surgery device – a staggeringly sophisticated nine-hundred-and-eighty-thousand-dollar robot, with three arms, two wrists, and a camera, all millimetres in diameter, which, controlled from a console, allows a surgeon to do almost any operation with no hand tremor and with only tiny incisions. A team of two surgeons and two nurses flew out to the manufacturer's headquarters, in Mountain View, California, for a full day of training on the machine. And they did get to practice on a pig and on a human cadaver. (The company apparently buys the cadavers from the city of San Francisco.) But even this was hardly thorough training. They learned enough to grasp the principles of using the robot, to start getting a feel for using it, and to understand how to plan an operation. That was about it. Sooner or later, you just have to go home and give the thing a try on someone.

Patients do eventually benefit – often enormously – but the first few patients may not, and may even be harmed. Consider the experience reported by the pediatric cardiac-surgery unit of the renowned Great Ormond Street Hospital, in London, as detailed in the British Medical Journal last April. The doctors described their results from three hundred and twenty-five consecutive operations between 1978 and 1998 on babies with a severe heart defect known as transposition of the great arteries. Such children are born with their heart's outflow vessels transposed: the aorta emerges from the right side of the heart instead of the left and the artery to the lungs emerges from the left instead of the right. As a result, blood coming in is pumped right back out to the body instead of first to the lungs, where it can be oxygenated. The babies died blue, fatigued, never knowing what it was to get enough breath. For years, it wasn't technically feasible to switch the vessels to their proper positions. Instead, surgeons did something known as the Senning procedure: they created a passage inside the heart to let blood from the lungs cross backward to the right heart. The Senning procedure allowed children to live into adulthood. The weaker right heart, however, cannot sustain the body's entire blood flow as long as the left. Eventually, these patients' hearts failed, and although most survived to adulthood, few lived to old age.

By the nineteen-eighties, a series of technological advances made it possible to do a switch operation safely, and this became the favored procedure. In 1986, the Great Ormond Street surgeons made the changeover themselves, and their report shows that it was unquestionably an improvement. The annual death rate after a successful switch procedure was less than a quarter that of the Senning, resulting in a life expectancy of sixty-three years instead of forty-seven. But the price of learning to do it was appalling. In their first seventy switch operations, the doctors had a twenty-five-per-cent surgical death rate, compared with just six per cent with the Senning procedure. Eighteen babies died, more than twice the number during the entire Senning era. Only with time did they master it: in their next hundred switch operations, five babies died.

As patients, we want both expertise and progress; we don't want to acknowledge that these are contradictory desires. In the words of one British public report, "There should be no learning curve as far as patient safety is concerned." But this is entirely wishful thinking.

Recently, a group of Harvard Business School researchers who have made a specialty of studying learning curves in industry decided to examine learning curves among surgeons instead of in semiconductor manufacture or airplane construction, or any of the usual fields their colleagues examine. They followed eighteen cardiac surgeons and their teams as they took on the new technique of minimally invasive cardiac surgery. This study, I was surprised to discover, is the first of its kind. Learning is ubiquitous in medicine, and yet no one had ever compared how well different teams actually do it.

The new heart operation – in which new technologies allow a surgeon to operate through a small incision between ribs instead of splitting the chest open down the middle – proved substantially more difficult than the conventional one. Because the incision is too small to admit the usual tubes and clamps for rerouting blood to the heart-bypass machine, surgeons had to learn a trickier method, which involved balloons and catheters placed through groin vessels. And the nurses, anesthesiologists, and perfusionists all had new roles to master. As you'd expect, everyone experienced a substantial learning curve. Whereas a fully proficient team takes three to six hours for such an operation, these teams took on average three times as long for their early cases. The researchers could not track complication rates in detail, but it would be foolish to imagine that they were not affected.

What's more, the researchers found striking disparities in the speed with which different teams learned. All teams came from highly respected institutions with experience in adopting innovations and received the same three-day training session. Yet, in the course of fifty cases, some teams managed to halve their operating time while others improved hardly at all. Practice, it turned out, did not necessarily make perfect. The crucial variable was how the surgeons and their teams practiced.

Richard Bohmer, the only physician among the Harvard researchers, made several visits to observe one of the quickest-learning teams and one of the slowest, and he was startled by the contrast. The surgeon on the fast-learning team was actually quite inexperienced compared with the one on the slow-learning team. But he made sure to pick team members with whom he had worked well before and to keep them together through the first fifteen cases before allowing any new members. He had the team go through a dry run before the first case, then deliberately scheduled six operations in the first week, so little would be forgotten in between. He convened the team before each case to discuss it in detail and afterward to debrief. He made sure results were tracked carefully. And Bohmer noticed that the surgeon was not the stereotypical Napoleon with a knife. Unbidden, he told Bohmer, "The surgeon needs to be willing to allow himself to become a partner [with the rest of the team] so he can accept input." At the other hospital, by contrast, the surgeon chose his operating team almost randomly and did not keep it together. In the first seven cases, the team had different members every time, which is to say that it was no team at all. And the surgeon had no pre-briefings, no debriefings, no tracking of ongoing results.

The Harvard Business School study offered some hopeful news. We can do things that have a dramatic effect on our rate of improvement – like being more deliberate about how we train, and about tracking progress, whether with students and residents or with senior surgeons and nurses. But the study's other implications are less reassuring. No matter how accomplished, surgeons trying something new got worse before they got better, and the learning curve proved longer, and was affected by a far more complicated range of factors, than anyone had realized.

This, I suspect, is the reason for the physician's dodge: the "I just assist" rap; the "We have a new procedure for this that you are perfect for" speech; the "You need a central line" without the "I am still learning how to do this." Sometimes we do feel obliged to admit when we're doing something for the first time, but even then we tend to quote the published complication rates of experienced surgeons. Do we ever tell patients that, because we are still new at something, their risks will inevitably be higher, and that they'd likely do better with doctors who are more experienced? Do we ever say that we need them to agree to it anyway? I've never seen it. Given the stakes, who in his right mind would agree to be practiced upon?

Many dispute this presumption. “Look, most people understand what it is to be a doctor,” a health policy expert insisted, when I visited him in his office not long ago. “We have to stop lying to our patients. Can people take on choices for societal benefit?” He paused and then answered his question. “Yes,” he said firmly.

It would certainly be a graceful and happy solution. We’d ask patients – honestly, openly – and they’d say yes. Hard to imagine, though. I noticed on the expert’s desk a picture of his child, born just a few months before, and a completely unfair question popped into my mind. “So did you let the resident deliver?” I asked.

There was silence for a moment. “No,” he admitted. “We didn’t even allow residents in the room.”

One reason I doubt whether we could sustain a system of medical training that depended on people saying “Yes, you can practice on me” is that I myself have said no. When my eldest child, Walker, was eleven days old, he suddenly went into congestive heart failure from what proved to be a severe cardiac defect. His aorta was not transposed, but a long segment of it had failed to grow at all. My wife and I were beside ourselves with fear – his kidneys and liver began failing, too – but he made it to surgery, the repair was a success, and although his recovery was erratic, after two and a half weeks he was ready to come home.

We were by no means in the clear, however. He was born a healthy six pounds plus but now, a month old, he weighed only five, and would need strict monitoring to insure that he gained weight. He was on two cardiac medications from which he would have to be weaned. And in the longer term, the doctors warned us, his repair would prove inadequate. As Walker grew, his aorta would require either dilation with a balloon or replacement by surgery. They could not say precisely when and how many such procedures would be necessary over the years. A pediatric cardiologist would have to follow him closely and decide.

Walker was about to be discharged, and we had not indicated who that cardiologist would be. In the hospital, he had been cared for by a full team of cardiologists, ranging from fellows in specialty training to attendings who had practiced for decades. The day before we took Walker home, one of the young fellows approached me, offering his card and suggesting a time to bring Walker to see him. Of those on the team, he had put in the most time caring for Walker. He saw Walker when we brought him in inexplicably short of breath, made the diagnosis, got Walker the drugs that stabilized him, coordinated with the surgeons, and came to see us twice a day to answer our questions. Moreover, I knew, this was how fellows always got their patients. Most families don’t know the subtle gradations among players, and after a team has saved their child's life they take whatever appointment they're handed.

But I knew the differences. "I'm afraid we're thinking of seeing Dr. Newburger," I said. She was the hospital's associate cardiologist-in-chief, and a published expert on conditions like Walker's. The young physician looked crestfallen. It was nothing against him, I said. She just had more experience, that was all.

"You know, there is always an attending backing me up," he said. I shook my head.

I know this was not fair. My son had an unusual problem. The fellow needed the experience. As a resident, I of all people should have understood this. But I was not torn about the decision. This was my child. Given a choice, I will always choose the best care I can for him. How can anybody be expected to do otherwise? Certainly, the future of medicine should not rely on it.

In a sense, then, the physician's dodge is inevitable. Learning must be stolen, taken as a kind of bodily eminent domain. And it was, during Walker's stay – on many occasions, now that I think back on it. A resident intubated him. A surgical trainee scrubbed in for his operation. The cardiology fellow put in one of his central lines. If I had the option to have someone more experienced, I would have taken it. But this was simply how the system worked – no such choices were offered – and so I went along.

The advantage of this coldhearted machinery is not merely that it gets the learning done. If learning is necessary but causes harm, then above all it ought to apply to everyone alike. Given a choice, people wriggle out, and such choices are not offered equally. They belong to the connected and the knowledgeable, to insiders over outsiders, to the doctor's child but not the truck driver's. If everyone cannot have a choice, maybe it is better if no one can.

It is 2 P.M. I am in the intensive-care unit. A nurse tells me Mr. G.'s central line has clotted off. Mr. G. has been in the hospital for more than a month now. He is in his late sixties, from South Boston, emaciated, exhausted, holding on by a thread – or a line, to be precise. He has several holes in his small bowel, and the bilious contents leak out onto his skin through two small reddened openings in the concavity of his abdomen. His only chance is to be fed by vein and wait for these fistulae to heal. He needs a new central line.

I could do it, I suppose. I am the experienced one now. But experience brings a new role: I am expected to teach the procedure instead. "See one, do one, teach one," the saying goes, and it is only half in jest.

There is a junior resident on the service. She has done only one or two lines before. I tell her about Mr. G. I ask her if she is free to do a new line. She misinterprets this as a question. She says she still has patients to see and a case coming up later. Could I do the line? I tell her no. She is unable to hide a grimace. She is burdened, as I was burdened, and perhaps frightened, as I was frightened.

She begins to focus when I make her talk through the steps – a kind of dry run, I figure. She hits nearly all the steps, but forgets about checking the labs and about Mr. G.'s nasty allergy to heparin, which is in the flush for the line. I make sure she registers this, then tell her to get set up and page me.

I am still adjusting to this role. It is painful enough taking responsibility for one's own failures. Being handmaiden to another's is something else entirely. It occurs to me that I could have broken open a kit and had her do an actual dry run. Then again maybe I can't. The kits must cost a couple of hundred dollars each. I'll have to find out for next time.

Half an hour later, I get the page. The patient is draped. The resident is in her gown and gloves. She tells me that she has saline to flush the line with and that his labs are fine.

"Have you got the towel roll?" I ask.

She forgot the towel roll. I roll up a towel and slip it beneath Mr.G.'s back. I ask him if he's all right. He nods. After all he's been through, there is only resignation in his eyes.

The junior resident picks out a spot for the stick. The patient is hauntingly thin. I see every rib and fear that the resident will puncture his lung. She injects the numbing medication. Then she puts the big needle in, and the angle looks all wrong. I motion for her to reposition. This only makes her more uncertain. She pushes in deeper and I know she does not have it. She draws back on the syringe: no blood. She takes out the needle and tries again. And again the angle looks wrong. This time, Mr. G. feels the jab and jerks up in pain. I hold his arm. She gives him more numbing medication. It is all I can do not to take over. But she cannot learn without doing, I tell myself. I decide to let her have one more try.

How We Listen

Aaron Copland

Chapter 2 in *What to Listen for in Music.* New York: McGraw-Hill, 1988. Originally published in 1939.

***Aaron Copland** (1900-1990) was an American composer and conductor. He had formal musical education in Paris and Rome, but also sought to create music in a distinctively American idiom that would reach out to the ordinary person and not just the upper classes. His ballets* Appalachian Spring *and* Rodeo *are among his most well-known works, but Copland also wrote chamber music, operas and film scores.*

***Why we are reading this:** We all think we know how to listen to music. In this essay, Copland argues that we can listen to music on at least three different levels – the sensory, expressive, and "sheerly musical" levels. The sensory level ("sensuous plane" in Copland's wording) is the simplest and easiest way to listen, and the one used by most people most of the time. The second, expressive, plane can be more complex and controversial – this is where one reflects upon the "meaning" of the music. Whatever the meaning of music might be, Copland suggests that it is not just in words that might be sung, but is embedded in the music itself. The third realm involves thinking about music in a more technical sense, using one's understanding of the techniques and methods that go into composing and performing music. His essay reminds us that as our experience and knowledge grow, we can learn to understand music more deeply. His examples come mostly from the European classical music tradition. He mentions the composers Bach, Mozart, Beethoven, Tchaikovsky, Ravel, and Stravinsky... but also Duke Ellington, suggesting that he believes that these ways of listening are universal and applicable to all forms of music. What do you think? Do these levels make sense to you? Does this help you understand what is going on when you listen to your favorite kinds of music? Are there other ways to listen that Copland has not mentioned?*

We all listen to music according to our separate capacities. But, for the sake of analysis, the whole listening process may become clearer if we break it up into its component parts, so to speak. In a certain sense we all listen to music on three separate planes. For lack of a better terminology, one might name these: (1) the sensuous plane, (2) the expressive plane, (3) the sheerly musical plane. The only advantage to be gained from mechanically splitting up the listening process into these hypothetical planes is the clearer view to be had of the way in which we listen.

The simplest way of listening to music is to listen for the sheer pleasure of the musical sound itself. That is the sensuous plane. It is the plane on which we hear music without thinking, without considering it in any way. One turns on the radio while doing something else and absent-mindedly bathes in the sound. A kind of brainless but attractive state of mind is engendered by the mere sound appeal of the music. You may be sitting in a room reading this book. Imagine one note struck on the piano. Immediately that one note is enough to change the atmosphere of the room – providing that the sound element in music is a powerful and mysterious agent, which it would be foolish to deride or belittle.

The surprising thing is that many people who consider themselves qualified music lovers abuse that plane in listening. They go to concerts in order to lose themselves. They use music as a consolation or an escape. They enter an ideal world where one doesn't have to think of the realities of everyday life. Of course they aren't thinking about the music either. Music allows them to leave it, and they go off to a place to dream, dreaming because of and apropos of the music yet never quite listening to it.

Yes, the sound appeal of music is a potent and primitive force, but you must not allow it to usurp a disproportionate share of your interest. The sensuous plane is an important one in music, a very important one, but it does not constitute the whole story.

There is no need to digress further on the sensuous plane. Its appeal to every normal human being is self-evident. There is, however, such a thing as becoming more sensitive to the different kinds of sound stuff as used by various composers. For all composers do not use that sound stuff in the same way. Don't get the idea that the value of music is commensurate with its sensuous appeal or that the loveliest sounding music is made by the greatest composer. If that were so, Ravel would be a greater creator than Beethoven. The point is that the sound element varies with each composer, that his usage of sound forms an integral part of his style and must be taken into account when listening. The reader can see, therefore, that a more conscious approach is valuable even on this primary plane of music listening.

The second plane on which music exists is what I have called the expressive one. Here, immediately, we tread on controversial ground. Composers have a way of shying away from any discussion of music's expressive side. Did not Stravinsky himself proclaim that his music was an "object," a "thing," with a life of its own, and with no other meaning than its own purely musical existence? This intransigent attitude of Stravinsky's may be due to the fact that so many people have tried to read different meanings into so many pieces. Heaven knows it is difficult enough to say precisely what it is that a piece of music means, to say it definitely, to say it finally so that everyone is satisfied with your explanation. But that should not lead one to the other extreme of denying to music the right to be "expressive."

My own belief is that all music has an expressive power, some more and some less, but that all music has a certain meaning behind the notes and that the meaning behind the notes constitutes, after all, what the piece is saying, what the piece is about. The whole problem can be stated quite simply by asking, "Is there a meaning to music?" My answer to that would be, "Yes." And "Can you state in so many words what the meaning is?" My answer to that would be, "No." Therein lies the difficulty.

Simple-minded souls will never be satisfied with the answer to the second of these questions. They always want music to have a meaning, and the more concrete it is the better they like it. The more the music reminds them of a train, a storm, a funeral, or any other familiar conception the more expressive it appears to be to them. This popular idea of music's meaning – stimulated and abetted by the usual run of musical commentator – should be discouraged wherever and whenever it is met. One timid lady once confessed to me that she suspected something seriously lacking in her appreciation of music because of her inability to connect it with anything definite. That is getting the whole thing backward, of course.

Still, the question remains, How close should the intelligent music lover wish to come to pinning a definite meaning to any particular work? No closer than a general concept, I should say. Music expresses, at different moments, serenity or exuberance, regrets or triumph, fury or delight. It expresses each of these moods, and many others, in a numberless variety of subtle shadings and differences. It may even express a state of meaning for which there exists no adequate word in any language. In that case, musicians often like to say that it has only a purely musical meaning. They sometimes go further and say that *all* music has only a purely musical meaning. What they really mean is that no appropriate word can be found to express the music's meaning and that, even if it could, they do not feel the need of finding it.

But whatever the professional musician may hold, most musical novices still search for specific words with which to pin down their musical reactions. That is why they always find Tschaikovsky easier to "understand" than Beethoven. In the first place, it is easier to pin a meaning-word on a Tschaikovsky piece than on a Beethoven one. Much easier. Moreover, with the Russian composer, every time you come back to a piece of his it almost always says the same thing to you, whereas with Beethoven it is often quite difficult to put your finger right on what he is saying. And any musician will tell you that that is why Beethoven is the greater composer. Because music which always says the same thing to you will necessarily soon become dull music, but music whose meaning is slightly different with each hearing has a greater chance of remaining alive.

Listen, if you can, to the forty-eight fugue themes of Bach's *Well Tempered Clavichord.* Listen to each theme, one after another. You will soon realize that each theme mirrors a different world of feeling. You will also soon realize that the more beautiful a theme seems to you the harder it is to find any word that will describe it to your complete satisfaction. Yes, you will certainly know whether it is a gay theme or a sad one. You will be able, in other words, in your own mind, to draw a frame of emotional feeling around your theme. Now study the sad one a little closer. Try to pin down the exact quality of its sadness. Is it pessimistically sad or resignedly sad; is it fatefully sad or smilingly sad?

Let us suppose that you are fortunate and can describe to your own satisfaction in so many words the exact meaning of your chosen theme. There is still no guarantee that anyone else will be satisfied. Nor need they be. The important thing is that each one feel for himself the specific expressive quality of a theme or, similarly, an entire piece of music. And if it is a great work of art, don't expect it to mean exactly the same thing to you each time you return to it.

Themes or pieces need not express only one emotion, of course. Take such a theme as the first main one of the *Ninth Symphony,* for example. It is clearly made up of different elements. It does not say only one thing. Yet anyone hearing it immediately gets a feeling of strength, a feeling of power. It isn't a power that comes simply because the theme is played loudly. It is a power inherent in the theme itself. The extraordinary strength and vigor of the theme results in the listener's receiving an impression that a forceful statement has been made. But one should never try to boil it down to "the fateful hammer of life," etc. That is where the trouble begins. The musician, in his exasperation, says it means nothing but the notes themselves, whereas the nonprofessional is only too anxious to hang on to any explanation that gives him the illusion of getting closer to the music's meaning. Now, perhaps, the reader will know better what I mean when I say that music does have an expressive meaning but that we cannot say in so many words what that meaning is.

The third plane on which music exists is the sheerly musical plane. Besides the pleasurable sound of music and the expressive feeling that it gives off, music does exist in terms of the notes themselves and of their manipulation. Most listeners are not sufficiently conscious of this third plane. Professional musicians, on the other hand, are, if anything, too conscious of the mere notes themselves. They often fall into the error of becoming so engrossed with their arpeggios and staccatos that they forget the deeper aspects of the music they are performing. But from the layman's standpoint, it is not so much a matter of getting over bad habits on the sheerly musical plane as of increasing one's awareness of what is going on, in so far as the notes are concerned.

When the man in the street listens to the "notes themselves" with any degree of concentration, he is most likely to make some mention of the melody. Either he hears a pretty melody or he does not, and he generally lets it go at that. Rhythm is likely to gain his attention next, particularly if it seems exciting. But harmony and tone color are generally taken for granted, if they are thought of consciously at all. As for music's having a definite form of some kind, that idea seems never to have occurred to him.

It is very important for all of us to become more alive to music on its sheerly musical plane. After all, an actual musical material is being used. The intelligent listener must be prepared to increase his awareness of the musical material and what happens to it. He must hear the melodies, the rhythms, the harmonies, the tone colors in a more conscious fashion. But above all he must, in order to follow the line of the composer's thought, know something of the principles of musical form. Listening to all of these elements is listening on the sheerly musical plane.

Let me repeat that I have split up mechanically the three separate planes on which we listen merely for the sake of greater clarity. Actually, we never listen on one or the other of these planes. What we do is to correlate them – listening in all three ways at the same time. It takes no mental effort, for we do it instinctively. Perhaps an analogy with what happens to us when we visit the theater will make this instinctive correlation clearer. In the theater, you are aware of the actors and actresses, costumes and sets, sounds and movements. All these give one the sense that the theater is a pleasant place to be in. They constitute the sensuous plane in our theatrical reactions.

The expressive plane in the theater would be derived from the feeling that you get from what is happening on the stage. You are moved to pity, excitement, or gayety. It is this general feeling, generated aside from the particular words being spoken, a certain emotional something which exists on the stage, that is analogous to the expressive quality in music.

The plot and plot development is equivalent to our sheerly musical plane. The playwright creates and develops a character in just the same way that a composer creates and develops a theme. According to the degree of your awareness of the way in which the artist in either field handles his material you will become a more intelligent listener. It is easy enough to see that the theatergoer never is conscious of any of these elements separately. He is aware of them all at the same time. The same is true of music listening. We simultaneously and without thinking listen on all three planes.

In a sense, the ideal listener is both inside and outside the music at the same moment, judging it and enjoying it, wishing it would go one way and watching it go another – almost like the composer at the moment he composes it; because in order to write his music, the composer must also be inside and outside his music, carried away by it and yet coldly critical of it. A subjective and objective attitude is implied in both creating and listening to music.

What the reader should strive for, then, is a more *active* kind of listening. Whether you listen to Mozart or Duke Ellington, you can deepen your understanding of music only by being a more conscious and aware listener – not someone who is just listening, but someone who is listening *for* something.

We Are All Bound Up Together

Frances Ellen Watkins Harper

From *Lift Every Voice: African American Oratory, 1787-1900*. Edited by Philip Sheldon Foner and Robert J. Branham. Tuscaloosa: University of Alabama Press, 1998, pp. 456-460. Spelling modernized.

Frances Ellen Watkins Harper *(1825-1911) was an African American poet, writer, and lecturer. Born free in Baltimore in 1825, she published her first book of poetry at age 20. By the time of the Civil War (1861-1865), she was a well-known anti-slavery activist. After the war she campaigned for women's suffrage, equal rights for African Americans, and the prohibition of alcohol. In these movements, the alliance between white and black activists was sometimes strained. Harper attended major women's rights conventions alongside leading white suffragists like Elizabeth Cady Stanton and Susan B. Anthony, but she was often the only African American present or permitted to speak. When Congress proposed the Fifteenth Amendment in 1869, which guaranteed the vote to all men regardless of race but did not address women's suffrage, the women's movement fragmented. Harper and most African American suffragists, as well as black male activists like Frederick Douglass, supported the amendment as a step forward for racial equality. However, some white suffragists, including Stanton and Anthony, chose to oppose it because it failed to enfranchise women, whether black and white. Some were motivated by white racism, insulted that black men would get the vote before white women. Political alliances that span gender, race, and class lines have often proved fragile at critical moments like this.*

Why we are reading this: *Black and white women have shared the experience of discrimination and disenfranchisement, yet black women have also faced discrimination and hostility on the basis of race, often from the white women with whom they seemingly shared so much. This is the essence of what some modern writers call intersectionality – the intersection of different forms of identity and oppression based on gender, class, race, sexuality, and other characteristics. When Frances Harper spoke to the Eleventh National Women's Rights Convention in New York in May 1866, she sought to communicate this situation to her largely white and female audience. Harper frankly describes the dual oppression of sexism and racism that afflicted black women, emphasizing mutual interests with white women, yet challenging them to recognize their own complicity in systems of racial oppression.*

I feel I am something of a novice upon this platform. Born of a race whose inheritance has been outrage and wrong, most of my life had been spent in battling against those wrongs. But I did not feel as keenly as others, that I had these rights, in common with other women, which are now demanded. About two years ago, I stood within the shadows of my home. A great sorrow had fallen upon my life. My husband had died suddenly, leaving me a widow, with four children, one my own, and the others stepchildren. I tried to keep my children together. But my husband died in debt; and before he had been in his grave three months, the administrator hadswept the very milk-crocks and wash tubs from my hands. I was a farmer's wife and made butter for the Columbus market; but what could I do, when they had swept all away? They left me one thing – and that was a looking glass! Had I died instead of my husband, how different would have been the result! By this time he would have had another wife, it is likely; and no administrator would have gone into his house, broken up his home, and sold his bed, and taken away his means of support.

I took my children in my arms, and went out to seek my living. While I was gone; a neighbor to whom I had once lent five dollars, went before a magistrate and swore that he believed I was a non-resident, and laid an attachment on my very bed. And I went back to Ohio with my orphan children in my arms, without a single feather bed in this wide world, that was not in the custody of the law. I say, then, that justice is not fulfilled so long as woman is unequal before the law.

We are all bound up together in one great bundle of humanity, and society cannot trample on the weakest and feeblest of its members without receiving the curse in its own soul. You tried that in the case of the negro. You pressed him down for two centuries; and in so doing you crippled the moral strength and paralyzed the spiritual energies of the white men of the country. When the hands of the black were fettered, white men were deprived of the liberty of speech and the freedom of the press. Society cannot afford to neglect the enlightenment of any class of its members. At the South, the legislation of the country was in behalf of the rich slaveholders, while the poor white man was neglected. What is the consequence today? From that very class of neglected poor white men, comes the man who stands today, with his hand upon the helm of the nation. He fails to catch the watchword of the hour, and throws himself, the incarnation of meanness, across the pathway of the nation. My objection to Andrew Johnson is not that he has been a poor white man; my objection is that he keeps "poor whites" all the way through. (Applause.)

That is the trouble with him.[1]

This grand and glorious revolution which has commenced, will fail to reach its climax of success, until throughout the length and breadth of the American Republic, the nation shall be so color-blind, as to know no man by the color of his skin or the curl of his hair. It will then have no privileged class, trampling upon and outraging the unprivileged classes, but will be then one great privileged nation, whose privilege will be to produce the loftiest manhood and womanhood that humanity can attain.

I do not believe that giving the woman the ballot is immediately going to cure all the ills of life. I do not believe that white women are dew-drops just exhaled from the skies. I think that like men they may be divided into three classes, the good, the bad, and the indifferent. The good would vote according to their convictions and principles; the bad, as dictated by prejudice or malice; and the indifferent will vote on the strongest side of the question, with the winning party.

You white women speak here of rights. I speak of wrongs. I, as a colored woman, have had in this country an education which has made me feel as if I were in the situation of Ishmael, my hand against every man, and every man's hand against me. Let me go tomorrow morning and take my seat in one of your street cars – I do not know that they will do it in New York, but they will in Philadelphia – and the conductor will put up his hand and stop the car rather than let me ride.

A Lady – They will not do that here.

Mrs. Harper – They do in Philadelphia. Going from Washington to Baltimore this Spring, they put me in the smoking car. (Loud Voices – "Shame.") Aye, in the capital of the nation, where the black man consecrated himself to the nation's defense, faithful when the white man was faithless, they put me in the smoking car! They did it once; but the next time they tried it, they failed; for I would not go in. I felt the fight in me; but I don't want to have to fight all the time. Today I am puzzled where to make my home. I would like to make it in Philadelphia, near my own friends and relations. But if I want to ride in the streets of Philadelphia, they send me to ride on the platform with the driver. (Cries of "Shame.") Have women nothing to do with this? Not long since, a colored woman took her seat in an Eleventh Street car in Philadelphia, and the conductor stopped the car, and told the rest of the passengers to get out, and left the car with her in it alone, when they took it back to the station. One day I took my seat in a car, and the conductor came to me and told me to take

[1] Andrew Johnson succeeded Abraham Lincoln as president after the latter's assassination in April 1865. Pres. Johnson sought to undermine the Freedmen's Bureau, which provided material assistance for former slaves, and opposed congressional legislation to extend full civil rights to African Americans.

another seat. I just screamed "murder." The man said if I was black I ought to behave myself. I knew that if he was white he was not behaving himself. Are there not wrongs to be righted?

In advocating the cause of the colored man, since the Dred Scott decision, I have sometimes said I thought the nation had touched bottom. But let me tell you there is a depth of infamy lower than that. It is when the nation, standing upon the threshold of a great peril, reached out its hands to a feebler race, and asked that race to help it, and when the peril was over, said, You are good enough for soldiers, but not good enough for citizens. When Judge Taney said that the men of my race had no rights which the white man was bound to respect, he had not seen the bones of the black man bleaching outside of Richmond. He had not seen the thinned ranks and the thickened graves of the Louisiana Second, a regiment which went into battle nine hundred strong, and came out with three hundred. He had not stood at Olustee and seen defeat and disaster crushing down the pride of our banner, until word was brought to Col. Hallowell, "The day is lost; go in and save it;" and black men stood in the gap, beat back the enemy, and saved your army.[2] (Applause.)

We have a woman in our country who has received the name of "Moses,"[3] not by lying about it, but by acting it out (applause) – a woman who has gone down into the Egypt of slavery and brought out hundreds of our people into liberty. The last time I saw that woman, her hands were swollen. That woman who had led one of Montgomery's most successful expeditions, who was brave enough and secretive enough to act as a scout for the American army, had her hands all swollen from a conflict with a brutal conductor, who undertook to eject her from her place. That woman, whose courage and bravery won a recognition from our army and from every black man in the land, is excluded from every thoroughfare of travel. Talk of giving women the ballot box? Go on. It is a normal school, and the white women of this country need it. While there exists this brutal element in society which tramples upon the feeble and treads down the weak, I tell you that if there is any class of people who need to be lifted out of their airy nothings and selfishness, it is the white women of America. (Applause.)

---

[2] At the Battle of Olustee (or Battle of Ocean Pond) in Florida on February 20, 1864, the (African American) 54th Massachusetts Regiment halted the Confederate rout of Union forces.

[3] Harriett Tubman (1822-1913), abolitionist and conductor on the Underground Railway.

The Solitude of Self: Speech to the House Judiciary Committee

Elizabeth Cady Stanton

From *Hearing of the Woman Suffrage Association Before the Committee on Judiciary*, January 18, 1892 (Elizabeth Cady Stanton Papers, Library of Congress), pp. 1-5. Slightly edited for clarity.

Elizabeth Cady Stanton *(1815-1902) was an American suffragist, abolitionist, and writer who devoted her life to the idea that men and women should have equal rights. She campaigned ceaselessly for a constitutional amendment granting women the right to vote in all elections – an achievement that she sadly did not live long enough to see, since the long-sought Nineteenth Amendment was adopted only in 1920.*

Why we are reading this: *Men and women may live in the same country, town, or family, share the same language and culture, and generally inhabit the same space – and yet have experiences and viewpoints that differ in striking and systematic ways. True and honest communication across gender boundaries is notoriously difficult and has provided fodder for countless plays, novels, and songs over the centuries. When one seeks to unmake a hierarchical system and needs to find allies among the politically dominant gender, things can be even harder. Elizabeth Cady Stanton was attempting such a form of political communication in this speech, delivered in early 1892. Moving beyond her life-long campaign to gain the vote for women, Stanton seeks to help an all-male Congressional committee understand things from a woman's point of view. She argues that the facts of women's lives – their intellectual and spiritual independence, their self-sovereignty, and their ability to know the world just as well as any man – require rights and freedoms equal to those of men, including property rights, access to a liberal education, and entrance into all occupations and realms of social life. This speech is sometimes considered the birth of modern feminism. What parts of her argument do you find the most persuasive?*

Mr. Chairman and gentlemen of the committee: We have been speaking before Committees of the Judiciary for the last twenty years and we have gone over all the arguments in favor of a sixteenth amendment which are familiar to all you gentlemen; therefore, it will not be necessary that I should repeat them again.[1]

The point I wish plainly to bring before you on this occasion is the individuality of each human soul; our Protestant idea, the right of individual conscience and judgment; our republican idea, individual citizenship. In discussing the rights of woman, we are to consider, first, what belongs to her as an individual, in a world of her own, the arbiter of her own destiny, an imaginary Robinson Crusoe, with her woman Friday on a solitary island. Her rights under such circumstances are to use allher faculties for her own safety and happiness.

Secondly, if we consider her as a citizen, as a member of a great nation, she must have the same rights as all other members, according to the fundamental principles of our Government.

Thirdly, viewed as a woman, an equal factor in civilization, herrights and duties are still the same – individual happiness and development.

Fourthly, it is only the incidental relations of life, such as mother, wife, sister, daughter, which may involve some special duties and training. In the usual discussion in regard to woman's sphere, such men as Herbert Spencer, Frederic Harrison, and Grant Allen uniformly subordinate her rights and duties as an individual, as a citizen, as a woman, to the necessities of these incidental relations, some of which a large class of women may never assume. In discussing the sphere of man we do not decide his rights as an individual, as a citizen, as a man by his duties as a father, a husband, a brother, or a son, relations some of which he may never fill. Moreover he would be better fitted for these very relations and whatever special work he might choose to do to earn his bread by the complete development of all his faculties as an individual.

Just so with woman. The education that will fit her to discharge the duties in the largest sphere of human usefulness will best fit her for whatever special work she may be compelled to do.

The isolation of every human soul and the necessity of self-dependence must give each individual the right to choose his own surroundings.

The strongest reason for giving woman all the opportunities for higher education, for the full development of her faculties, her forces of mind and body; for giving her the most enlarged freedom of thought and action; a complete emancipation from all forms of bondage, of custom, dependence, superstition; from all the crippling influences of fear, is the solitude and personal responsibility of her own individual life. The strongest reason

[1] Complete women's suffrage was proposed to the Senate as the Sixteenth amendment in 1878, but it sat in committee for years before being rejected in 1887. At the time of this speech there was no suffrage amendment before the Senate.

why we ask for woman a voice in the government under which she lives; in the religion she is asked to believe; equality in social life, where she is the chief factor; a place in the trades and professions, where she may earn her bread, is because of her birthright to self-sovereignty; because, as an individual, she must rely on herself. No matter how much women prefer to lean, to be protected and supported, nor how much men desire to have them do so, they must make the voyage of life alone, and for safety in an emergency, they must know something of the laws of navigation. To guide our own craft, we must be captain, pilot, engineer; with chart and compass to stand at the wheel; to watch the winds and waves, and know when to take in the sail, and to read the signs in the firmament over all. It matters not whether the solitary voyager is man or woman. Nature having endowed them equally, leaves them to their own skill and judgment in the hour of danger, and, if not equal to the occasion, alike they perish.

To appreciate the importance of fitting every human soul for independent action, think for a moment of the immeasurable solitude of self. We come into the world alone, unlike all who have gone before us, we leave it alone under circumstances peculiar to ourselves. No mortal ever has been, no mortal ever will be like the soul just launched on the sea of life. There can never again be just such a combination of prenatal influences; never again just such environments as make up the infancy, youth and manhood of this one. Nature never repeats herself, and the possibilities of one human soul will never be found in another. No one has ever found two blades of ribbon grass alike, and no one will ever find two human beings alike. Seeing, then, what must be the infinite diversity in human character, we can in a measure appreciate the loss to a nation when any class of the people is uneducated and unrepresented in the government. We ask for the complete development of every individual, first, for his own benefit and happiness. In fitting out an army, we give each soldier his own knapsack, arms, powder, his blanket, cup, knife, fork and spoon. We provide alike for all their individual necessities, then each man bears his own burden.

Again, we ask complete individual development for the general good; for the consensus of the competent on the whole round of human interests; on all questions of national life, and here each man must bear his share of the general burden. It is sad to see how soon friendless children are left to bear their own burdens, before they can analyze their feelings; before they can even tell their joys and sorrows, they are thrown on their own resources. The great lesson that nature seems to teach us at all ages in self-dependence, self-protection, self-support. What a touching instance of a child's solitude; of that hunger of the heart for love and recognition, in the case of the little girl who helped to dress a Christmas tree for the children of the family in which she served. On finding there was no present for herself she slipped away in the darkness and spent the night in an open field sitting on a stone, and when found in the morning was weeping as if her heart would break. No mortal will ever know the thoughts that passed through the mind of that friendless child in the long hours of that cold night, with only the silent stars to keep her company. The mention of her case in the daily papers moved many generous hearts to send her presents, but in the hours of her keenest suffering she was thrown wholly on herself for consolation.

In youth our most bitter disappointments, our brightest hopes and ambitions are known only to ourselves; even our friendship and love we never fully share with another; there is something of every passion, in every situation, we conceal. Even so in our triumphs and our defeats. The successful candidate for the Presidency and his opponent each have a solitude peculiarly his own, and good form forbids either to speak of his pleasure or regret. The solitude of the king on his throne and the prisoner in his cell differs in character and degree, but it is solitude nevertheless.

We ask no sympathy from others in the anxiety and agony of a broken friendship or shattered love. When death sunders our nearest ties, alone we sit in the shadow of our affliction. Alike amid the greatest triumphs and darkest tragedies of life, we walk alone. On the divine heights of human attainment, eulogized and worshiped as a hero or saint, we stand alone. In ignorance, poverty and vice, as a pauper or criminal, alone we starve or steal; alone we suffer the sneers and rebuffs of our fellows; alone we are hunted and hounded through dark courts and alleys, in by-ways and highways; alone we stand in the judgment seat; alone in the prison cell we lament our crimes and misfortunes; alone we expiate them on the gallows. In hours like these we realize the awful solitude of individual life, its pains, its penalties, its responsibilities, hours in which the youngest and most helpless are thrown on their own resources for guidance and consolation. Seeing, then, that life must ever be a march and a battle that each soldier must be equipped for his own protection, it is the height of cruelty to rob the individual of a single natural right.

To throw obstacles in the way of a complete education is like putting out the eyes; to deny the rights of property, like cutting off the hands. To refuse political equality is to rob the ostracized of all self-respect; of credit in the market place; of recompense in the world of work, of a voice in choosing those who make and administer the law, a choice in the jury before whom they are tried, and in the judge who decides their punishment. Shakespeare's play of Titus and Andronicus contains a terrible satire on woman's position in the nineteenth century – "Rude men" (the play tells us) "seized the king's daughter, cut out her tongue, cut off her hands, and then bade her go call for water and wash her hands." What a picture of woman's position. Robbed of her natural rights, handicapped by law and custom at every turn, yet compelled to fight her own battles, and in the emergencies of life to fall back on herself for protection.

The girl of sixteen, thrown on the world to support herself, to make her own place in society, to resist the temptations that surround her and maintain a spotless integrity, must do all this by native force or superior education. She does not acquire this power by being trained to trust others and distrust herself. If she wearies of the struggle, finding it hard work to swim upstream, and allows herself to drift with the current, she will find plenty of company, but not one to share her misery in the hour of her deepest humiliation. If she tries to retrieve her position, to conceal the past, her life is hedged about with fears lest willing hands should tear the veil from what she fain would hide. Young and friendless, *she* knows the bitter solitude of self.

The young wife and mother, at the head of some establishment, with a kind husband to shield her from the adverse winds of life, with wealth, fortune and position, has a certain harbor of safety, secure against the ordinary ills of life. But to manage a household, have a desirable influence in society, keep her friends and the affections of her husband, train her children and servants well, she must have rare common sense, wisdom, diplomacy, and a knowledge of human nature. To do all this, she needs the cardinal virtues and the strong points of character that the most successful statesman possesses.

An uneducated woman trained to dependence, with no resources in herself, must make a failure of any position in life. But society says women do not need a knowledge of the world, the liberal training that experience in public life must give, all the advantages of collegiate education; but when for the lack of all this, the woman's happiness is wrecked, alone she bears her humiliation; and the solitude of the weak and the ignorant is indeed pitiable. In the wild chase for the prizes of life, they are ground to powder.

In age, when the pleasures of youth are passed, children grown up, married and gone, the hurry and bustle of life in a measure over, when the hands are weary of active service, when the old armchair and the fireside are the chosen resorts, then men and women alike must fall back on their own resources. If they cannot find companionship in books, if they have no interest in the vital questions of the hour, no interest in watching the consummation of reforms with which they might have been identified, they soon pass into their dotage. The more fully the faculties of the mind are developed and kept in use, the longer the period of vigor and active interest in all around us continues. If from a lifelong participation in public affairs, a woman feels responsible for the laws regulating our system of education, the discipline of our jails and prisons, the sanitary condition of our private homes, public buildings and thoroughfares, an interest in commerce, finance, our foreign relations, in any or all these questions, her solitude will at least be respectable, and she will not be driven to gossip or scandal for entertainment.

The chief reason for opening to every soul the doors to the whole round of human duties and pleasures is the individual development thus attained, the resources thus provided under all circumstances to mitigate the solitude that at times must come to everyone. I once asked Prince Kropotkin, a Russian nihilist, how he endured his long years in prison, deprived of books, pen, ink, and paper. "Ah," he said, "I thought out many questions in which I had a deep interest. In the pursuit of an idea I took no note of time. When tired of solving knotty problems I recited all the beautiful passages in prose or verse I had ever learned. I became acquainted with myself and my own resources. I had a world of my own, a vast empire, that no Russian jailor or Czar could invade." Such is the value of liberal thought and broad culture when shut off from all human companionship, bringing comfort and sunshine within even the four walls of a prison cell.

As women ofttimes share a similar fate, should they not have all the consolation that the most liberal education can give? Their suffering in the prisons of St. Petersburg; in the long, weary marches to Siberia, and in the mines, working side by side with men, surely call for all the self-support that the most exalted sentiments of heroism can give. When suddenly roused at midnight, with the startling cry of "fire! fire!" to find the house over their heads in flames, do women wait for men to point the way to safety? And are the men, equally bewildered and half suffocated with smoke, in a position to do more than try to save themselves?

At such times the most timid women have shown a courage and heroism in saving their husbands and children that has surprised everybody. Inasmuch, then, as woman shares equally the joys and sorrows of time and eternity, is it not the height of presumption in man to propose to represent her at the ballot box and the throne of grace, to do her voting in the state, her praying in the church, and to assume the position of high priest at the family altar?

Nothing strengthens the judgment and quickens the conscience like individual responsibility. Nothing adds such dignity to character as the recognition of one's self-sovereignty; the right to an equal place, everywhere conceded; a place earned by personal merit, not an artificial attainment by inheritance, wealth, family and position. Seeing, then, that the responsibilities of life rest equally on man and woman, that their destiny is the same, they need the same preparation for time and eternity. The talk of sheltering woman from the fierce storms of life is the sheerest mockery, for they beat on her from every point of the compass, just as they do on man, and with more fatal results, for he has been trained to protect himself, to resist, and to conquer. Such are the facts in human experience, the responsibilities of individual sovereignty. Rich and poor, intelligent and ignorant, wise and foolish, virtuous and vicious, man and woman, it is ever the same, each soul must depend wholly on itself.

Whatever the theories may be of woman's dependence on man, in the supreme moments of her life he cannot bear her burdens. Alone she goes to the gates of death to give life to every man that is born into the world. No one can share her fears, no one can mitigate her pangs; and if her sorrow is greater than she can bear, alone she passes beyond the gates into the vast unknown.

From the mountain tops of Judea long ago, a heavenly voice bade his disciples, "Bear ye one another's burden," but humanity has not yet risen to that point of self-sacrifice and if ever so willing, how few the burdens are that one soul can bear for another. In the highways of Palestine; in prayer and fasting on the solitary mountain top; in the Garden of Gethsemane; before the judgment seat of Pilate; betrayed by one of His trusted disciples at His last supper; in His agonies on the cross, even Jesus of Nazareth, in those last sad days on earth, felt the awful solitude of self. Deserted by man, in agony he cries, "My God! My God! why hast Thou forsaken me?" And so it ever must be in the conflicting scenes of life, in the long, weary march, each one walks alone. We may have many friends, love, kindness, sympathy and charity to smooth our pathway in everyday life, but in the tragedies and triumphs of human experience, each mortal stands alone.

But when all artificial trammels are removed, and women are recognized as individuals, responsible for their own environments, thoroughly educated for all positions in life they may be called to fill; with all the resources in themselves that liberal thought and broad culture can give; guided by their own conscience and judgment; trained to self-protection by a healthy development of the muscular system, and skill in the use of weapons of defense, and stimulated to self-support by a knowledge of the business world and the pleasure that pecuniary independence must ever give; when women are trained in this way they will, in a measure, be fitted for those hours of solitude that come alike to all, whether prepared or otherwise. As in our extremity we must depend on ourselves, the dictates of wisdom point to complete individual development.

In talking of education, how shallow the argument that each class must be educated for the special work it proposes to do, and that all those faculties not needed in this special work must lie dormant and utterly wither for want of use, when, perhaps, these will be the very faculties needed in life's greatest emergencies. Some say, "Where is the use of drilling girls in the languages, the sciences, in law, medicine, theology? As wives, mothers, housekeepers, cooks, they need a different curriculum from boys who are to fill all positions. The chief cooks in our great hotels and ocean steamers are men. In our large cities, men run the bakeries; they make our bread, cake and pies. They manage the laundries; they are now considered our best milliners and dressmakers. Because some men fill these departments of usefulness, shall we regulate the curriculum in Harvard and Yale to their present necessities? If not, why this talk in our best colleges of a curriculum for girls who are crowding into the trades and professions, teachers in all our public schools, rapidly filling many lucrative and honorable positions in life? They are showing, too, their calmness and courage in the most trying hours of human experience."

You have probably all read in the daily papers of the terrible storm in the Bay of Biscay when a tidal wave made such havoc on the shore, wrecking vessels, unroofing houses, and carrying destruction everywhere. Among other buildings the woman's prison was demolished. Those who escaped saw men struggling to reach the shore. They promptly by clasping hands made a chain of themselves and pushed out into the sea, again and again, at the risk of their lives, until they had brought six men to shore, carried them to a shelter, and did all in their power for their comfort and protection.

What special school training could have prepared these women for this sublime moment in their lives? In times like this humanity rises above all college curriculums and recognizes Nature as the greatest of all teachers in the hour of danger and death. Women are already the equals of men in the whole realm of thought, in art, science, literature and government. With telescopic vision they explore the starry firmament and bring back the history of the planetary world. With chart and compass they pilot ships across the mighty deep, and with skillful finger send electric messages around the globe. In galleries of art the beauties of nature and the virtues of humanity are immortalized by them on canvas and by their inspired touch dull blocks of marble are transformed into angels of light.

In music they speak again the language of Mendelssohn, Beethoven, Chopin, Schumann, and are worthy interpreters of their great thoughts. The poetry and novels of the century are theirs, and they have touched the keynote of reform, in religion, politics and social life. They fill the editor's and professor's chair, plead at the bar of justice, walk the wards of the hospital, speak from the pulpit and the platform. Such is the type of womanhood that an enlightened public sentiment welcomes today, and such the triumph of the facts of life over the false theories of the past.

Is it, then, consistent to hold the developed woman of this day within the same narrow political limits as the dame with the spinning wheel and knitting needle occupied in the past? No, no! Machinery has taken the labors of woman as well as man on its tireless shoulders; the loom and the spinning wheel are but dreams of the past; the pen, the brush, the easel, the chisel, have taken their places, while the hopes and ambitions of women are essentially changed.

We see reason sufficient in the outer conditions of human beings for individual liberty and development, but when we consider the self-dependence of every human soul, we see the need of courage, judgment and the exercise of every faculty of mind and body, strengthened and developed by use, in woman as well as man.

Whatever may be said of man's protecting power in ordinary conditions, amid all the terrible disasters by land and sea, in the supreme moments of danger, alone woman must ever meet the horrors of the situation; the Angel of Death even makes no royal pathway for her. Man's love and sympathy enter only into the sunshine of our lives. In that solemn solitude of self, that links us with the immeasurable and the eternal, each soul lives alone forever. A recent writer says: "I remember once, in crossing the Atlantic, to have gone upon the deck of the ship at midnight, when a dense black cloud enveloped the sky, and the great deep was roaring madly under the lashes of demoniac winds. My feeling was notof danger or fear (which is a base surrender of the immortal soul) but of utter desolation and loneliness; a little speck of life shut in by a tremendous darkness. Again I remember to have climbed the slopes of the Swiss Alps, up beyond the point where vegetation ceases, and the stunted conifers no longer struggle against the unfeeling blasts. Around me lay a huge confusion of rocks, out of which the gigantic ice peaks shot into the measureless blue of the heavens, and again my only feeling was the awful solitude."

And yet, there is a solitude which each and every one of us has always carried with him, more inaccessible than the ice-cold mountains, more profound than the midnight sea; the solitude of self. Our inner being, which we call ourself, no eye nor touch of man or angel has ever pierced. It is more hidden than the caves of the gnome; the sacred adytum of the oracle; the hidden chamber of Eleusinian mystery, for to it only omniscience is permitted to enter.

Such is individual life. Who, I ask you, can take, dare take, on himself the rights, the duties, the responsibilities of another human soul?

Yellow Woman

Leslie Marmon Silko

From Leslie Marmon Silko, *Storyteller.* New York: Arcade Publishing, 1981, pp. 54-62. The story was first published in 1974.

Leslie Marmon Silko (b. 1948) *is a key figure in modern Native American literature, author of three novels, a memoir, and numerous short stories. Born in New Mexico and raised on the Laguna Pueblo Indian reservation, she learned Laguna traditional stories from her grandparents and other family members. As a writer and story teller she has sought to preserve and pass on these cultural traditions while making her audience aware of the dangers of racism, sexism, violence, and white cultural imperialism. One feature of her writing is to take Laguna Pueblo stories and recast them in a modern setting. Her best-known work is the novel* Ceremony, *published in 1977.*

Why we are reading this*: Short stories, novels, and other works of fiction are not only popular entertainment but a wonderful way to enter into someone else's world and gain access to a wider range of human experiences and cultures. Story telling is an ancient part of human culture, practiced by our ancestors for countless centuries before writing was invented. Far from being a static tradition, stories in oral cultures are told and retold over the generations, changing and developing with each retelling. In this spirit, Silko has adopted a popular tale from Pueblo oral culture, that of Kochininako ("Yellow Woman"), and retold it in her own way. In the traditional stories, Yellow Woman wanders away from her husband and family in the pueblo and is either abducted or voluntarily goes away with a spirit from the mountain known as a ka'tsina (sometimes called Whirlwind Man). In some versions of the story, Yellow Woman is killed, either by her husband or the ka'tsina. In other versions, Yellow Woman overcomes peril through her sensuality, returning home with renewed spirit and bringing her tribe great benefit. Silko incorporated Yellow Woman ideas into several of her novels and short stories, where the character serves as a liberated woman and role model who overcomes racism and injustice, not by violence or destruction, but through peace and caring. In the story below, the narrator is a modern woman who is bewildered to find herself living out the Yellow Woman stories her grandfather used to tell. Can myths, legends, and other stories help us process and understand our own situations and everyday lives? How do our stories about the past shape our perceptions and behavior in the present? In what ways are we connected to, and shaped by, the people who came before us?*

What Whirlwind Man Told Kochininako, Yellow Woman

I myself belong to the wind
and so it is we will travel swiftly
this whole world
with dust and with windstorms.

My thigh clung to his with dampness, and I watched the sun rising up through the tamaracks and willows. The small brown water birds came to the river and hopped across the mud, leaving brown scratches in the alkali-white crust. They bathed in the river silently. I could hear the water, almost at our feet where the narrow fast channel bubbled and washed green ragged moss and fern leaves. I looked at him beside me, rolled in the red blanket on the white river sand. I cleaned the sand out of the cracks between my toes, squinting because the sun was above the willow trees. I looked at him for the last time, sleeping on the white river sand.

I felt hungry and followed the river south the way we had come the afternoon before, following our footprints that were already blurred by lizard tracks and bug trails. The horses were still lying down, and the black one whinnied when he saw me but he did not get up – maybe it was because the corral was made out of thick cedar branches and the horses had not yet felt the sun like I had. I tried to look beyond the pale red mesas to the pueblo. I knew it was there, even if I could not see it, on the sandrock hill above the river, the same river that moved past me now and had reflected the moon last night.

The horse felt warm underneath me. He shook his head and pawed the sand. The bay whinnied and leaned against the gate trying to follow, and I remembered him asleep in the red blanket beside the river. I slid off the horse and tied him close to the other horse, I walked north with the river again, and the white sand broke loose in footprints over footprints.

"Wake up."

He moved in the blanket and turned his face to me with his eyes still closed. I knelt down to touch him.

"I'm leaving."

He smiled now, eyes still closed. "You are coming with me, remember?" He sat up now with his bare dark chest and belly in the sun.

"Where?"

"To my place."

"And will I come back?"

He pulled his pants on. I walked away from him, feeling him behind me and smelling the willows.

"Yellow Woman," he said.

I turned to face him. "Who are you?" I asked.

He laughed and knelt on the low, sandy bank, washing his face in the river. "Last night you guessed my name, and you knew why I had come."

I stared past him at the shallow moving water and tried to remember the night, but I could only see the moon in the water and remember his warmth around me.

"But I only said that you were him and that I was Yellow Woman – I'm not really her – I have my own name and I come from the pueblo on the other side of the mesa. Your name is Silva and you are a stranger I met by the river yesterday afternoon."

He laughed softly. "What happened yesterday has nothing to do with what you will do today, Yellow Woman."

"I know – that's what I'm saying – the old stories about the ka'tsina spirit and Yellow Woman can't mean us."

My old grandpa liked to tell those stories best. There is one about Badger and Coyote who went hunting and were gone all day, and when the sun was going down they found a house. There was a girl living there alone, and she had light hair and eyes and she told them that they could sleep with her. Coyote wanted to be with her all night so he sent Badger into a prairie-dog hole, telling him he thought he saw something in it. As soon as Badger crawled in, Coyote blocked up the entrance with rocks and hurried back to Yellow Woman.

"Come here," he said gently.

He touched my neck and I moved close to him to feel his breathing and to hear his heart. I was wondering if Yellow Woman had known who she was – if she knew that she would become part of the stories. Maybe she'd had another name that her husband and relatives called her so that only the ka'tsina from the north and the storytellers would know her as Yellow Woman. But I didn't go on; I felt him all around me, pushing me down into the white river sand.

Yellow Woman went away with the spirit from the north and lived with him and his relatives. She was gone for a long time, but then one day she came back and she brought twin boys.

"Do you know the story?"

"What story?" He smiled and pulled me close to him as he said this. I was afraid lying there on the red blanket. All I could know was the way he felt, warm, damp, his body beside me. This is the way it happens in the stories, I was thinking, with no thought beyond the moment she meets the ka'tsina spirit and they go.

"I don't have to go. What they tell in stories was real only then, back in time immemorial, like they say."

He stood up and pointed at my clothes tangled in the blanket. "Let's go," he said.

I walked beside him, breathing hard because he walked fast, his hand around my wrist. I had stopped trying to pull away from him, because his hand felt cool and the sun was high, drying the river bed into alkali. I will see someone, eventually I will see someone, and then I will be certain that he is only a man – some man from nearby – and I will be sure that I am not Yellow Woman. Because she is from out of time past and I live now and I've been to school and there are highways and pickup trucks that Yellow Woman never saw.

It was an easy ride north on horseback. I watched the change from the cottonwood trees along the river to the junipers that brushed past us in the foothills, and finally there were only piñons, and when I looked up at the rim of the mountain plateau I could see pine trees growing on the edge. Once I stopped to look down, but the pale sandstone had disappeared and the river was gone and the dark lava hills were all around. He touched my hand, not speaking, but always singing softly a mountain song and looking into my eyes.

I felt hungry and wondered what they were doing at home now – my mother, my grandmother, my husband, and the baby. Cooking breakfast, saying, "Where did she go? – maybe kidnapped." And Al going to the tribal police with the details: "She went walking along the river."

The house was made with black lava rock and red mud. It was high above the spreading miles of arroyos and long mesas. I smelled a mountain smell of pitch and buck brush. I stood there beside the black horse, looking down on the small, dim country we had passed, and I shivered.

"Yellow Woman, come inside where it's warm."

He lit a fire in the stove. It was an old stove with a round belly and an enamel coffeepot on top. There was only the stove, some faded Navajo blankets, and a bedroll and cardboard box. The floor was made of smooth adobe plaster, and there was one small window facing east. He pointed at the box.

"There's some potatoes and the frying pan." He sat on the floor with his arms around his knees pulling them close to his chest and he watched me fry the potatoes. I didn't mind him watching me because he was always watching me – he had been watching me since I came upon him sitting on the river bank trimming leaves from a willow twig with his knife. We ate from the pan and he wiped the grease from his fingers on his Levi's.

"Have you brought women here before?" He smiled and kept chewing, so I said, "Do you always use the same tricks?"

"What tricks?" He looked at me like he didn't understand.

"The story about being a ka'tsina from the mountains. The story about

Yellow Woman."

Silva was silent; his face was calm.

"I don't believe it. Those stories couldn't happen now," I said.

He shook his head and said softly, "But someday they will talk about us, and they will say, 'Those two lived long ago when things like that happened.'"

He stood up and went out. I ate the rest of the potatoes and thought about things – about the noise the stove was making and the sound of the mountain wind outside. I remembered yesterday and the day before, and then I went outside.

I walked past the corral to the edge where the narrow trail cut through the black rim rock. I was standing in the sky with nothing around me but the wind that came down from the blue mountain peak behind me. I could see faint mountain images in the distance miles across the vast spread of mesas and valleys and plains. I wondered who was over there to feel the mountain wind on those sheer blue edges – who walks on the pine needles in those blue mountains.

"Can you see the pueblo?" Silva was standing behind me.

I shook my head. "We're too far away."

"From here I can see the world." He stepped out on the edge. "The Navajo reservation begins over there." He pointed to the east. "The Pueblo boundaries are over here." He looked below us to the south, where the narrow trail seemed to come from. "The Texans have their ranches over there, starting with that valley, the Concho Valley. The Mexicans run some cattle over there too."

"Do you ever work for them?"

"I steal from them," Silva answered. The sun was dropping behind us and the shadows were filling the land below. I turned away from the edge that dropped forever into the valleys below.

"I'm cold," I said, "I'm going inside." I started wondering about this man who could speak the Pueblo language so well but who lived on a mountain and rustled cattle. I decided that this man Silva must be Navajo, because Pueblo men didn't do things like that.

"You must be a Navajo."

Silva shook his head gently. "Little Yellow Woman," he said, "you never give up, do you? I have told you who I am. The Navajo people know me, too." He knelt down and unrolled the bedroll and spread the extra blankets out on a piece of canvas. The sun was down, and the only light in the house came from outside – the dim orange light from sundown.

I stood there and waited for him to crawl under the blankets.

"What are you waiting for?" he said, and I lay down beside him. He undressed me slowly like the night before beside the river – kissing my face gently and running his hands up and down my belly and legs. He took off my pants and then he laughed.

"Why are you laughing?"

"You are breathing so hard."

I pulled away from him and turned my back to him.

He pulled me around and pinned me down with his arms and chest. "You don't understand, do you, little Yellow Woman? You will do what I want."

And again he was all around me with his skin slippery against mine, and I was afraid because I understood that his strength could hurt me. I lay underneath him and I knew that he could destroy me. But later, while he slept beside me, I touched his face and I had a feeling – the kind of feeling for him that overcame me that morning along the river. I kissed him on the forehead and he reached out for me.

When I woke up in the morning he was gone. It gave me a strange feeling because for a long time I sat there on the blankets and looked around the little house for some object of his – some proof that he had been there or maybe that he was coming back. Only the blankets and the cardboard box remained. The .30-30 that had been leaning in the corner was gone, and so was the knife I had used the night before. He was gone, and I had my chance to go now. But first I had to eat, because I knew it would be a long walk home.

I found some dried apricots in the cardboard box, and I sat down on a rock at the edge of the plateau rim. There was no wind and the sun warmed me. I was surrounded by silence. I drowsed with apricots in my mouth, and I didn't believe that there were highways or railroads or cattle to steal.

When I woke up, I stared down at my feet in the black mountain dirt. Little black ants were swarming over the pine needles around my foot. They must have smelled the apricots. I thought about my family far below me. They would be wondering about me, because this had never happened to me before. The tribal police would file a report. But if old Grandpa weren't dead he would tell them what happened – he would laugh and say, "Stolen by a ka'tsina, a mountain spirit. She'll come home – they usually do." There are enough of them to handle things. My mother and grandmother will raise the baby like they raised me. Al will find someone else, and they will go on like before, except that there will be a story about the day I disappeared while I was walking along the river. Silva had come for me; he said he had. I did not decide to go. I just went. Moonflowers blossom in the sand hills before dawn, just as I followed him. That's what I was thinking as I wandered along the trail through the pine trees.

It was noon when I got back. When I saw the stone house I remembered that I had meant to go home. But that didn't seem important any more, maybe because there were little blue flowers growing in the meadow behind the stone house and the gray squirrels were playing in the pines next to the house. The horses were standing in the corral, and there was a beef carcass hanging on the shady side of a big pine in front of the house. Flies buzzed around the clotted blood that hung from the carcass. Silva was washing his hands in a bucket full of water. He must have heard me coming because he spoke to me without turning to face me.

"I've been waiting for you."

"I went walking in the big pine trees."

I looked into the bucket full of bloody water with brown-and-white animal hairs floating in it. Silva stood there letting his hand drip, examining me intently.

"Are you coming with me?"

"Where?" I asked him.

"To sell the meat in Marquez."

"If you're sure it's O.K."

"I wouldn't ask you if it wasn't," he answered.

He sloshed the water around in the bucket before he dumped it out and set the bucket upside down near the door. I followed him to the corral and watched him saddle the horses. Even beside the horses he looked tall, and I asked him again if he wasn't Navajo. He didn't say anything; he just shook his head and kept cinching up the saddle.

"But Navajos are tall."

"Get on the horse," he said, "and let's go."

The last thing he did before we started down the steep trail was to grab the .30-30 from the corner. He slid the rifle into the scabbard that hung from his saddle.

"Do they ever try to catch you?" I asked.

"They don't know who I am."

"Then why did you bring the rifle?"

"Because we are going to Marquez where the Mexicans live."

The trail leveled out on a narrow ridge that was steep on both sides like an animal spine. On one side I could see where the trail went around the rocky gray hills and disappeared into the southeast where the pale sandrock mesas stood in the distance near my home. On the other side was a trail that went west, and as I looked far into the distance I thought I saw the little town. But Silva said no, that I was looking in the wrong place, that I just thought I saw houses. After that I quit looking off into the distance; it was hot and the wildflowers were closing up their deep-yellow petals. Only the waxy cactus flowers bloomed in the bright sun, and I saw every color that a cactus blossom can be; the white ones and the red ones were still buds, but the purple and the yellow were blossoms, open full and the most beautiful of all.

Silva saw him before I did. The white man was riding a big gray horse, coming up the trail towards us. He was traveling fast and the gray horse's feet sent rocks rolling off the trail into the dry tumbleweeds. Silva motioned for me to stop and we watched the white man. He didn't see us right away, but finally his horse whinnied at our horses and he stopped. He looked at us briefly before he lapped the gray horse across the three hundred yards that separated us. He stopped his horse in front of Silva, and his young fat face was shadowed by the brim of his hat. He didn't look mad, but his small, pale eyes moved from the blood-soaked gunny sacks hanging from my saddle to Silva's face and then back to my face.

"Where did you get the fresh meat?" the white man asked.

"I've been hunting," Silva said, and when he shifted his weight in the saddle the leather creaked.

"The hell you have, Indian. You've been rustling cattle. We've been looking for the thief for a long time."

The rancher was fat, and sweat began to soak through his white cowboy shirt and the wet cloth stuck to the thick rolls of belly fat. He almost seemed to be panting from the exertion of talking, and he smelled rancid, maybe because Silva scared him.

Silva turned to me and smiled. "Go back up the mountain, Yellow Woman."

The white man got angry when he heard Silva speak in a language he couldn't understand. "Don't try anything, Indian. Just keep riding to Marquez. We'll call the state police from there."

The rancher must have been unarmed because he was very frightened and if he had a gun he would have pulled it out then. I turned my horse around and the rancher yelled, "Stop!" I looked at Silva for an instant and there was something ancient and dark – something I could feel in my stomach – in his eyes, and when I glanced at his hand I saw his finger on the trigger of the .30-30 that was still in the saddle scabbard. I slapped my horse across the flank and the sacks of raw meat swung against my knees as the horse leaped up the trail. It was hard to keep my balance, and once I thought I felt the saddle slipping backward; it was because of this that I could not look back.

I didn't stop until I reached the ridge where the trail forked. The horse was breathing deep gasps and there was a dark film of sweat on its neck. I looked down in the direction I had come from, but I couldn't see the place. I waited. The wind came up and pushed warm air past me. I looked up at the sky, pale blue and full of thin clouds and fading vapor trails left by jets.

I think four shots were fired – I remember hearing four hollow explosions that reminded me of deer hunting. There could have been more shots after that, but I couldn't have heard them because my horse was running again and the loose rocks were making too much noise as they scattered around his feet.

Horses have a hard time running downhill, but I went that way instead of uphill to the mountain because I thought it was safer. I felt better with the horse running southeast past the round gray hills that were covered with cedar trees and black lava rock. When I got to the plain in the distance I could see the dark green patches of tamaracks that grew along the river; and beyond the river I could see the beginning of the pale sandrock mesas. I stopped the horse and looked back to see if anyone was coming; then I got off the horse and turned the horse around, wondering if it would go back to its corral under the pines on the mountain. It looked back at me for a moment and then plucked a mouthful of green tumbleweeds before it trotted back up the trail with its ears pointed forward, carrying its head daintily to one side to avoid stepping on the dragging reins. When the horse disappeared over the last hill, the gunny sacks full of meat were still swinging and bouncing.

I walked toward the river on a wood-hauler's road that I knew would eventually lead to the paved road. I was thinking about waiting beside the road for someone to drive by, but by the time I got to the pavement I had decided it wasn't very far to walk if I followed the river back the way Silva and I had come.

The river water tasted good, and I sat in the shade under a cluster of silvery willows. I thought about Silva, and I felt sad at leaving him; still, there was something strange about him, and I tried to figure it out all the way back home.

I came back to the place on the river bank where he had been sitting the first time I saw him. The green willow leaves that he had trimmed from the branch were still lying there, wilted in the sand. I saw the leaves and I wanted to go back to him – to kiss him and to touch him – but the mountains were too far away now. And I told myself, because I believe it, he will come back sometime and be waiting again by the river.

I followed the path up from the river into the village. The sun was getting low, and I could smell supper cooking when I got to the screen door of my house. I could hear their voices inside – my mother was telling my grandmother how to fix the Jell-O and my husband, Al, was playing with the baby. I decided to tell them that some Navajo had kidnaped me, but I was sorry that old Grandpa wasn't alive to hear my story because it was the Yellow Woman stories he liked to tell best.

O Me! O Life!

Walt Whitman

From Walt Whitman, *Leaves of Grass*. Brooklyn, 1855.

Walt Whitman *(1819-1892) was a famous poet, journalist, and essay writer. He was born in Long Island, New York, and finished his formal schooling at age eleven, at which time he became an apprentice for a printer. He worked as a journalist for a number of years and eventually became more interested in poetry. His collection of poems* Leaves of Grass *is still considered to include some of the best American poetry, even though it was considered quite risqué during his lifetime. His affinity with deism and transcendentalism can be seen in his poems.*

Why we are reading this: *We often learn important things about the world when we look through someone else's eyes. Many of the readings in this anthology are meant to introduce you to points of view you might not have considered before. Consider poetry, which can provide insight into the experience of others and startling new ways of looking at the world. Whitman's poem opens with a person in anguish over eternal existential questions. The speaker finds bedrock in the affirmation of existence itself. The "answer" to life's questions revolves around a metaphor wherein each of us is somehow an actor or playwright in a massive ongoing theatrical play. What will your verse be?*

Oh me! Oh life! of the questions of these recurring,
Of the endless trains of the faithless, of cities fill'd with the foolish,
Of myself forever reproaching myself, (for who more foolish than I, and who more faithless?)
Of eyes that vainly crave the light, of the objects mean, of the struggle ever renew'd,
Of the poor results of all, of the plodding and sordid crowds I see around me,
Of the empty and useless years of the rest, with the rest me intertwined,
The question, O me! so sad, recurring – What good amid these, O me, O life?

Answer.

That you are here – that life exists and identity,
That the powerful play goes on, and you may contribute a verse.

Afterimages

Audre Lorde

In *Chosen Poems: Old and New*. New York: Norton, 1982.

Audre Lorde *(1934-1992) was an African American poet, writer, feminist, librarian, teacher, and civil rights activist. Born to Caribbean immigrant parents in New York City, Lorde became a masterful poet, often conveying anger and outrage at the social injustice she witnessed. In her prose works, she was an important innovator and theorist of black feminism, lesbianism, personal identity, and intersectionality.*

Why we are reading this: *Poetry can give us access to someone else's memories, perspectives, and subjective view of the world. In this poem, written in 1981, the poet reflects on her memories of two traumatic events. The first was the murder of Emmett Till, a fourteen-year-old black boy from Chicago who was visiting relatives in the small town of Money, Mississippi, in the summer of 1955. Some accounts say that he flirted or whistled at a white woman working in a small grocery store, but others say he did nothing of the sort. Whatever happened, his actions or perhaps his mere presence enraged local white supremacists. Four days later, the woman's husband and his half-brother abducted, tortured, and murdered Till, dumping his body in the nearby Tallahatchie river. The two men were acquitted by an all-white jury. They later admitted to the crime in a magazine interview but were never held responsible by the law. Between the 1880s and 1960s, over 3,000 African Americans were lynched in the United States, including more than 500 in Mississippi, but this particular case became notorious. Till's mother insisted that he be given an open-casket funeral in Chicago and allowed news photographs of his mutilated body to be published in newspapers and magazines around the country and abroad. The murder, photographs, and subsequent trial directed attention to the injustices suffered by African Americans in the U.S. South and helped galvanize the Civil Rights movement. Recent killings of African Americans by police officers under the eye of cellphone cameras have had a similar transformational effect. The second event referenced in the poem is the devastating flood of the Pearl River in April 1979, which placed most of Jackson, the state capital of Mississippi, under water and forced more than 17,000 people from their homes. Audre Lorde experienced both events from a distance, through the mediation of journalism and television. She imagines a metaphysical connection between these two events and offers insight into the workings of memory and imagination.*

I

However the image enters
its force remains within
my eyes
rockstrewn caves where dragonfish evolve
wild for life, relentless and acquisitive
learning to survive
where there is no food
my eyes are always hungry
and remembering
however the image enters
its force remains.
A white woman stands bereft and empty
a black boy hacked into a murderous lesson
recalled in me forever
like a lurch of earth on the edge of sleep
etched into my visions
food for dragonfish that learn
to live upon whatever they must eat
fused images beneath my pain.

II

The Pearl River floods through the streets of Jackson
A Mississippi summer televised.
Trapped houses kneel like sinners in the rain
a white woman climbs from her roof to a passing boat
her fingers tarry for a moment on the chimney
now awash
tearless and no longer young, she holds
a tattered baby's blanket in her arms.
In a flickering afterimage of the nightmare rain
a microphone
thrust up against her flat bewildered words
    "we jest come from the bank yestiddy
        borrowing money to pay the income tax
        now everything's gone.
        I never knew it could be so hard."
Despair weighs down her voice like Pearl River mud
caked around the edges
her pale eyes scanning the camera for help or explanation

unanswered
she shifts her search across the watered street, dry-eyed
"hard, but not this hard."
Two tow-headed children hurl themselves against her
hanging upon her coat like mirrors
until a man with ham-like hands pulls her aside
snarling "She ain't got nothing more to say!"
and that lie hangs in his mouth
like a shred of rotting meat.

III

I inherited Jackson, Mississippi.
For my majority it gave me Emmett Till
his 15 years puffed out like bruises
on plump boy-cheeks
his only Mississippi summer
whistling a 21 gun salute to Dixie
as a white girl passed him in the street
and he was baptized my son forever
in the midnight waters of the Pearl.

His broken body is the afterimage of my 21st year
when I walked through a northern summer
my eyes averted
from each corner's photographies
newspapers protest posters magazines
Police Story, Confidential, True
the avid insistence of detail
pretending insight or information
the length of gash across the dead boy's loins
his grieving mother's lamentation
the severed lips, how many burns
his gouged out eyes
sewed shut upon the screaming covers
louder than life
all over
the veiled warning, the secret relish
of a black child's mutilated body
fingered by street-corner eyes
bruise upon livid bruise
and wherever I looked that summer

I learned to be at home with children's blood
with savored violence
with pictures of black broken flesh
used, crumpled, and discarded
lying amid the sidewalk refuse
like a raped woman's face.

A black boy from Chicago
whistled on the streets of Jackson, Mississippi
testing what he'd been taught was a manly thing to do
his teachers
ripped his eyes out his sex his tongue
and flung him to the Pearl weighted with stone
in the name of white womanhood
they took their aroused honor
back to Jackson
and celebrated in a whorehouse
the double ritual of white manhood
confirmed.

IV

> "If earth and air and water do not judge them who are
> we to refuse a crust of bread?"

Emmett Till rides the crest of the Pearl, whistling
24 years his ghost lay like the shade of a raped woman
and a white girl has grown older in costly honor
(what did she pay to never know its price?)
now the Pearl River speaks its muddy judgment
and I can withhold my pity and my bread.

"Hard, but not this hard."
Her face is flat with resignation and despair
with ancient and familiar sorrows
a woman surveying her crumpled future
as the white girl besmirched by Emmett's whistle
never allowed her own tongue
without power or conclusion
unvoiced
she stands adrift in the ruins of her honor
and a man with an executioner's face

pulls her away.

Within my eyes
the flickering afterimages of a nightmare rain
a woman wrings her hands
beneath the weight of agonies remembered
I wade through summer ghosts
betrayed by vision
hers and my own
becoming dragonfish to survive
the horrors we are living
with tortured lungs
adapting to breathe blood.

A woman measures her life's damage
my eyes are caves, chunks of etched rock
tied to the ghost of a black boy
whistling
crying and frightened
her tow-headed children cluster
like little mirrors of despair their
father's hands upon them
and soundlessly
a woman begins to weep.

Consider the Lobster

David Foster Wallace

In *Gourmet*, August 2004. Reprinted in David Foster Wallace, *Consider the Lobster and Other Essays*. New York: Little, Brown and Company, 2005.

***David Foster Wallace** (1962-2008) was an American novelist, short story author, essayist and journalist, generally considered one of the most significant writers of the latter part of the twentieth century. Known for his dry humor, as well as a fascination with footnotes, Wallace was particularly fond of taking mundane or by-the-way events and facts of life (cruises, mid-level tennis players, state fairs) and placing them in front of the audience for consideration. His most well-known novel is* Infinite Jest *(1996).*

***Why we are reading this:** The final reading in our anthology is an essay by David Foster Wallace. The essay is a popular and flexible genre that dates back to the late 1500s, though it has antecedents in the ancient world. Essays are generally short works of non-fiction in which an author reflects on a particular issue from one or more perspectives, sometimes making a coherent argument, but sometimes leaving things more open. You may have been asked to write an essay more than once in your education. Expect to write more.*

Asked by Gourmet *magazine in 2004 to write a light account of the annual Maine Lobster Festival, Wallace unexpectedly embarks upon a deep scientific, philosophical, and whimsical investigation into whether it is ethical to boil lobsters alive and eat them. His quest involves a detailed exploration of the world of the lobster. Among other things, he wonders: Do lobsters feel pain when we boil them? How might we answer this question? Can we see the world from a lobster's point of view? These are indeed interesting questions. But note the important fact that he stops to ask them. While Wallace says some entertaining things about tourists in Maine, he himself does not go through life as a tourist, waiting to be entertained, merely a passive consumer of life and lobsters. He pursues his questions to the end, even when they become uncomfortable and begin to challenge his own eating preferences and moral position. What do you find interesting in this essay? Is this essay disturbing? Does Wallace's intellectual journey in here resonate with any of the texts you have read earlier in this anthology? Are you prepared to go through college (and life) as something more than a tourist?*

Consider the Lobster

For 56 years, the Maine Lobster Festival has been drawing crowds with the promise of sun, fun, and fine food. One visitor would argue that the celebration involves a whole lot more.

The enormous, pungent, and extremely well marketed Maine Lobster Festival is held every late July in the state's midcoast region, meaning the western side of Penobscot Bay, the nerve stem of Maine's lobster industry. What's called the midcoast runs from Owl's Head and Thomaston in the south to Belfast in the north. (Actually, it might extend all the way up to Bucksport, but we were never able to get farther north than Belfast on Route 1, whose summer traffic is, as you can imagine, unimaginable.) The region's two main communities are Camden, with its very old money and yachty harbor and five-star restaurants and phenomenal B&Bs, and Rockland, a serious old fishing town that hosts the Festival every summer in historic Harbor Park, right along the water.[1]

Tourism and lobster are the midcoast region's two main industries, and they're both warm-weather enterprises, and the Maine Lobster Festival represents less an intersection of the industries than a deliberate collision, joyful and lucrative and loud. The assigned subject of this article is the 56th Annual MLF, July 30 to August 3, 2003, whose official theme was "Lighthouses, Laughter, and Lobster." Total paid attendance was over 80,000, due partly to a national CNN spot in June during which a Senior Editor of a certain other epicurean magazine hailed the MLF as one of the best food-themed festivals in the world. 2003 Festival highlights: concerts by Lee Ann Womack and Orleans, annual Maine Sea Goddess beauty pageant, Saturday's big parade, Sunday's William G. Atwood Memorial Crate Race, annual Amateur Cooking Competition, carnival rides and midway attractions and food booths, and the MLF's Main Eating Tent, where something over 25,000 pounds of fresh-caught Maine lobster is consumed after preparation in the World's Largest Lobster Cooker near the grounds' north entrance. Also available are lobster rolls, lobster turnovers, lobster sauté, Down East lobster salad, lobster bisque, lobster ravioli, and deep-fried lobster dumplings. Lobster Thermidor is obtainable at a sit-down restaurant called The Black Pearl on Harbor Park's northwest wharf. A large all-pine booth sponsored by the Maine Lobster Promotion Council has free pamphlets with recipes, eating tips, and Lobster Fun Facts. The winner of Friday's Amateur Cooking Competition prepares

---

[1] There's a comprehensive native apothegm: "Camden by the sea, Rockland by the smell."

Saffron Lobster Ramekins, the recipe for which is available for public downloading at www.mainelobsterfestival.com. There are lobster T-shirts and lobster bobblehead dolls and inflatable lobster pool toys and clamp-on lobster hats with big scarlet claws that wobble on springs. Your assigned correspondent saw it all, accompanied by one girlfriend and both his own parents – one of which parents was actually born and raised in Maine, albeit in the extreme northern inland part, which is potato country and a world away from the touristic midcoast.[2]

For practical purposes, everyone knows what a lobster is. As usual, though, there's much more to know than most of us care about – it's all a matter of what your interests are. Taxonomically speaking, a lobster is a marine crustacean of the family Homaridae, characterized by five pairs of jointed legs, the first pair terminating in large pincerish claws used for subduing prey. Like many other species of benthic carnivore, lobsters are both hunters and scavengers. They have stalked eyes, gills on their legs, and antennae. There are dozens of different kinds worldwide, of which the relevant species here is the Maine lobster, *Homarus americanus*. The name "lobster" comes from the Old English *loppestre*, which is thought to be a corrupt form of the Latin word for locust combined with the Old English *loppe*, which meant spider.

Moreover, a crustacean is an aquatic arthropod of the class Crustacea, which comprises crabs, shrimp, barnacles, lobsters, and freshwater crayfish. All this is right there in the encyclopedia. And an arthropod is an invertebrate member of the phylum Arthropoda, which phylum covers insects, spiders, crustaceans, and centipedes/millipedes, all of whose main commonality, besides the absence of a centralized brain-spine assembly, is a chitinous exoskeleton composed of segments, to which appendages are articulated in pairs.

The point is that lobsters are basically giant sea-insects.[3] Like most arthropods, they date from the Jurassic period, biologically so much older than mammalia that they might as well be from another planet. And they are – particularly in their natural brown-green state, brandishing their claws like weapons and with thick antennae awhip – not nice to look at. And it's true that they are garbagemen of the sea, eaters of dead stuff,[4] although they'll also eat some live shellfish, certain kinds of injured fish, and sometimes each other.

But they are themselves good eating. Or so we think now. Up until

---

[2] N.B. All personally connected parties have made it clear from the start that they do not want to be talked about in this article.

[3] Midcoasters' native term for a lobster is, in fact, "bug," as in "Come around on Sunday and we'll cook up some bugs."

[4] Factoid: Lobster traps are usually baited with dead herring.

sometime in the 1800s, though, lobster was literally low-class food, eaten only by the poor and institutionalized. Even in the harsh penal environment of early America, some colonies had laws against feeding lobsters to inmates more than once a week because it was thought to be cruel and unusual, like making people eat rats. One reason for their low status was how plentiful lobsters were in old New England. "Unbelievable abundance" is how one source describes the situation, including accounts of Plymouth pilgrims wading out and capturing all they wanted by hand, and of early Boston's seashore being littered with lobsters after hard storms – these latter were treated as a smelly nuisance and ground up for fertilizer. There is also the fact that premodern lobster was often cooked dead and then preserved, usually packed in salt or crude hermetic containers. Maine's earliest lobster industry was based around a dozen such seaside canneries in the 1840s, from which lobster was shipped as far away as California, in demand only because it was cheap and high in protein, basically chewable fuel.

Now, of course, lobster is posh, a delicacy, only a step or two down from caviar. The meat is richer and more substantial than most fish, its taste subtle compared to the marine-gaminess of mussels and clams. In the U.S. pop-food imagination, lobster is now the seafood analog to steak, with which it's so often twinned as Surf 'n' Turf on the really expensive part of the chain steak house menu.

In fact, one obvious project of the MLF, and of its omnipresently sponsorial Maine Lobster Promotion Council, is to counter the idea that lobster is unusually luxe or rich or unhealthy or expensive, suitable only for effete palates or the occasional blow-the-diet treat. It is emphasized over and over in presentations and pamphlets at the Festival that Maine lobster meat has fewer calories, less cholesterol, and less saturated fat than chicken.[5] And in the Main Eating Tent, you can get a "quarter" (industry shorthand for a 1 ¼ -pound lobster), a 4-ounce cup of melted butter, a bag of chips, and a soft roll w/ butter-pat for around $12.00, which is only slightly more expensive than supper at McDonald's.

Be apprised, though, that the Main Eating Tent's suppers come in Styrofoam trays, and the soft drinks are iceless and flat, and the coffee is convenience-store coffee in yet more Styrofoam, and the utensils are plastic (there are none of the special long skinny forks for pushing out the tail meat, though a few savvy diners bring their own). Nor do they give you near enough napkins, considering how messy lobster is to eat,

---

[5] Of course, the common practice of dipping the lobster meat in melted butter torpedoes all these happy fat-specs, which none of the Council's promotional stuff ever mentions, any more than potato-industry PR talks about sour cream and bacon bits.

especially when you're squeezed onto benches alongside children of various ages and vastly different levels of fine-motor development – not to mention the people who've somehow smuggled in their own beer in enormous aisle-blocking coolers, or who all of a sudden produce their own plastic tablecloths and try to spread them over large portions of tables to try to reserve them (the tables) for their little groups. And so on. Any one example is no more than a petty inconvenience, of course, but the MLF turns out to be full of irksome little downers like this – see for instance the Main Stage's headliner shows, where it turns out that you have to pay $20 extra for a folding chair if you want to sit down; or the North Tent's mad scramble for the NyQuil-cup-size samples of finalists' entries handed out after the Cooking Competition; or the much-touted Maine Sea Goddess pageant finals, which turn out to be excruciatingly long and to consist mainly of endless thanks and tributes to local sponsors. What the Maine Lobster Festival really is is a midlevel county fair with a culinary hook, and in this respect it's not unlike Tidewater crab festivals, Midwest corn festivals, Texas chili festivals, etc., and shares with these venues the core paradox of all teeming commercial demotic events: It's not for everyone.[6] Nothing against the aforementioned euphoric Senior Editor,

---

[6] In truth, there's a great deal to be said about the differences between working-class Rockland and the heavily populist flavor of its Festival versus comfortable and elitist Camden with its expensive view and shops given entirely over to $200 sweaters and great rows of Victorian homes converted to upscale B&Bs. And about these differences as two sides of the great coin that is U.S. tourism. Very little of which will be said here, except to amplify the above-mentioned paradox and to reveal your assigned correspondent's own preferences. I confess that I have never understood why so many people's idea of a fun vacation is to don flip-flops and sunglasses and crawl through maddening traffic to loud hot crowded tourist venues in order to sample a "local flavor" that is by definition ruined by the presence of tourists. This may (as my Festival companions keep pointing out) all be a matter of personality and hardwired taste: The fact that I just do not like tourist venues means that I'll never understand their appeal and so am probably not the one to talk about it (the supposed appeal). But, since this note will almost surely not survive magazine-editing anyway, here goes:

As I see it, it probably really is good for the soul to be a tourist, even if it's only once in a while. Not good for the soul in a refreshing or enlivening way, though, but rather in a grim, steely-eyed, let's-look-honestly-at-the-facts-and-find-some-way-to-deal-with-them way. My personal experience has not been that traveling around the country is broadening or relaxing, or that radical changes in place and context have a salutary effect, but rather that intranational tourism is radically constricting, and humbling in the hardest way – hostile to my fantasy of being a real individual, of living somehow outside and above it all. (Coming up is the part that my companions find especially unhappy and repellent, a sure way to

but I'd be surprised if she'd spent much time here in Harbor Park, watching people slap canal-zone mosquitoes as they eat deep-fried Twinkies and watch Professor Paddywhack, on six-foot stilts in a raincoat with plastic lobsters protruding from all directions on springs, terrify their children.

Lobster is essentially a summer food. This is because we now prefer our lobsters fresh, which means they have to be recently caught, which for both tactical and economic reasons takes place at depths of less than 25 fathoms. Lobsters tend to be hungriest and most active (i.e., most trappable) at summer water temperatures of 45–50°F. In the autumn, some Maine lobsters migrate out into deeper water, either for warmth or to avoid the heavy waves that pound New England's coast all winter. Some burrow into the bottom. They might hibernate; nobody's sure. Summer is also lobsters' molting season – specifically early- to mid-July. Chitinous arthropods grow by molting, rather the way people have to buy bigger clothes as they age and gain weight. Since lobsters can live to be over 100, they can also get to be quite large, as in 20 pounds or more – though truly senior lobsters are rare now, because New England's waters are so heavily trapped.[7] Anyway, hence the culinary distinction between hard- and soft-shell lobsters, the latter sometimes a.k.a. shedders. A soft-shell lobster is one that has recently molted. In midcoast restaurants, the summer menu often offers both kinds, with shedders being slightly cheaper even though they're easier to dismantle and the meat is allegedly sweeter. The reason for the discount is that a molting lobster uses a layer of seawater for insulation while its new shell is hardening, so there's slightly less actual meat when you crack open a shedder, plus a redolent gout of water that gets all over everything and can sometimes jet out lemonlike and catch a tablemate right in the eye. If it's winter or you're buying lobster someplace far from New England, on the other hand, you can almost bet that the lobster is a hard-shell, which for obvious reasons travel better.

As an à la carte entrée, lobster can be baked, broiled, steamed, grilled, sautéed, stir-fried, or microwaved. The most common method, though, is

---

spoil the fun of vacation travel.) To be a mass tourist, for me, is to become a pure late-date American: alien, ignorant, greedy for something you cannot ever have, disappointed in a way you can never admit. It is to spoil, by way of sheer ontology, the very unspoiledness you are there to experience. It is to impose yourself on places that in all noneconomic ways would be better, realer, without you. It is, in lines and gridlock and transaction after transaction, to confront a dimension of yourself that is as inescapable as it is painful: As a tourist, you become economically significant but existentially loathsome, an insect on a dead thing.

[7] Datum: In a good year, the U.S. industry produces around 80 million pounds of lobster, and Maine accounts for more than half that total.

boiling. If you're someone who enjoys having lobster at home, this is probably the way you do it, since boiling is so easy. You need a large kettle w/ cover, which you fill about half full with water (the standard advice is that you want 2.5 quarts of water per lobster). Seawater is optimal, or you can add two tbsp salt per quart from the tap. It also helps to know how much your lobsters weigh. You get the water boiling, put in the lobsters one at a time, cover the kettle, and bring it back up to a boil. Then you bank the heat and let the kettle simmer – ten minutes for the first pound of lobster, then three minutes for each pound after that. (This is assuming you've got hard-shell lobsters, which, again, if you don't live between Boston and Halifax, is probably what you've got. For shedders, you're supposed to subtract three minutes from the total.) The reason the kettle's lobsters turn scarlet is that boiling somehow suppresses every pigment in their chitin but one. If you want an easy test of whether the lobsters are done, you try pulling on one of their antennae – if it comes out of the head with minimal effort, you're ready to eat.

A detail so obvious that most recipes don't even bother to mention it is that each lobster is supposed to be alive when you put it in the kettle. This is part of lobster's modern appeal: It's the freshest food there is. There's no decomposition between harvesting and eating. And not only do lobsters require no cleaning or dressing or plucking (though the mechanics of actually eating them are a different matter), but they're relatively easy for vendors to keep alive. They come up alive in the traps, are placed in containers of seawater, and can, so long as the water's aerated and the animals' claws are pegged or banded to keep them from tearing one another up under the stresses of captivity,[8] survive right up until they're boiled. Most of us have been in supermarkets or restaurants that feature tanks of live lobster, from which you can pick out your supper while it watches you point. And part of the overall spectacle of the Maine Lobster Festival is that you can see actual lobstermen's vessels docking at the wharves along the northeast grounds and unloading freshly caught

---

[8] N.B. Similar reasoning underlies the practice of what's termed "debeaking" broiler chickens and brood hens in modern factory farms. Maximum commercial efficiency requires that enormous poultry populations be confined in unnaturally close quarters, under which conditions many birds go crazy and peck one another to death. As a purely observational side-note, be apprised that debeaking is usually an automated process and that the chickens receive no anesthetic. It's not clear to me whether most gourmet readers know about debeaking, or about related practices like dehorning cattle in commercial feedlots, cropping swine's tails in factory hog farms to keep psychotically bored neighbors from chewing them off, and so forth. It so happens that your assigned correspondent knew almost nothing about standard meat-industry operations before starting work on this article.

product, which is transferred by hand or cart 100 yards to the great clear tanks stacked up around the Festival's cooker – which is, as mentioned, billed as the World's Largest Lobster Cooker and can process over 100 lobsters at a time for the Main Eating Tent.

So then here is a question that's all but unavoidable at the World's Largest Lobster Cooker, and may arise in kitchens across the U.S.: Is it all right to boil a sentient creature alive just for our gustatory pleasure? A related set of concerns: Is the previous question irksomely PC or sentimental? What does "all right" even mean in this context? Is it all just a matter of individual choice?

As you may or may not know, a certain well-known group called People for the Ethical Treatment of Animals thinks that the morality of lobster-boiling is not just a matter of individual conscience. In fact, one of the very first things we hear about the MLF ...well, to set the scene: We're coming in by cab from the almost indescribably odd and rustic Knox County Airport[9] very late on the night before the Festival opens, sharing the cab with a wealthy political consultant who lives on Vinalhaven Island in the bay half the year (he's headed for the island ferry in Rockland). The consultant and cabdriver are responding to informal journalistic probes about how people who live in the midcoast region actually view the MLF, as in is the Festival just a big-dollar tourist thing or is it something local residents look forward to attending, take genuine civic pride in, etc. The cabdriver – who's in his seventies, one of apparently a whole platoon of retirees the cab company puts on to help with the summer rush, and wears a U.S.-flag lapel pin, and drives in what can only be called a very deliberate way – assures us that locals do endorse and enjoy the MLF, although he himself hasn't gone in years, and now come to think of it no one he and his wife know has, either. However, the demilocal consultant's been to recent Festivals a couple times (one gets the impression it was at his wife's behest), of which his most vivid impression was that "you have to line up for an ungodly long time to get your lobsters, and meanwhile there are all these ex–flower children coming up and down along the line handing out pamphlets that say the lobsters die in terrible pain and you shouldn't eat them."

And it turns out that the post-hippies of the consultant's recollection were activists from PETA. There were no PETA people in obvious view at the 2003 MLF,[10] but they've been conspicuous at many of the recent

[9] The terminal used to be somebody's house, for example, and the lost-luggage-reporting room was clearly once a pantry.

[10] It turned out that one Mr. William R. Rivas-Rivas, a high-ranking PETA official out of the group's Virginia headquarters, was indeed there this year, albeit solo, working the Festival's main and side entrances on Saturday, August 2, handing

Festivals. Since at least the mid-1990s, articles in everything from *The Camden Herald* to *The New York Times* have described PETA urging boycotts of the MLF, often deploying celebrity spokespeople like Mary Tyler Moore for open letters and ads saying stuff like "Lobsters are extraordinarily sensitive" and "To me, eating a lobster is out of the question." More concrete is the oral testimony of Dick, our florid and extremely gregarious rental-car guy, to the effect that PETA's been around so much in recent years that a kind of brittlely tolerant homeostasis now obtains between the activists and the Festival's locals, e.g.: "We had some incidents a couple years ago. One lady took most of her clothes off and painted herself like a lobster, almost got herself arrested. But for the most part they're let alone. [Rapid series of small ambiguous laughs, which with Dick happens a lot.] They do their thing and we do our thing."

This whole interchange takes place on Route 1, 30 July, during a four-mile, 50-minute ride from the airport[11] to the dealership to sign car-rental papers. Several irreproducible segues down the road from the PETA anecdotes, Dick – whose son-in-law happens to be a professional lobsterman and one of the Main Eating Tent's regular suppliers – articulates what he and his family feel is the crucial mitigating factor in the whole morality-of-boiling-lobsters-alive issue: "There's a part of the brain in people and animals that lets us feel pain, and lobsters' brains don't

---

out pamphlets and adhesive stickers emblazoned with "Being Boiled Hurts," which is the tagline in most of PETA's published material about lobster. I learned that he'd been there only later, when speaking with Mr. Rivas-Rivas on the phone. I'm not sure how we missed seeing him *in situ* at the Festival, and I can't see much to do except apologize for the oversight – although it's also true that Saturday was the day of the big MLF parade through Rockland, which basic journalistic responsibility seemed to require going to (and which, with all due respect, meant that Saturday was maybe not the best day for PETA to work the Harbor Park grounds, especially if it was going to be just one person for one day, since a lot of diehard MLF partisans were off-site watching the parade (which, again with no offense intended, was in truth kind of cheesy and boring, consisting mostly of slow homemade floats and various midcoast people waving at one another, and with an extremely annoying man dressed as Blackbeard ranging up and down the length of the crowd saying "Arrr" over and over and brandishing a plastic sword at people, etc.; plus it rained)).

[11] The short version regarding why we were back at the airport after already arriving the previous night involves lost luggage and a miscommunication about where and what the local National Car Rental franchise was – Dick came out personally to the airport and got us, out of no evident motive but kindness. (He also talked nonstop the entire way, with a very distinctive speaking style that can be described only as manically laconic; the truth is that I now know more about this man than I do about some members of my own family.)

have this part."

Besides the fact that it's incorrect in about 11 different ways, the main reason Dick's statement is interesting is that its thesis is more or less echoed by the Festival's own pronouncement on lobsters and pain, which is part of a Test Your Lobster IQ quiz that appears in the 2003 MLF program courtesy of the Maine Lobster Promotion Council: "The nervous system of a lobster is very simple, and is in fact most similar to the nervous system of the grasshopper. It is decentralized with no brain. There is no cerebral cortex, which in humans is the area of the brain that gives the experience of pain."

Though it sounds more sophisticated, a lot of the neurology in this latter claim is still either false or fuzzy. The human cerebral cortex is the brain-part that deals with higher faculties like reason, metaphysical self-awareness, language, etc. Pain reception is known to be part of a much older and more primitive system of nociceptors and prostaglandins that are managed by the brain stem and thalamus.[12] On the other hand, it is true that the cerebral cortex is involved in what's variously called suffering, distress, or the emotional experience of pain – i.e., experiencing painful stimuli as unpleasant, very unpleasant, unbearable, and so on.

Before we go any further, let's acknowledge that the questions of whether and how different kinds of animals feel pain, and of whether and why it might be justifiable to inflict pain on them in order to eat them, turn out to be extremely complex and difficult. And comparative neuroanatomy is only part of the problem. Since pain is a totally subjective mental experience, we do not have direct access to anyone or anything's pain but our own; and even just the principles by which we can infer that others experience pain and have a legitimate interest in not feeling pain involve hard-core philosophy – metaphysics, epistemology, value theory, ethics. The fact that even the most highly evolved nonhuman mammals can't use language to communicate with us about their subjective mental experience is only the first layer of additional complication in trying to extend our reasoning about pain and morality to animals. And everything gets progressively more abstract and convolved as we move farther and farther out from the higher-type mammals into cattle and swine and dogs and cats and rodents, and then birds and fish, and finally invertebrates like lobsters.

The more important point here, though, is that the whole animal-

---

[12] To elaborate by way of example: The common experience of accidentally touching a hot stove and yanking your hand back before you're even aware that anything's going on is explained by the fact that many of the processes by which we detect and avoid painful stimuli do not involve the cortex. In the case of the hand and stove, the brain is bypassed altogether; all the important neurochemical action takes place in the spine.

cruelty-and-eating issue is not just complex, it's also uncomfortable. It is, at any rate, uncomfortable for me, and for just about everyone I know who enjoys a variety of foods and yet does not want to see herself as cruel or unfeeling. As far as I can tell, my own main way of dealing with this conflict has been to avoid thinking about the whole unpleasant thing. I should add that it appears to me unlikely that many readers of *Gourmet* wish to think hard about it, either, or to be queried about the morality of their eating habits in the pages of a culinary monthly. Since, however, the assigned subject of this article is what it was like to attend the 2003 MLF, and thus to spend several days in the midst of a great mass of Americans all eating lobster, and thus to be more or less impelled to think hard about lobster and the experience of buying and eating lobster, it turns out that there is no honest way to avoid certain moral questions.

There are several reasons for this. For one thing, it's not just that lobsters get boiled alive, it's that you do it yourself – or at least it's done specifically for you, on-site.[13] As mentioned, the World's Largest Lobster Cooker, which is highlighted as an attraction in the Festival's program, is right out there on the MLF's north grounds for everyone to see. Try to imagine a Nebraska Beef Festival[14] at which part of the festivities is watching trucks pull up and the live cattle get driven down the ramp and slaughtered right there on the World's Largest Killing Floor or something – there's no way.

The intimacy of the whole thing is maximized at home, which of

---

[13] Morality-wise, let's concede that this cuts both ways. Lobster-eating is at least not abetted by the system of corporate factory farms that produces most beef, pork, and chicken. Because, if nothing else, of the way they're marketed and packaged for sale, we eat these latter meats without having to consider that they were once conscious, sentient creatures to whom horrible things were done. (N.B. PETA distributes a certain video – the title of which is being omitted as part of the elaborate editorial compromise by which this note appears at all – in which you can see just about everything meat-related you don't want to see or think about. (N.B. Not that PETA's any sort of font of unspun truth. Like many partisans in complex moral disputes, the PETA people are fanatics, and a lot of their rhetoric seems simplistic and self-righteous. Personally, though, I have to say that I found this unnamed video both credible and deeply upsetting.))

[14] Is it significant that "lobster," "fish," and "chicken" are our culture's words for both the animal and the meat, whereas most mammals seem to require euphemisms like "beef" and "pork" that help us separate the meat we eat from the living creature the meat once was? Is this evidence that some kind of deep unease about eating higher animals is endemic enough to show up in English usage, but that the unease diminishes as we move out of the mammalian order? (And is "lamb"/"lamb" the counterexample that sinks the whole theory, or are there special, biblico-historical reasons for that equivalence?)

course is where most lobster gets prepared and eaten (although note already the semiconscious euphemism "prepared," which in the case of lobsters really means killing them right there in our kitchens). The basic scenario is that we come in from the store and make our little preparations like getting the kettle filled and boiling, and then we lift the lobsters out of the bag or whatever retail container they came home in ... whereupon some uncomfortable things start to happen. However stuporous the lobster is from the trip home, for instance, it tends to come alarmingly to life when placed in boiling water. If you're tilting it from a container into the steaming kettle, the lobster will sometimes try to cling to the container's sides or even to hook its claws over the kettle's rim like a person trying to keep from going over the edge of a roof. And worse is when the lobster's fully immersed. Even if you cover the kettle and turn away, you can usually hear the cover rattling and clanking as the lobster tries to push it off. Or the creature's claws scraping the sides of the kettle as it thrashes around. The lobster, in other words, behaves very much as you or I would behave if we were plunged into boiling water (with the obvious exception of screaming).[15] A blunter way to say this is that the lobster acts as if it's in terrible pain, causing some cooks to leave the kitchen altogether and to take one of those little lightweight plastic oven timers with them into another room and wait until the whole process is over.

There happen to be two main criteria that most ethicists agree on for determining whether a living creature has the capacity to suffer and so has genuine interests that it may or may not be our moral duty to consider.[16] One is how much of the neurological hardware required for pain-experience the animal comes equipped with – nociceptors,

---

[15] There's a relevant populist myth about the high-pitched whistling sound that sometimes issues from a pot of boiling lobster. The sound is really vented steam from the layer of seawater between the lobster's flesh and its carapace (this is why shedders whistle more than hard-shells), but the pop version has it that the sound is the lobster's rabbitlike death scream. Lobsters communicate via pheromones in their urine and don't have anything close to the vocal equipment for screaming, but the myth's very persistent – which might, once again, point to a low-level cultural unease about the boiling thing.

[16] "Interests" basically means strong and legitimate preferences, which obviously require some degree of consciousness, responsiveness to stimuli, etc. See, for instance, the utilitarian philosopher Peter Singer, whose 1974 *Animal Liberation* is more or less the bible of the modern animal-rights movement: "It would be nonsense to say that it was not in the interests of a stone to be kicked along the road by a schoolboy. A stone does not have interests because it cannot suffer. Nothing that we can do to it could possibly make any difference to its welfare. A mouse, on the other hand, does have an interest in not being kicked along the road, because it will suffer if it is."

prostaglandins, neuronal opioid receptors, etc. The other criterion is whether the animal demonstrates behavior associated with pain. And it takes a lot of intellectual gymnastics and behaviorist hairsplitting not to see struggling, thrashing, and lid-clattering as just such pain-behavior. According to marine zoologists, it usually takes lobsters between 35 and 45 seconds to die in boiling water. (No source I could find talked about how long it takes them to die in superheated steam; one rather hopes it's faster.)

There are, of course, other fairly common ways to kill your lobster on-site and so achieve maximum freshness. Some cooks' practice is to drive a sharp heavy knife point-first into a spot just above the midpoint between the lobster's eyestalks (more or less where the Third Eye is in human foreheads). This is alleged either to kill the lobster instantly or to render it insensate – and is said at least to eliminate the cowardice involved in throwing a creature into boiling water and then fleeing the room. As far as I can tell from talking to proponents of the knife-in-the-head method, the idea is that it's more violent but ultimately more merciful, plus that a willingness to exert personal agency and accept responsibility for stabbing the lobster's head honors the lobster somehow and entitles one to eat it. (There's often a vague sort of Native American spirituality-of-the-hunt flavor to pro-knife arguments.) But the problem with the knife method is basic biology: Lobsters' nervous systems operate off not one but several ganglia, a.k.a. nerve bundles, which are sort of wired in series and distributed all along the lobster's underside, from stem to stern. And disabling only the frontal ganglion does not normally result in quick death or unconsciousness. Another alternative is to put the lobster in cold salt water and then very slowly bring it up to a full boil. Cooks who advocate this method are going mostly on the analogy to a frog, which can supposedly be kept from jumping out of a boiling pot by heating the water incrementally. In order to save a lot of research-summarizing, I'll simply assure you that the analogy between frogs and lobsters turns out not to hold.

Ultimately, the only certain virtues of the home-lobotomy and slow-heating methods are comparative, because there are even worse/crueler ways people prepare lobster. Time-thrifty cooks sometimes microwave them alive (usually after poking several extra vent holes in the carapace, which is a precaution most shellfish-microwavers learn about the hard way). Live dismemberment, on the other hand, is big in Europe: Some chefs cut the lobster in half before cooking; others like to tear off the claws and tail and toss only these parts in the pot.

And there's more unhappy news respecting suffering-criterion number one. Lobsters don't have much in the way of eyesight or hearing, but they do have an exquisite tactile sense, one facilitated by hundreds of thousands of tiny hairs that protrude through their carapace. "Thus," in the words of T.M. Prudden's industry classic *About Lobster*, "it is that although encased in what seems a solid, impenetrable armor, the lobster can receive stimuli and impressions from without as readily as if it possessed a soft and delicate skin." And lobsters do have nociceptors,[17] as well as invertebrate versions of the prostaglandins and major neurotransmitters via which our own brains register pain.

Lobsters do not, on the other hand, appear to have the equipment for making or absorbing natural opioids like endorphins and enkephalins, which are what more advanced nervous systems use to try to handle intense pain. From this fact, though, one could conclude either that lobsters are maybe even *more* vulnerable to pain, since they lack mammalian nervous systems' built-in analgesia, or, instead, that the absence of natural opioids implies an absence of the really intense pain-sensations that natural opioids are designed to mitigate. I for one can detect a marked upswing in mood as I contemplate this latter possibility: It could be that their lack of endorphin/enkephalin hardware means that lobsters' raw subjective experience of pain is so radically different from mammals' that it may not even deserve the term *pain*. Perhaps lobsters are more like those frontal-lobotomy patients one reads about who report experiencing pain in a totally different way than you and I. These patients evidently do feel physical pain, neurologically speaking, but don't dislike it – though neither do they like it; it's more that they feel it but don't feel anything *about* it – the point being that the pain is not distressing to them or something they want to get away from. Maybe lobsters, who are also without frontal lobes, are detached from the neurological-registration-of-injury-or-hazard we call pain in just the same way. There is, after all, a difference between (1) pain as a purely neurological event, and (2) actual suffering, which seems crucially to involve an emotional component, an awareness of pain as unpleasant, as something to fear/dislike/want to avoid.

Still, after all the abstract intellection, there remain the facts of the frantically clanking lid, the pathetic clinging to the edge of the pot. Standing at the stove, it is hard to deny in any meaningful way that this is a living creature experiencing pain and wishing to avoid/escape the painful experience. To my lay mind, the lobster's behavior in the kettle appears to be the expression of a *preference*; and it may well be that an ability to form

---

[17] This is the neurological term for special pain receptors that are (according to Jane A. Smith and Kenneth M. Boyd's *Lives in the Balance*) "sensitive to potentially damaging extremes of temperature, to mechanical forces, and to chemical substances which are released when body tissues are damaged."

preferences is the decisive criterion for real suffering.[18] The logic of this (preference → suffering) relation may be easiest to see in the negative case. If you cut certain kinds of worms in half, the halves will often keep crawling around and going about their vermiform business as if nothing had happened. When we assert, based on their post-op behavior, that these worms appear not to be suffering, what we're really saying is that there's no sign that the worms know anything bad has happened or would *prefer* not to have gotten cut in half.

Lobsters, however, are known to exhibit preferences. Experiments have shown that they can detect changes of only a degree or two in water temperature; one reason for their complex migratory cycles (which can often cover 100-plus miles a year) is to pursue the temperatures they like best.[19] And, as mentioned, they're bottom-dwellers and do not like bright light: If a tank of food lobsters is out in the sunlight or a store's fluorescence, the lobsters will always congregate in whatever part is darkest. Fairly solitary in the ocean, they also clearly dislike the crowding that's part of their captivity in tanks, since (as also mentioned) one reason why lobsters' claws are banded on capture is to keep them from attacking

---

[18] "Preference" is maybe roughly synonymous with "interest," but it is a better term for our purposes because it's less abstractly philosophical – "preference" seems more personal, and it's the whole idea of a living creature's personal experience that's at issue.

[19] Of course, the most common sort of counterargument here would begin by objecting that "like best" is really just a metaphor, and a misleadingly anthropomorphic one at that. The counterarguer would posit that the lobster seeks to maintain a certain optimal ambient temperature out of nothing but unconscious instinct (with a similar explanation for the low-light affinities about to be mentioned in the main text). The thrust of such a counterargument will be that the lobster's thrashings and clankings in the kettle express not unpreferred pain but involuntary reflexes, like your leg shooting out when the doctor hits your knee. Be advised that there are professional scientists, including many researchers who use animals in experiments, who hold to the view that nonhuman creatures have no real feelings at all, only "behaviors." Be further advised that this view has a long history that goes all the way back to Descartes, although its modern support comes mostly from behaviorist psychology.

To these what-look-like-pain-are-really-only-reflexes counterarguments, however, there happen to be all sorts of scientific and pro-animal-rights counter-counterarguments. And then further attempted rebuttals and redirects, and so on. Suffice to say that both the scientific and the philosophical arguments on either side of the animal-suffering issue are involved, abstruse, technical, often informed by self-interest or ideology, and in the end so totally inconclusive that as a practical matter, in the kitchen or restaurant, it all still seems to come down to individual conscience, going with (no pun) your gut.

one another under the stress of close-quarter storage.

In any event, at the Festival, standing by the bubbling tanks outside the World's Largest Lobster Cooker, watching the fresh-caught lobsters pile over one another, wave their hobbled claws impotently, huddle in the rear corners, or scrabble frantically back from the glass as you approach, it is difficult not to sense that they're unhappy, or frightened, even if it's some rudimentary version of these feelings ...and, again, why does rudimentariness even enter into it? Why is a primitive, inarticulate form of suffering less urgent or uncomfortable for the person who's helping to inflict it by paying for the food it results in? I'm not trying to give you a PETA-like screed here – at least I don't think so. I'm trying, rather, to work out and articulate some of the troubling questions that arise amid all the laughter and saltation and community pride of the Maine Lobster Festival. The truth is that if you, the Festival attendee, permit yourself to think that lobsters can suffer and would rather not, the MLF can begin to take on aspects of something like a Roman circus or medieval torture-fest.

Does that comparison seem a bit much? If so, exactly why? Or what about this one: Is it not possible that future generations will regard our own present agribusiness and eating practices in much the same way we now view Nero's entertainments or Aztec sacrifices? My own immediate reaction is that such a comparison is hysterical, extreme – and yet the reason it seems extreme to me appears to be that I believe animals are less morally important than human beings;[20] and when it comes to defending such a belief, even to myself, I have to acknowledge that (a) I have an obvious selfish interest in this belief, since I like to eat certain kinds of animals and want to be able to keep doing it, and (b) I have not succeeded in working out any sort of personal ethical system in which the belief is truly defensible instead of just selfishly convenient.

Given this article's venue and my own lack of culinary sophistication, I'm curious about whether the reader can identify with any of these reactions and acknowledgments and discomforts. I am also concerned not to come off as shrill or preachy when what I really am is confused. Given the (possible) moral status and (very possible) physical suffering of the animals involved, what ethical convictions do gourmets evolve that allow them not just to eat but to savor and enjoy flesh-based viands (since of course refined *enjoyment*, rather than just ingestion, is the whole point of

---

[20] Meaning a *lot* less important, apparently, since the moral comparison here is not the value of one human's life vs. the value of one animal's life, but rather the value of one animal's life vs. the value of one human's taste for a particular kind of protein. Even the most diehard carniphile will acknowledge that it's possible to live and eat well without consuming animals.

gastronomy)? And for those gourmets who'll have no truck with convictions or rationales and who regard stuff like the previous paragraph as just so much pointless navel-gazing, what makes it feel okay, inside, to dismiss the whole issue out of hand? That is, is their refusal to think about any of this the product of actual thought, or is it just that they don't want to think about it? Do they ever think about their reluctance to think about it? After all, isn't being extra aware and attentive and thoughtful about one's food and its overall context part of what distinguishes a real gourmet? Or is all the gourmet's extra attention and sensibility just supposed to be aesthetic, gustatory?

These last couple queries, though, while sincere, obviously involve much larger and more abstract questions about the connections (if any) between aesthetics and morality, and these questions lead straightaway into such deep and treacherous waters that it's probably best to stop the public discussion right here. There are limits to what even interested persons can ask of each other.